FAIR PLAY

Other Intelligence Titles from Potomac Books

The Castro Obsession: U.S. Covert Operations Against Cuba,
1959–1965
by Don Bohning

CIA Inc: Espionage and the Craft of Business Intelligence
by F. W. Rustmann Jr.

Flawed Patriot: The Rise and Fall of CIA Legend Bill Harvey
by Bayard Stockton

Hide and Seek: Intelligence, Law Enforcement, and the Stalled
War on Terrorist Finance
by John A. Cassara

Silent Warfare: Understanding the World of Intelligence, Third Edition
by Abram N. Shulsky and Gary J. Schmitt

Spymaster: My Life in the CIA
by Ted Shackley with Richard A. Finney

Why Secret Intelligence Fails
by Michael A. Turner

FAIR PLAY

THE MORAL DILEMMAS OF SPYING

JAMES M. OLSON

Potomac Books, Inc.
Washington, D.C.

Library of Congress Cataloging-in-Publication Data
Olson, James M., 1941–
   Fair play : the moral dilemmas of spying / James M. Olson.—1st ed.
      p. cm.
   Includes bibliographical references and index.
   ISBN 1-57488-949-4 (hardcover : alk. paper)
   1. Intelligence service—United States. 2. Espionage—Moral and ethical aspects. 3. Espionage—Case studies. 4. United States. Central Intelligence Agency. I. Title.
   JK468.I6O47 2006
   172'.4—dc22
                              2006012890

Printed in the United States of America on acid-free paper that meets the American National Standards Institute Z39-48 Standard.

Potomac Books, Inc.
22841 Quicksilver Drive
Dulles, Virginia 20166

First Edition

10 9 8 7 6 5 4 3

To Meredith, Jeremy, Joshua, and Hillary—

the best support team any spy ever had.

CONTENTS

PREFACE

The stereotype of spying is that it is a cold, hard, and dirty business where almost anything goes. As the protagonist in James Hilton's *Random Harvest* put it, "The primary aim is to frustrate the enemy's knavish tricks. Anything that does so is the thing to do, even if it seems a bit knavish itself." The United States has certainly been no stranger to "knavery" in its espionage and covert action operations around the world. However, U.S. intelligence does not and should not operate in a moral vacuum. As we will see in this book, U.S. attitudes toward spying have varied considerably over the years. In times of danger, Americans have been tolerant of more aggressive spying, even behavior many would consider "dirty tricks." When the external threat has seemed less imminent, the moral standards have tightened. Some Americans have finessed the issue by taking the view that what happens in the shadows should stay in the shadows. Their directive to the U.S. intelligence community is, in effect, "get the job done but don't tell us the details." That look-the-other-way attitude, I believe, is unhelpful—and not the way the United States should be doing business.

What constitutes acceptable moral behavior in any given operational situation has too often been left to the judgment of individual intelligence officers, their supervisors, or other senior officials. This has been a recipe for confusion, abuse, and cover-up. No profession, particularly one that can hide behind a veil of secrecy, should police itself. Attempts to codify what is morally permissible have generally failed because of the murkiness of the spy world and the shifting attitudes of U.S. government decision-makers and the public. What might have been considered morally unthinkable before the age of terror is now palatable to large numbers of Americans. Some U.S. politicians and editorial writers believe the intelligence community should be "unleashed" to fight the war on terror. Others believe unconstrained intelligence activity would undermine American values and make us no better than those we are fighting.

The current situation of no clear guidelines is unfair and unwise. Few U.S. politicians in either the legislative or the executive branches have been eager to put their name on laws or other documents that can in any way be perceived as "stretching" the moral limits. Members of the CIA, FBI, NSA, military, and other U.S. intelligence agencies are being told to penetrate terrorist cells and to prevent future attacks against Americans. If they do not do that, they will be held accountable and will suffer the consequences— maybe even losing their jobs. But no one is willing to tell them the rules. "Go do it," they are told, "but if after the fact we decide you went too far, we will have your heads." This is not a formula that encourages risk-taking by intelligence practitioners, and the end result is that the overall effectiveness of the war on terror suffers.

U.S. intelligence is the servant of the American people. What it does in the United States and abroad it does in their name and on their behalf. In our open and democratic society, spies should not be making their own rules. The American people should have a voice in how U.S. intelligence operates and what the moral limits are. Ordinary citizens have no need to know the details of specific operations, sources, or methods, but they should have input on how our country conducts itself overseas and at home as it fights the war on terror. The first step, I believe, is for them to know what the world of intelligence is *really* like and what the moral issues intelligence professionals often face are. That's my objective here. Public awareness must be raised before the country can have a well-informed, serious, and nonpartisan debate on the moral dilemmas of spying. I hope my book opens some eyes and causes some hard thinking.

Acknowledgments

My first thanks go to the students of the Master's Program in International Affairs at the George Bush School of Government and Public Service at Texas A&M University in College Station, Texas. They were my sounding board in formulating and refining the moral issues associated with intelligence operations that eventually took shape in this book. Their comments in the classroom, in the corridors, in my office, and over lunch were invaluable to me in understanding how these future public servants, many of whom will one day be working in national security jobs, analyze these complex moral dilemmas.

I must also acknowledge the strong support and encouragement I received in writing this book from Dean Dick Chilcoat, Associate Dean for International Affairs Chuck Hermann, and all my colleagues on the faculty at the Bush School. I could not have asked for an environment that was more supportive or conducive to research and writing.

This book would not have been possible without the thoughtful input of many "commentators" from around the country. I used earlier associations in the intelligence community and elsewhere to prevail upon several of them; others, however, I knew only by reputation or were referred to by mutual acquaintances. In a few cases, not unexpectedly, I was turned down cold. Other people I approached for comments chose not to go on the record with their views on these controversial topics and graciously declined. That's fine. For those who did respond, I wish to express my heartfelt appreciation.

Next, I would like to thank the Publications Review Board (PRB) of the Central Intelligence Agency, to which I was required on the basis of my CIA secrecy agreement to submit the manuscript in advance. I was aware from the beginning that my book would be walking close to the line between what would and would not be permitted, but I thought it was important that I portray the real world of spying as accurately as possible. The last thing I would ever want to do would be to compromise past, current, or future U.S. intelligence operations, sources, or methods. I tried to be as careful as I could in writing this book to avoid that. At the same time, I did not want to short-change the reader by glossing over the realities of spying, using incorrect terminology, or hiding behind generalities. The PRB worked with me professionally and cooperatively to achieve what I believe turned out to be a good balance. In most instances, the requested changes were slight, and I simply revised the text accordingly. In other cases, where the changes were more significant, I chose to use blacked out spaces to show where deletions occurred. I hasten to add that I understand the CIA's rationale for making the deletions (most of them anyway), and I do not object.

Finally, I would like to expand on my dedication at the front of the book. There is no way I could have done what I did in my career without the love and support of my wife Meredith, my son Jeremy, my son Joshua, and my daughter Hillary. They were always there—and still are. I hope they know how much meaning they give to my life and how much they inspire me.

Introduction: A Career Under Cover

God is not averse to deceit in a holy cause.
—Aeschylus

Hateful to me as the gates of hell,
Is he who, hiding one thing in his heart,
Utters another.
—Homer

When I was growing up in Iowa, I wanted at various times to be a lighthouse keeper, a catcher for the New York Yankees, a fishing guide, an actuary, or a lawyer. Never would I have dreamed that I would actually turn out to be a spy.[1*]

I was born in the small town of Le Mars, Iowa, but was raised in West Des Moines, a suburb of the capital Des Moines. After graduating from high school, I went to the University of Iowa in Iowa City, the only school to which I applied. My test scores seemed to indicate that I had a quantitative bent, so I completed a double major in mathematics and economics. My heart was not in either of those subjects, however. In my freshman year I took a Russian course and discovered that I had a passion and aptitude for foreign language study. Beginning with my sophomore year I studied French, eventually earning a paid technical assistantship in the French department. Language courses gobbled up all my electives but proved to be far more enjoyable to me than my classes in differential equations and econometrics. I was not yet thinking in terms of ever using foreign languages professionally; my motivation at the time was simply to be able to read foreign literature in the original, something I continue to enjoy to this day.

---

* The numbered notes are found in the chapter at the end of the book called "Spying 101: Notes." These notes amplify the text and should be read in parallel with the main body of the book. For ease in reference, the notes section is separated by a divider.

Two events in my college years had a decisive influence on the future direction of my life. The first involved my cousin and best friend Mike Joynt, who was also a student at the University of Iowa. Mike had joined the U.S. Navy Reserve right out of high school, and during our freshman year he suggested that I might like to take a look at it also. I enlisted and was accepted into the Reserve Officer Candidate program. Mike and I attended weekly drills at the Navy Reserve Center in Iowa City and spent our summers in training. When we graduated, we were commissioned as ensigns. I served aboard guided missile destroyers and frigates, deploying several times to the Mediterranean, the North Atlantic, and the Caribbean. My knowledge of French came in handy, and I accompanied the commodore as his interpreter when he made calls on French naval officers and government officials. For several weeks I was assigned as the American liaison officer aboard the French flagship *Le Cassard* during joint exercises with the U.S. Navy. These experiences in the Navy reinforced my interest in foreign languages and travel. They also planted the seed for an eventual career in public service.

The second influential event of my college years was the receipt of a Christmas present from my uncle Dr. Robert Joynt. Bob gave me a copy of Allen Dulles's book *The Craft of Intelligence*. This was my first exposure of any kind to the world of intelligence. The book fascinated me, but it did not quite seem real. Even if spying existed as Dulles described it, it would certainly be out of reach for a boy from Iowa. It hadn't yet occurred to me that espionage could ever be a realistic career choice. Much later, when the opportunity unexpectedly presented itself, the positive impressions of the CIA that I had from *The Craft of Intelligence* came back and clearly influenced my decision.

I loved the Navy but eventually decided not to stay. The main reason was the lifestyle. I could see how much time the married officers in the wardroom spent away from their wives and children. Although I was a bachelor at the time, I hoped to have a normal family life someday and decided that a career as a Navy officer would not allow me to do that. My wife, incidentally, thinks it's hilarious that I left the Navy because I wanted a normal family life and ended up in the CIA, a career that did not make for what most people would call a normal family life. More on that later.

I used the GI Bill and my savings to attend the College of Law at the University of Iowa. I was happy to go back to my roots in the heartland and was convinced that my foreign adventures were a thing of the past. My life goals were now very clear: I would finish law school and practice in a small county-seat town in Iowa. I would serve my community and perhaps even run for local office. I would find a nice Iowa girl, marry, and raise a family in what I thought then (and still do) was the ideal family setting, small-town rural America. It would be a good life.

That all changed one Friday afternoon during my last semester of law school when I was sitting in my dormitory room at the University of Iowa and the phone rang. The voice on the phone said he was calling "to discuss a career opportunity that might be of interest" to me. That caught my attention because I was actively job hunting. I had interviewed with law firms in Clinton, Atlantic, and Dubuque and was leaning toward Clinton. Clinton is a nice little Mississippi River town, and the law firm there was offering a membership in the local country club as part of its package. The caller that Friday was vague about the nature of the job, saying only that it would involve "serving our country." He invited me to a meeting the next day at the Hotel Savery in downtown Des Moines, about a two-hour drive from Iowa City.

When I think back on that phone call now, I am surprised I even went to the meeting. Maybe the world was safer then and we were less suspicious by nature, but today I doubt many young people would go to a meeting like that knowing so few details. I remember thinking that the caller was probably from the U.S. Navy. I was still in the Navy Reserve and guessed that the Navy probably wanted to know if I would be interested in coming back on active duty for some special classified project. It sounded exciting, and I was anxious to hear what the Navy had to say.

It was not the Navy. The person I met in the lobby of the Hotel Savery was a CIA recruiter from Kansas City. He was never clear about how I had come to his attention, but I assume now (I still don't know for sure) that I had either crossed paths with a CIA spotter on campus[2] or had simply been flagged by the CIA because of my Navy service and knowledge of Russian and French. It has also occurred to me that my applications to other government agencies, which I was filling out in case the Iowa law firms didn't work out, had somehow been noticed by the CIA.

The recruiter and I talked in a corner of the lobby for about two hours, and I was intrigued by what I heard. I knew virtually nothing about the CIA beyond the Dulles book and would not have thought of applying on my own. Yet that afternoon I was asked to make a formal application for CIA employment.

One of the other government agencies to which I applied was the FBI. Three of us from the Iowa law school went through the processing together, dealing with an FBI special agent who worked in Cedar Rapids, the nearest FBI resident office. It seemed very strange to me, but the first thing we did for the FBI was take a spelling test. Apparently, J. Edgar Hoover had expressed unhappiness with the quality of spelling at the bureau and had decreed that poor spellers should be screened out from the beginning. By correctly spelling "accommodation," "supersede," "subpoena," and a long list of other words, I was able to advance to further processing. In fact, I was still in the running after the interviews, medical examination, and background investigation. I was not sure if I was really interested in an FBI career, but, again, I wanted to have something else to turn to if Clinton, Atlantic, and Dubuque fell through.

Shortly after my meeting with the Kansas City recruiter, I applied to the CIA. It turned out, unbeknownst to me, that my simultaneous applications to the FBI and the CIA were on a collision course. Tensions between the FBI and CIA are often exaggerated today and, in fact, relations are quite good now, but in the late 1960s the two agencies barely communicated with each other. The paranoia of Hoover at the FBI and James Jesus Angleton at the CIA reigned supreme and resulted in bizarre interagency policies in both organizations. CIA and FBI personnel were on occasion actually disciplined for sharing information or, even worse, for cooperating (horror of horrors) with their cross-town rival.

My CIA processing was going slowly. I had passed the CIA's aptitude testing, the medical and psychological screening, and the polygraph, but the background investigation was not completed yet, probably because I had spent so much time overseas. The slow pace concerned me because graduation was approaching and I needed a job—soon. I had exhausted my Navy savings and GI Bill benefits and could not postpone getting an income for very long. I had a solid job offer from the Clinton law firm, so I was not desperate, but I was still eager to play out whatever government options I might have.

With graduation from law school just two weeks away, I phoned my FBI contact in Cedar Rapids to inquire about the status of my application. He said, "Jim, everything looks good, but a slight problem has come up. We have learned that you have also applied to the CIA, so we need you to withdraw your application from the CIA and to send us a copy of your withdrawal letter by registered mail. Then we can continue your FBI processing." The FBI-CIA rivalry had smacked me directly. I replied, "Sir, will I have a firm job offer from the FBI if I do that?" He was noncommittal; he would only say that "everything looked good" but no final decision could be made "until the CIA was out of the picture." I thought the FBI's position was ridiculous and, besides, I had still not gotten over how rinky-dink its spelling test was, so I withdrew my FBI application. I have the greatest respect for the FBI and am sure I would have had a fine career there, but things worked out differently.

The CIA offer came through just in time. I had graduated and had passed the bar exam. The Clinton law firm was pressing me for an answer. So, what would it be? Law in beautiful downtown Clinton, Iowa, or spying overseas?

(It's an indication of how much I love Iowa that this was such a tough decision for me. The now-hackneyed lines from the movie *Field of Dreams* ring true for all of us Hawkeyes: "Is this heaven?" "No, it's Iowa.") After a lot of thought, I accepted the position in the CIA's Career Training Program. As I packed my little red Volkswagen for the trip east, I had the firm intention of doing this "CIA thing" for only a few years and then, I guaranteed myself, I would return to Iowa to pursue my original dream. I never made it to Clinton, but I often think how different my life would have been if I had. I discovered very early on that the CIA was where I belonged. Service to our country and the art of espionage had gotten into my blood, and I quickly realized that this was what I wanted to do with my life. When my wife and I look back now on our life together in the CIA, we have no regrets. Instead, we have a nice warm feeling knowing that we were privileged to serve something we believed in and, we hope, to have made a difference.

I'll never forget the thrill of seeing my first CIA salary check in the mailbox. I felt rich making $9,600 a year.[3]

In the years before I joined the CIA, I had seen America go through some difficult times—some horrible times—but I still had no doubts about our government or the honorable nature of what I was doing. Like most of my fellow CIA trainees at the time, I felt lucky to be there. We believed that expansionist, oppressive, and atheistic Communism was antithetical to our values and freedoms and had to be defeated. For most of us, service in the CIA was more of a calling or a crusade than a job. CIA officer Duane "Dewey" Clarridge refers to those of us on the operational side of the CIA as the "president's centurions," and I think he's right. We felt like soldiers, ready to march off against our country's enemies.

My Career Training Program[4] class was not scheduled to start immediately, so I was assigned orientation classes and interim jobs for my first few months. My first adviser and mentor was Frank Friberg, a CIA veteran who had been the CIA chief in Helsinki when the famous Soviet defector Anatoly Golitsyn[5] had walked in, in 1960. I was absolutely in awe of Frank. Not only was he a legend in the CIA, but he was also a kind and patient teacher. Frank arranged for me to have two interim assignments at CIA headquarters before starting my training at "the Farm," our remote undercover training facility in Virginia. Every morning, I had one-on-one language instruction to perfect my Russian skills. In the afternoon, I worked in the French office analyzing French companies suspected of illegally trading with the Chinese. That meant that after lunch every day I walked across headquarters from the operational side, where I was assigned, to the analytical side, where the French company files were kept.

As luck would have it, the French analytical section was right next to the German analytical section. As I walked past the German section on my way to the French section every day, I could not help noticing, out of the corner of my eye (spies have to have good peripheral vision), a lovely young lady working there as a German analyst. Over time, I noticed that this German analyst had a friend in the French section, named Fran, whom I had met. After watching all of this from afar for several weeks, I finally summoned up enough courage to ask Fran about her friend. She said, "Oh, you must mean Meredith." That was the first time I had heard her name. After clumsily determining that Meredith was not seeing anyone else regularly and getting her phone number from Fran, I made what we call a "cold call." I figured my chances of success were no better than 10 percent. "You don't know me," I said, "but I have been working in the French section and was wondering if you might be interested in dinner and a movie some evening." She said yes. I was flabbergasted.

Our dating was complicated because I was soon to enter full-time training. The first few months were in the Washington area and consisted of generic intelligence training for all new officers. After that, we would go to the Farm for a long stretch of operational training. I was amazed that so many "big names" from inside and outside the government came to speak to us. Back then we entered the Career Training Program without any firm idea of what we would end up doing later on. After the basic training, we were each taken aside and asked where we thought we could make the greatest contribution to the Agency's mission. I told the panel I had been a communications officer in the Navy and could help in that area. That was the wrong answer; what would be my second choice? I said I had enjoyed research and writing in law school, so I thought I could be an analyst. Apparently I was wrong again. The senior officer on the panel asked how I would like to be an operator. In the short time I had been at the CIA, I had come to the conclusion that I was probably not cut out for operational work. I did not see myself as a James Bond type—in fact, far from it. But the panel was telling me that my psychological profile and training reports indicated otherwise. They actually knew me better than I knew myself. And how right they were. It's hard to believe now that I could ever have considered any other career path. It turned out that I loved being a case officer, and I am very grateful that the panel overruled me.

The training at the Farm[6] was tough. We had classes and exercises all day and then wrote our reports at night, often until three or four in the morning. One of the highlights of the training for me was a fantastic lecture by the legendary CIA case officer George Kisevalter, who had handled both the Pyotr Popov and Oleg Penkovsky cases.[7] I hung on every word Kisevalter said. I think he inspired all of us. There was also a great tradition at the

Farm of just hanging out at the bar in the student lounge with people like Kisevalter and other veterans of the business. It was heady stuff for us trainees, and we probably learned as much at the bar as we did in the class-rooms. My classmates were from all over the country, but a majority were from the prestigious schools of the Northeast. Though it's different now, when I joined the CIA, a recruit from Iowa was still something of a novelty. CIA training is a bonding experience, and I made lifelong friends at the Farm. Two of my best friends were ████████ paramilitary types being trained for covert action operations. John, Ray, and I played basketball in the gym every night together before dinner. We also teamed up on several of the group exercises. When we graduated, John and Ray were assigned to the CIA's secret war in Laos ████████. I learned later that shortly after they arrived, both were killed, one by a Pathet Lao sniper and the other in a helicopter crash. That was the part of a CIA career that never got easy: we all lost friends.

Our weekends were usually free, and we couldn't wait to get back to Washington to see our wives or girlfriends (we were almost exclusively male in those years).[8] I'll never forget, though, one of the married trainees who usually stayed at the Farm on weekends "to get in a little more time on the obstacle course." I couldn't decide whether Harry was super dedicated or just plain crazy. It can be a fine line sometimes. I knew one thing for sure: there would be no obstacle courses for me on weekends. I had important business in Washington—Meredith.

Meredith and I spent our entire career together in the CIA. She was from Ellensburg, Washington, and had joined the CIA for the same patri-otic reasons I had. In Meredith's case, though, there was an extra, more personal motivation. When she was in high school in Ellensburg, a cryptog-rapher for the National Security Agency named William Martin defected to the Soviet Union. Martin was originally from Ellensburg, and his betrayal was a cause of great shame for the town. Meredith, young and idealistic, decided that one day she would do what she could to restore, if only in a small way, the good name of her hometown. After graduating from Gonzaga University in Spokane with a degree in political science, she sent off an application to the CIA.

Meredith had been at the CIA for about eighteen months when we met. She was just about ready to return to Washington State to go to graduate school, but changed her mind when we began dating seriously. After our marriage, Meredith received operational training, and over our time in the CIA supported clandestine operations in countless ways. She learned French, Russian, German, and Spanish. Although Meredith always gave her first priority to our home and to raising our three children, she completed the denied-area tradecraft course and worked inside the CIA office in Moscow.

Our three children, Jeremy, Joshua, and Hillary, who were all born overseas, were not aware that Meredith and I were in the CIA until they were in high school. Until then, they thought we were simply whatever our cover was. Meredith and I had a variety of covers over the years, both official and nonofficial.[9] The CIA leaves it up to its officers whether they tell their children the truth. Some of our CIA friends went through their entire careers under cover, retired under cover, and never told their children they were in the CIA. That works best for them, for whatever reason, and that's fine. It's their decision. Most of us, however, prefer to tell our children the truth because we're not comfortable lying to them forever and we're proud of what we are really doing. If we do tell them, though, we obviously can't do it when they're too young. First, they might not be able to keep the secret. And second, if they are too small, we are concerned that it might be frightening for them to know they are part of a CIA family living in potentially dangerous circumstances. For that reason, most CIA officers wait until their children are in their late high school or early college years before telling them the truth.

As one would expect, children react in different ways. Meredith and I have a friend in the CIA who told us that when he told his daughter the truth, her reaction was to run to her room, slam her door, jump on her bed, and cry nonstop for several hours. Her dad and mom had lied to her, and she was brokenhearted. They had not trusted her. She felt betrayed by her own parents. Unfortunately, this sense of betrayal is not uncommon among CIA children when they find out the truth.

Other CIA friends of ours, John and Nancy, had a different experience when they told their teenaged daughter, Leslie, that they were in the CIA. Leslie reacted with "relief." I asked John, "What do you mean by relief?" He said that when they told Leslie they had been in the CIA for all those years, she said, "Thank goodness, Dad, that's what it is, because I had always sensed there was this big family secret, and I was afraid you and Mom . . . were brother and sister!"

Meredith and I broke the news to our children when we were in Vienna, Austria. Our CIA office there had been doing some aggressive covert action against some ████ terrorists who were operating in and through Vienna. To this day we do not know how, but somehow the terrorists found out the CIA was behind their problems and that I was the CIA chief in Vienna. They sent me a letter, which they ominously mailed to the address at which Meredith and I were living with our three children there. I will never forget that letter. It started out "Dear Infidel Dog" (I could tell right off it wasn't going to be friendly). It was a serious death threat against me by name, against Meredith by name, and against each of our three children by name. That was frightening. We took immediate precautions, of course, for the safety of our family, particularly the children. We also decided that under the circumstances we should tell our oldest, Jeremy, who was then sixteen, that we were a CIA family and needed his help. He should always watch out for his brother and sister and make sure they stayed together. He should make sure they always got on the same school bus. He should be alert to his surroundings, and if he noted anyone following or watching them, he should get in touch with someone in a position of authority right away. Jeremy reacted with pride, as we had hoped he would, and when Joshua and Hillary were a little older and we told them the truth, they also reacted with pride.

Speaking of pride, Meredith and I are very proud of our children. Jeremy served as an officer in the U.S. Marine Corps and is now working in campus ministry in Houston. Joshua was an officer in the U.S. Navy and is now in graduate school preparing for a career in teaching. Hillary and her husband Jeff are missionaries in Ethiopia, where they run a combination clinic and orphanage. On balance, I think our children benefited greatly from living overseas for most of their childhood years. They learned foreign languages and cultures and became comfortable with diversity. They became adaptable. For long stretches, they often had only one another as friends, so they became very close, and it is gratifying for us as parents to see how their closeness has continued. The only real problem, according to our children, is that they are stumped when someone asks them "where are you from?" They have lived in so many different places that they're not sure how to answer that question. The CIA operational lifestyle is definitely not for every family, but from what I have seen and experienced, a successful family life and a clandestine service career are not incompatible.

Most of my CIA operations are still classified. I am permitted to say, however, that I served under official cover in Moscow, Vienna, and Mexico City. My targets were the Soviet KGB, terrorists, narcotics traffickers, nuclear proliferators, North Korea, Iran, Libya, Cuba, and other threats to our nation's security. I had an exciting and rewarding career. I recruited and handled agents, planned and executed technical operations, participated in exfiltrations, helped to catch spies, and worked with many friendly liaison services.

Two specific operations in which I have been publicly identified as having had a role were the GTTAW[10] cable-tapping operation in Moscow and the Clayton Lonetree espionage case in Vienna. My participation in those operations has been described accurately in the excellent book *The Main Enemy* by Milt Bearden and James Risen, but I would like to add a few details here.

GTTAW was an incredible operation. The United States used satellite imaging to watch the Soviets dig a trench alongside a highway outside Moscow and then install communications cables in it. This trench led to two high-priority intelligence targets for the CIA, one ████████████████████ a sensitive military research and development center. It was clear from the images that these underground cables would be used to carry communications to and from the target facilities. The Soviets, in accordance with standard practice, installed manholes about every fifty yards along the line for servicing and maintenance. The CIA experts anticipated that these manholes would be locked and possibly alarmed. It seemed like an extremely tall order, but the CIA's Directorate of Science and Technology decided to go after the underground cables.

The CIA and a contractor built a mock-up of the cable line and a manhole for training purposes. I was one of three CIA officers selected to undergo this training. I'll never forget our first briefing, when we were "read in" on the operation. I thought to myself, "They must be kidding. This is really pie in the sky. We'll never do it." GTTAW was, in fact, the most ingenious and audacious operation I had ever seen. The three of us started training at the mock-up site the next day.

I was immediately intimidated by one of the other trainees. He showed up in full commando camouflage, complete with combat boots, beret, and ascot. I was in jeans, sneakers, and a sweatshirt. Only one of us was going to get the actual assignment in Moscow, and it seemed obvious to me who that would be. Well, I decided, I was going to give it my best shot anyway. We trained on manhole entry techniques for hour after hour, with every possible contingency thrown in. At one point, we were even blindfolded to see if we could complete an entry and a simulated tap just by feel alone. We got so we could do it, but in one of the blindfolded drills I ran into an unexpected snag. The instructors, without my knowledge, had wedged screws all around the manhole's flange to make the task of removing the manhole cover difficult, if not impossible. The purpose of the drill, I'm sure, was to see how quickly and effectively we adjusted to unforeseen complications. When I couldn't use my hook to lift the manhole cover, I felt with my hands around the flange and detected the screws. The only suitable tool I had was a large pocketknife, so I took it out and used it to pry out the screws. The knife slipped, however, and badly cut into my left index finger. I could feel that it was bleeding a lot, so I wrapped a handkerchief around it and finished the exercise. Once that was done, I was rushed by a security officer to a hospital emergency room, where my finger was stitched up. I think some of the GTTAW instructors were impressed by my decision to carry on with the exercise despite the injury, but, nevertheless, I was marked down on the critique sheet (and quite appropriately so) for "having left telltale blood at the operational site."

When I arrived in Moscow, the decision for me to do the actual operation was based on timing and on my ability to break KGB surveillance.[11] Meredith and I had seen some exploitable flaws in our surveillance coverage by the KGB and thought we could use those gaps to our operational advantage. On the day in question, with Meredith's help, I broke surveillance, assumed a disguise, and worked my way toward the manhole. It was easy, just like the training. I received the Intelligence Medal of Merit for my part in the GTTAW operation, but I honestly felt I didn't deserve it. The people who were far more deserving of recognition were the CIA engineers who designed the innovative tap technology and devised the means for getting so much data out of the hole and safely back to the CIA without being detected by the Soviets. Their work was what made GTTAW the remarkable intelligence achievement it was.

Sergeant Clayton Lonetree, USMC, was a marine security guard at the U.S. embassy in Vienna. He had served previously at the U.S. embassy in Moscow, where he had broken strict regulations by becoming involved with an attractive young Russian woman named Violetta. Violetta, not surprisingly, was cooperating with the KGB and set up the lovesick marine for recruitment.[12] Lonetree was never an enthusiastic spy for the KGB, but he was in way over his head and did what he thought he had to do to keep Violetta happy and safe. He gave the KGB some relatively low-level documents from the Moscow embassy and accepted small payments in return. When Lonetree was transferred to Vienna, the KGB followed. The KGB's handling of Lonetree in Moscow had been professional, sensitive, slow, and patient, just what Lonetree needed psychologically to avoid being spooked. In Vienna, however, Lonetree was turned over to a boorish KGB American-targets officer who was anything but subtle. He saw in Lonetree a potential penetration of the important U.S. embassy and CIA office in Vienna, and he pushed his prized agent too hard. Lonetree was scared to death and didn't know where to turn. He feared that the KGB would order him to do things he didn't want to do and would then forcibly defect him to the USSR. He loved Violetta but knew he didn't want to spend the rest of his life in Russia as a defector and traitor.

In his confusion and desperation, Lonetree approached me at the ambassador's Christmas party in 1986 to confess what he had done. I believe he had some misguided notion that he could redeem himself by serving as a double agent[13] for the CIA. He told me at the party that "he knew who I was because *they* had told him who I was." I arranged for Lonetree to meet with me the next day outside the embassy so we could begin a series of discreet debriefings. It was immediately apparent that Lonetree was too confused and distraught to pull off a double agent role convincingly. In addition, he was still infatuated with Violetta, so there would always be a problem of control. We turned Lonetree over to the Naval Investigative Service, which had criminal jurisdiction in the case, and he was sent off to the brig in Quantico, Virginia, for more questioning and eventual court-martial. Lonetree was sentenced to thirty years in prison but was released after serving only eight years. I think that was justice. Clayton Lonetree was a young man with problems who had been put into a situation he couldn't handle. He shouldn't have been a marine security guard in the first place, let alone put in key posts like Moscow and Vienna. He was easy prey for the KGB. Lonetree's drinking and emotional problems were not being addressed by the Marine Corps, and he received almost no supervision in Moscow, where he was certainly not the only marine fraternizing with Soviet women. After his conviction, Lonetree expressed remorse for what he had done and assisted conscientiously in the damage assessment. He was, of course, a traitor who committed an inexcusable crime, but the damage he did to the United States was slight and he paid his debt. I wish him well.

When Meredith and I were in Mexico City, I applied for the CIA's Officer-in-Residence Program,[14] which sends CIA officers to universities around the country to teach courses on intelligence. I had always thought I would like to have a second career in teaching someday, and this seemed like an ideal way to get some experience. I was initially selected to go to the Les Aspin School of Government at Marquette University in Milwaukee. The department head at Marquette told me, among other things, that I could coteach a course on the Cold War with George McGovern, who was a visiting professor there. I thought that would be an amazing opportunity and quite an honor. Meredith and I discreetly visited the campus and began looking at housing in the Milwaukee suburbs. We were all set to go.

In the meantime, however, a retired CIA officer named Mike Absher was trying to persuade the Agency to send an officer in residence to the brand new George Bush School of Government and Public Service at Texas A&M University. Mike had written to former President George Bush and had received an enthusiastic response. President Bush confirmed to the then-DCI George Tenet that, yes, he would very much like to have a CIA officer in residence assigned to his school. So, what happens when a former president and DCI make a request like that? The CIA does its best to comply. I was the only CIA officer approved for immediate assignment to a university, so the Agency asked Meredith and me to go down to Texas to take a look. We were told this was not a directed assignment; we could still go to Marquette if we wanted.

We liked what we saw at the Bush School from the start. International affairs was only a "track" in the public administration degree program at the time, but there were plans to expand international affairs into a separate degree program. The Bush School looked like an excellent fit for my background. Still, it was a tough decision because Meredith and I liked Marquette also, but in the end we decided to go to Texas A&M. I actually learned that my request to go to Texas A&M had been approved when I ran into George Tenet one day in the elevator at CIA headquarters. On the way up, George commented to me casually, "So, Jim, I see you're going to be an Aggie." It turned out to be the right decision. The Master's Program in International Affairs at the Bush School has grown rapidly. It attracts top graduate students from all over the United States and abroad who are interested in careers in intelligence, diplomacy, international economics, counterterrorism, homeland security, and related fields. Meredith and I definitely caught the "Aggie spirit." We learned to love Texas A&M's history, its values, traditions, and sports. When my two-and-a-half-year assignment as an officer in residence came to an end, I was eligible to retire from the CIA. The CIA proposed two nice jobs, one at headquarters and the other in the field, but the Bush School offered a full-time faculty position if I chose to stay. By then, I was hooked on teaching and wanted to continue working with Bush School students to help prepare them for exciting careers in national security. I honestly can't think of anything I could have done that would have been more fulfilling. Meredith, too, found a rewarding "second career" in College Station as a nurse. She graduated from the local Blinn College's nursing program and earned her RN, which was quite an accomplishment because she had been out of school for "a few years," and all her previous academic work had been in political science.

So now, from the relatively tranquil worlds of teaching and nursing, Meredith and I can look back on our previous lives. It's a good time for self-reflection. I consider myself a moral person—at least I hope I am. But I lied, cheated, manipulated, and deceived every day of my CIA career. I stole foreign countries' secrets whenever I could and undermined unfriendly governments. I induced foreign officials to commit treason against their countries. I saw and exploited the dark side of human nature more often than I care to remember. I believed then and still do that all these actions were in the service of a noble cause—but no one could have had the kind of career I did without at least some second thoughts.

So, what about the morality of what Meredith and I did in the CIA—and what our colleagues in the CIA and other U.S. intelligence agencies are doing right now? Are these actions contrary to our country's values and democratic principles or, on the other hand, are they supportive of those values and principles? What are the moral limits of spying? Who sets them? To what extent, if any, did the events of September 11, 2001, change the moral landscape? How far can and should we go in fighting and winning the War on Terrorism? These are controversial questions that need to be debated. How we answer them will not only define us as Americans but will also profoundly affect the way we are perceived by the rest of the world. The underlying question is this: What kind of country does America want to be?

At no time in my CIA career did I receive training in ethics or morality. At the Farm, for example, I cannot recall a single occasion when we discussed the morality of what we were doing. We simply accepted as given that we would do what we had to do to collect the intelligence our country needed. It was very much a case of "our country right or wrong." That has been modified to some extent today, but it is still hard for CIA instructors to get beyond ethical and moral generalities. It is relatively easy for them to teach the many regulations and executive orders that relate to intelligence activities, but the moral subtleties and ambiguities that arise in everyday spying operations continue to cause difficulty. Let's take a close look at them.

Perhaps we should start by consulting some of the great thinkers of the past.

── Philosophical and ── Historical Arguments

With a gentleman I am always a gentleman and a half,
and with a fraud I try to be a fraud and a half.
—BISMARCK

America is great because she is good, and if America
ever ceases to be good, America will cease to be great.
—ALEXIS DE TOCQUEVILLE

Thinkers from the beginning of recorded history have grappled with the problems of spying and public morality. What actions by a state are permissible in pursuing the state's interests? Are lying, cheating, manipulation, deception, coercion and other techniques of espionage and covert action justifiable in national self-defense? Who establishes the rules? Are there remedies for abuses? How, if at all, can spying be reconciled with the great philosophical, ethical, and religious traditions of the past?

What follows is by no means an exhaustive study of the topic; it is simply offered as a convenient and concise summary of the principal sources.

Bible

Then Joshua sent two spies from the camp at Acacia with orders to go and secretly explore the land of Canaan, especially the city of Jericho. When they came to the city, they were to spend the night in the house of a prostitute named Rahab. (Josh. 2:1)

The most pertinent biblical reference to spying is the story of the prostitute Rahab in the Book of Joshua. In preparation for his invasion of Canaan and his attack on the city of Jericho, Joshua sent two spies into the city. The spies were sheltered in the house of Rahab to protect them from the king of Jericho's men, who were searching for them. Rahab not only hid the spies under stalks of flax on the roof of her house, but also lied to the king's men about their whereabouts. She said that two unknown men had briefly stopped at her house but had left the city at sundown. On the basis of Rahab's lie, the king's men went looking for the spies in the wrong direction. Rahab then helped the spies to escape and told them where they could hide in the hills to avoid capture. Thanks to Rahab's assistance, the spies were able to complete their mission and to return safely to the Israelite camp.

In return for her kindness to the spies, Rahab and her family were spared when the Israelites captured and destroyed Jericho.

> But Joshua spared the lives of the prostitute Rahab and all her relatives, because she had hidden the two spies that he had sent to Jericho. Her descendants have lived in Israel to this day. (Josh. 6:25)

Rahab is considered a heroine of Israel. She is listed in Matthew's genealogy of Jesus as an ancestor of David (Matt. 1:5) and is exemplified in the Book of Hebrews as a paragon of faith (Heb. 11:31). There is no doubt that her actions were considered praiseworthy.

> You see, then, that it is by his actions that a person is put right with God, and not by his faith alone. It was the same with the prostitute Rahab. She was put right with God through her actions, by welcoming the Israelite spies and helping them to escape by a different road. (James 2:24–25)

It seems clear, then, that if the act of spying was considered inherently immoral in the Judeo-Christian faiths, the Bible would not have treated Rahab in this manner. She lied to protect the spies, but her lie was not condemned. Her lie was justified in the service of a greater good. It is likely that the intelligence collected by the spies was instrumental in the successful capture of Jericho and saved Israelite lives. That good offset the moral opprobrium of lying. If aiding the spies was deemed virtuous, then it is hard not to conclude that the act of spying itself was also moral.

The story of Rahab may have relevance to resolving other moral dilemmas of modern spying. Was Rahab not an early example of how intelligence operatives sometimes have to associate themselves with disreputable persons in order to accomplish a mission? Rahab was a prostitute and a social outcast, but she was also well positioned to assist in the spying venture. Her house was right on the walls of Jericho, which made it easier for the spies to enter and exit the city without being seen. Also, of course, Rahab was a good liar and had no scruples about deceiving the king's men. This analogy should not be stretched too far, but it does give context to some of the later "unholy alliances" of U.S. intelligence, for example, those with Reinhard Gehlen,[1] Manuel Noriega, Augusto Pinochet, Rafael Trujillo, Ngo Dinh Diem, and the Shah of Iran.

The apparently pro-spying message of the story of Rahab does not go unchallenged in the Bible. Other passages seem to contradict indirectly Rahab's pliable morality and make no clear exceptions for a greater good:

> Always be fair and just, so that you will occupy the land that the Lord your God is giving you and so that you will continue to live there. (Deut. 16:20)

> Therefore all that you wish men would do to you, so also you do to them. (Matt. 7:12)

It is not surprising that intelligence practitioners are more comfortable with the Rahab story than they are with Deuteronomy and Matthew.

Aristotle

Intelligence professionals will likewise search in vain for moral loopholes in Aristotle (384–22 B.C.). At first glance, Aristotle's theory of the mean would appear to offer flexibility in defining virtuous behavior. Every virtue exists on a continuum, says Aristotle, between extremes of opposing vices. The proper implementation of a virtue is therefore somewhere in between these two extremes, because each end is a vice. The virtue of courage, for example, might rest between the vice of foolhardiness at one extreme and the vice of pusillanimity at the other. The task of the ruler of practical wisdom is to determine the mean value for courage and to apply it.

This search for the mean would appear to offer variability or "wiggle room" in what constitutes virtue, but Aristotle slams the door shut in both *Politics* and *Nicomachean Ethics*. Aristotle's mean must be determined in a way that best promotes the achievement of a noble and virtuous end. What the mean is can vary from situation to situation depending on the threats, passions, and fears of the moment, but the end is always the same: *eudaimonia*, or a good life. This principle, Aristotle emphasizes, applies equally whether the actor is an individual or a city-state. All of a state's actions must aim toward the chief good of eudaimonia for its citizens, a life consisting of noble actions.

> . . . the best life, both for individuals and states, is the life of virtue. (*Politics* VII, 1)

In practice, therefore, Aristotle's theory of the mean is not a license for moral relativism. Any individual or state that engages in immoral practices becomes immoral itself, thus defeating any possibility of achieving a good life. A state that steals becomes a thief; a state that murders becomes a murderer. Aristotle is categorical in stating that certain actions, such as theft, murder, and adultery, are always morally wrong. He makes no exception for the good of the state.

Aristotle recognizes that no ruler is ever going to be perfect. No ruler will ever infallibly find the right intermediate between excess and defect in deciding on a course of action. Nevertheless, the good ruler must always strive toward the life of virtue.

> How can that which is not even lawful be the business of the states-man or the legislator? Unlawful it certainly is to rule without regard to justice, for there may be might where there is no right. (*Politics* VII, 2)

Justice, according to Aristotle, is not a function of who is more powerful or whose interests can best be served by a given course of action. He, in fact, condemns the following double standard:

> . . . what men affirm to be unjust and inexpedient in their own case they are not ashamed of practicing toward others; they demand just rule for themselves but where other men are concerned they care nothing about it. (*Politics* VII, 2)

In short, justice is universal; it is not situational. One cannot engage in actions against others that would be deemed unjust if conducted against oneself.

> If actions are, as we said, what gives life its character, no happy man can become miserable, for he will never do acts that are hateful and mean. (*Nicomachean Ethics*, Book I, 10)

What would Aristotle say about the aggressive techniques of modern day espionage and covert action? I'm afraid it is clear he would find them "hateful and mean."

Cicero

Marcus Tullius Cicero (106–43 B.C.) certainly admired Aristotle, particularly his emphasis on justice as a guiding principle in all things, but Cicero is far more flexible when it comes to matters of state. Cicero is too much the politician and too much the patriot to limit himself to idealistic absolutes. He aspires to what is absolutely good (*honestum*) whenever possible, but recognizes that this goal is sometimes in conflict with what is relatively good or useful (*utile*). "Expediency sometimes clashes with honesty" (*De Officiis* III, 3).

When there is a conflict between expediency and honesty, the right choice, according to Cicero, is the action that contributes better to the overall good of society or the state. It would be unfair, I think, to characterize Cicero as dishonest or a hypocrite, but he consistently puts the state's interests first and is willing to make moral compromises, when necessary, toward that end. "The safety of the people is the supreme law" (*De Legibus* III, 3, 8).

This does not mean that Cicero totally subjugates idealism to politics. He retains a keen sense of right and wrong, as illustrated in his famous analogy of the fox and the lion:

> While wrong may be done, then, in either of two ways, that is, by force or by fraud, both are bestial; fraud seems to belong to the cunning fox, force to the lion; both are wholly unworthy of man, but fraud is more contemptible. (*De Officiis* I, 41)

In theory, then, Cicero rejects fraud and force as "bestial" and unjust, "unworthy of man," but in practice he concedes that they sometimes are necessary for the good of the state. The needs of the country, for Cicero, are paramount, and any neglect of them by political leaders would be "unnatural." Cicero practiced what he preached. He deplored deceit in principle, as we have seen, but he instructed the Allobroges to use deceit to infiltrate the inner circle of Lucius Catiline by pretending to be sympathetic to the Catiline conspiracy. This was espionage, pure and simple, for the purpose of protecting the state. Cicero was even willing to stretch the law to counter what he saw as an imminent subversive threat. His order to have the five members of the Catiline conspiracy strangled to death was clearly extra-legal but still justifiable in Cicero's view on grounds of state security. Cicero was not a party to the assassination of Caesar, but he applauded it after it occurred and, in general, approved tyrannicide in his rhetoric and writing. In a famous quote, Cicero summarizes his belief that extraordinary means are acceptable when the survival of a state is being threatened, particularly when it is at war:

> *Inter arma enim silent leges.* In time of war, the laws fall silent. (*Pro Milone*, IV.)

Cicero is eager to reassure us, however, that he is not totally ruthless and that there are limits to his moral flexibility when it comes to defending the state. He is no Machiavelli, whom we'll discuss later in the chapter.

> For there are some acts either so repulsive or so wicked, that a wise
> man would not commit them, even to save his country . . . some of
> them are so shocking, so indecent, that it seems immoral even to men-
> tion them. The wise man, therefore, will not think of doing any such
> thing for the sake of his country; no more, will his country consent to
> have it done for her. (*De Officiis* I, 159)

Cicero does not enumerate these "repulsive" or "wicked" acts that should
never be done, even for one's country, but he is clearly establishing the same
kind of limit we refer to today as "shocking to the conscience." I believe
modern readers can find a great deal of relevance in Cicero as he struggles
with the identical problem we face today: how to reconcile morality with the
legitimate security interests of the state. How far can a state go before its
actions become "shocking" and "indecent"?

Saint Thomas Aquinas

Intelligence professionals who ponder such things often refer to Saint Thomas Aquinas (1225–74) for moral and ethical guidance. Aquinas provides us
with the most articulate formulation of what is known as the "just war"
doctrine, the attempt to codify when and how it is morally justifiable to
wage war. Spying is not explicitly mentioned by Aquinas or by his spiritual
predecessor Saint Augustine (354–430), but I do not think it is a stretch of
logic to assert that intelligence is an indispensable adjunct of a state's war-
making capability and therefore legitimately comes under the just war theory.
Spying as an integral part of war is as old as recorded history. Intelligence
operations help to determine what the threat is, where the enemy's vulnerabilities are, and how the war can be won. Political and military leaders, in
fact, need intelligence to know if the conditions for a "just war" exist in the
first place. As the U.S. Catholic bishops put it in their 1993 statement *The
Harvest of Justice is Sown in Peace*, "Any application of just war principles depends on the availability of accurate information not easily obtained in the
pressured political context in which such choices must be made."

In *Summa Theologica* II-II, question 40, Aquinas lists three conditions as
necessary for a war to be just:

1) The war must be declared by appropriate legal authority; it cannot
   be waged by individuals or usurpers.
2) A just cause is required, such as self-defense, defense of others,

recovery of something unjustly taken, or redress of a serious injury. (This provision is a significant departure from St. Augustine,
who does not recognize as morally justifiable the use of force for
defense of self or property.)

3) The state going to war must have a righteous intention, namely,
the restoration of peace or the promotion of some other good.
Revenge, greed, thirst for power, desire for territorial gain, and
hatred are not righteous intentions.

Later thinkers expand the just war doctrine to include additional conditions, all of which have been incorporated into modern international law
and conventions along with Aquinas's original three conditions:

4) The damage caused by going to war must be proportional to and
not exceed the good to be achieved.
5) The war must have a reasonable probability of success. It is morally wrong to cause damage and expend lives in a futile or hope-
less war.
6) Going to war must be a last resort. All nonmilitary means of achieving the same end must be exhausted before resorting to military force.
7) Every reasonable effort must be made to avoid harming innocent
civilians.

It is instructive, I think, to examine each of these conditions in the
context of U.S. espionage and covert action operations. U.S. intelligence
activities are legally authorized under U.S. law. Presidential findings, National
Security Council approvals, and congressional oversight are all a part of the
process. An intelligence operation, to be valid, must be undertaken for the
just cause of defending our country against an external threat. U.S. intelligence agencies should not carry out their operations for reasons of revenge,
hatred, or other base motives. The potential harm or loss from the operation must be outweighed by the potential gain. No intelligence operation
should be approved that does not have a reasonable expectation of success.
Spying should always be a last resort and should not be done if the information can be acquired by other means or, in the case of covert action, if the
desired outcome can be accomplished in another way. Finally, spying must
avoid targeting and harming innocents, that is, individuals who are totally
extraneous to whatever the legitimate operational objective is.

Aquinas makes clear that it is the public authorities that are responsible
for making these decisions. He states in *Summa Theologica* II-II, question 40,

Since responsibility for public action is committed to the rulers, they are charged with the defense of the city, the kingdom, or the province subject to them. And just as in punishing criminals they are justly defending the state with the civil arm against all internal disturbances . . . so also they are responsible to defend the state against external foes with war weapons.

As an update and confirmation of Aquinas's thinking on this point, the Catechism of the Catholic Church, published in 1992, includes the following in section 2309:

The strict conditions for legitimate defense by military force require rigorous consideration . . . The evaluation of these conditions for moral legitimacy belongs to the prudential judgment of those who have responsibility for the common good.

According to these authorities, therefore, U.S. decisions on the moral legitimacy of using "war weapons" against "external foes" should be made by the U.S. government, presumably with input in our democratic form of government from all U.S. citizens. Isn't intelligence, as discussed above, a "war weapon"? Shouldn't, then, the same guidelines that apply to war also apply to intelligence operations?

Machiavelli

Niccolo Machiavelli (1469–1527), the Florentine statesman and patriot, had little use for Aquinas or for Catholic theology in general. Machiavelli was a political realist who put the interests of the state above all else. The survival and prosperity of the state are the ultimate goals, and no legal, moral, or religious considerations should be allowed to get in the way:

A prince . . . cannot observe all those things for which men are esteemed, being often forced, in order to maintain the state, to act contrary to faith, friendship, humanity, and religion. Thus, he must be prepared to change as the winds of fortune and the alternations of circumstance dictate. As I have already said, he must stick to the good as long as he can, but being compelled by necessity, he must be ready to take the way of evil. (*The Prince*, XVIII)

What is so remarkable about Machiavelli is that he is totally unapologetic about his ruthless patriotism. A state must preserve itself, by war if necessary, and no other condition is necessary to make going to war for this purpose "just." In fact, a ruler is justified in going to war simply to advance his country's interests, even if the survival of the country is not at stake.

> No good man will ever reproach another who endeavors to defend his country, whatever be his mode of doing so. (*The History of Florence*, V, 2)

Machiavelli lived in a chaotic political period in Florence and saw no problem in a Florentine ruler resorting to cruelty and deceit if by doing so he could achieve his political objectives. The political end justified all means. Lying, cheating, stealing, and killing were all "good" if they contributed to the state's goals. Machiavelli wrote often of the "glorious crimes" and "honorable frauds" of "successful" rulers he admired. A clever ruler, though, should be careful to conceal his true nature by pretending to be virtuous, since a reputation for goodness strengthens the loyalty and support he receives from his citizenry. He should try to be good when it suits his purpose, but know how to be bad when circumstances require.

> Therefore a prince will not actually need to have all the qualities previously mentioned, but he must surely seem to have them. Indeed, I would go so far as to say that having them all and always conforming to them would be harmful, while appearing to have them would be useful. (*The Prince*, XVIII)

Spying is a major weapon in the state's exercise of power, according to Machiavelli. In his *Art of War*, he provides amazingly modern and sophisticated instructions on how to prevent spying by the enemy (counterintelligence), how to deceive the enemy (covert action), and how to learn its intentions (espionage). In Book Five he emphasizes intelligence collection and secrecy as necessary ingredients of going to war. In Book Six he describes several techniques for deceiving the enemy, including disinformation, double agents, and false truces. Machiavelli admires states that have successfully used intelligence techniques to defeat their adversaries:

> We see therefore that the Romans in the early beginning of their power already employed fraud, which it has ever been necessary for those to practice who from small beginnings wish to rise to the highest degree of power; and then it is the less censurable the more it is concealed. (*Discourses* II, 13)

Machiavelli summarizes his strong support for clandestine activity in the same treatise:

Cunning and deceit will every time serve a man better than force . . . I believe it to be most true that it seldom happens that men rise from low condition to high rank without employing either force or fraud, unless that rank should be attained either by gift or inheritance. Nor do I believe that force alone will ever be found to suffice, whilst it will often be the case that cunning alone serves the purpose. (*Discourses* II, 13)

In Machiavelli, we find an unbridled champion for even the most aggressive of intelligence techniques. He takes Cicero's ideas to the extreme. It is hard to imagine that Machiavelli would ever find any intelligence operation morally unacceptable if it could be argued that the state's interests would be served by carrying it out.

Kant

The German philosopher Immanuel Kant (1724–1804) brings the debate back to the other extreme. He establishes a very tough standard for determining whether an action is morally acceptable or not. In his *Foundations of the Metaphysics of Morals*, published in 1795, Kant argues that morality is a function of what he calls "good will." A person of good will always do his or her duty according to the moral law. Doing one's duty does not necessarily make one happy, but it does make one moral . . . and that should be the aim of anyone wanting to live a good life.

Good will depends on motive. To be moral, an action must be motivated by a pure desire to do the right thing, regardless of cost or inconvenience, and without any ulterior purpose. Kant summarizes his views on morality in his well-known Categorical Imperative.

The Categorical Imperative has two primary formulations. The first, called the Universal Law formulation, states, "Act only according to that maxim by which you can at the same time will that it should become a universal law." Good will, therefore, is "universalizable"; it is binding on all persons at all times. The test of whether an action is moral or not is whether it represents a principle that could be universally applied to everyone for the overall good of society. Telling a lie is therefore immoral because a society in which everyone lied would be unlivable. Stealing is immoral because a society in which there was no respect for personal property would be chaotic. No individual can make an exception for himself or herself in applying the rule. Self-interest, in fact, is a clear violation of the Categorical Imperative because it aims at some personal benefit to the exclusion of others.

This leads to the second formulation of the Categorical Imperative, the so-called Humanity formulation. It goes like this: "Act in such a way that you always treat humanity, whether in your own person or in the person of any other, never simply as a means, but always at the same time as an end." In other words, we must treat people with respect. We cannot use them for our own ends. We must always treat them with openness and honesty. It would be morally wrong for us to use coercion, deception, or manipulation against them to achieve our ends. Our actions toward others must be based on our genuine concern for their ends, not our own.

I am hard pressed to think of any espionage or covert action operation in which I was involved that passes this test. Intelligence, by definition, depends on deception and manipulation and, when necessary, coercion to attain its objectives. There is no other way. The recruitment cycle[2] is a clear example. Case officers are trained to exploit other people's weaknesses to draw them into espionage. Kant makes no exception for Machiavelli's *raison d'etat*; in fact, he makes it clear that no state can violate the human rights of others without violating the universal moral law. Furthermore, according to Kant, humanity is cosmopolitan, and no state can declare its ends superior to those of any other state.

There are no moral loopholes in the writings of Kant to justify intelligence operations. In fact, spying is singled out by Kant for special attention:

> Among these forbidden means are to be reckoned the appointment of subjects to act as spies, or engaging subjects or even strangers to act as assassins, or poisoners (in which class might well be included the so-called sharpshooters who lurk in ambush for individuals), or even employing agents to spread false news.
>
> In a word, it is forbidden to use any such malignant and perfidious means as would destroy the confidence which would be required to establish a lasting peace thereafter. (*The Science of Right* I, 57)

One can quibble with Kant's moral absolutism and his unwillingness to make distinctions between degrees of good and evil, but spies seeking a moral justification for their line of work will have to look elsewhere.

Realpolitik

Kant's idealism did not fare well in the rough and tumble world of nineteenth century European power politics. Napoleon's push for empire and glory for France had nothing to do with "good will" as defined by Kant and everything to do with the pursuit of pure national interest. It was the German Chancellor Otto von Bismarck (1815–98) who epitomized what became known as *realpolitik*, the advancement of national interests by all means necessary, even at the expense of doctrinal, religious, or ethical considerations. Bismarck's reputation for cold and calculating political realism was well deserved:

> Not by making speeches and counting majorities are the great questions of the time to be solved . . . but by iron and blood." (Speech to the Prussian Chamber of Deputies, September 30, 1862)

It was hard to argue with success. Bismarck had been preceded by masters of cunning and power politics who had done great things to expand the power and influence of their countries. Cardinal Richelieu (1558–1642) consolidated the power of the Bourbon monarchy in France by ruthlessly defeating his domestic opposition and waging war against the Hapsburgs. Frederick the Great of Prussia (1712–86) was guided by "necessity of state" in using force and guile when necessary to thwart Austrian ambitions, to share in the partition of Poland, and to make Prussia a leading European power. Austrian Foreign Minister Metternich (1773–1859) was a role model in deviousness as he tenaciously defended Austria's interests at the Congress of Vienna in 1815 and for the next thirty years. The key to successful statecraft was raw power, deceit, and war making. *Realpolitik* certainly seemed to advance a country's interests better than the Christian principles of forgiveness, meekness, and truthfulness. The moral and religious idealists had at least temporarily been routed by Machiavelli.

This dichotomy between how a state *should* theoretically act and how it feels it *must* act to defend its interests is frequently justified, even today, in terms of necessity. The needs of the state, according to this rationalization, prevail over moral constraints. As the French theologian Jean de Gerson put it way back in the fifteenth century, *"necessitas legem non habet"* (necessity has no law). *Raison d'etat, realpolitik,* and necessity are all iterations of this point of view. Modern manifestations of what continues to be a hotly debated philosophical and political conflict are expressed as realism vs. idealism, unilateralism vs. multilateralism, nationalism vs. internationalism, and national security vs. civil liberties.

The term *realpolitik* often has a pejorative ring to it today; it is seen as a stinging criticism. For example, to call any American political leader a practitioner of *realpolitik* would be a strong insult. But, labels aside, an America-first attitude is not unpopular with large numbers of Americans. If it's good for America, they urge, then why not do it? These people, in most cases, are sincerely guided by love of country and patriotism. The problem with their mindset, of course, is the cost. Love of country and patriotism are good, and a country must be defended against its enemies, but history has shown, in several different countries, that patriotism can degenerate into chauvinism, pride into arrogance, zeal into disregard for human rights, and dedication into fanaticism. That's our dilemma.

Terrorists practice *realpolitik*. To them any means, including the massacre of thousands of people at a time, are justified in the advancement of their cause. Should the United States respond with its own form of gloves-off *realpolitik*? Bismarck would have a ready answer for us: "I am accustomed to pay men back in their own coin."

Or should we take our counsel instead from the poet John Milton in *Paradise Lost*, Book IX, 171?

> *Revenge, at first though sweet,*
> *Bitter ere long back on itself recoils.*

Utilitarianism

The concept of utilitarianism, a new way of gauging whether an action is right or wrong, began to take shape in the mid-1700s. The British philosopher Francis Hutcheson (1694–1746) reasoned that since the ultimate goal of life is "happiness," all actions could be evaluated on the basis of how well they achieved that goal: "That action is best, which procures the greatest happiness for the greatest numbers."

This formulaic approach to analyzing human behavior was further developed by Jeremy Bentham (1748–1832), generally regarded as the "father of utilitarianism," who summarized his theory thus: "The greatest happiness of the greatest number is the foundation of morals and legislation."

Bentham believed that it was possible to calculate the degree to which a given action produced for those concerned either pleasure or happiness, on the one hand, or pain or unhappiness, on the other. Morality, therefore, was a kind of summing up of the overall effects of an act in terms of pleasure or pain. This basically hedonistic calculus was modified by the great utilitarian thinker John Stuart Mill (1806–73), who emphasized that nonphysical happiness was superior to physical happiness. Later utilitarian philosophers specified that abstract concepts like freedom, justice, knowledge, and beauty were valid components of happiness. The American economist Kenneth Arrow (born 1921) caused quite a stir when he outlined what was called "preference utilitarianism" in his classic work *Social Choice and Individual Values*, published in 1951. According to Arrow and other preference utilitarians, a group, society, or nation can decide for itself what constitutes "happiness," that is, the desired end of any action or series of actions. Communism and capitalism are equally valid choices under this theory, and pursuit of those ends would qualify as Bentham's "foundation of morals and legislation" for those societies.

The essence of utilitarianism is that no act is inherently right or wrong, moral or immoral. One must look first at the consequences of that act before making a value judgment. An act is good if it tends to promote happiness in a society or country. The motive of the person or state taking the action does not determine its rightness or wrongness. It is the end that matters.

Utilitarians argue that this standard is not as harsh and amoral as it seems, because in most cases actions generally considered to be "good" are what make a majority of people happy. But not always. It is too rigid, say the utilitarians, to apply a strict set of moral rules to decision making. Life is far more nuanced and complicated than that. Some lies, thefts, and even acts of violence can have good consequences and are therefore justifiable under utilitarian theory. It is easy to come up with examples. Who could object to telling a lie to avoid insult or to prevent easily avoidable anguish in a listener? Shouldn't lost and starving travelers be allowed to break into a remote cabin in the woods to steal food? And going farther, wouldn't most people agree that murdering a genocidal maniac to prevent him from slaughtering hundreds of thousands of innocent people would be a good and humane act?

Security, peace of mind, and freedom are important elements of "happiness" for most societies and nations. Both Bentham and Mill, in fact, elevated security to special status in their hierarchy of happiness. In his *Principles of the Civil Code*, published posthumously in 1843, Bentham wrote,

> When security and equality are in opposition, there should be no hesitation; equality should give way. The first [security] is the foundation of life, of subsistence, of abundance, of happiness; everything depends on it.

Mill made the same point, just as strongly, in *On Liberty*, published in 1859:

> The sole end for which mankind are warranted, individually or collectively, in interfering with the liberty of action of any of their number, is self-protection.

Since defense and national security are paramount values for many utilitarians, it is not surprising that they tend toward an end-justifies-the-means approach in these matters. To reach that point, these so-called "radical" utilitarians must deal with two major criticisms.

First, as many nonutilitarians and some "milder" utilitarians contend, all individuals and nations are equal and deserve equal treatment. In their view, utilitarianism cannot be applied exclusively and unilaterally to one group or nation. The radicals respond that Bentham and Mill clearly intended for utilitarianism to apply not to mankind as a whole, but to a given society or population. Utilitarianism, as "the foundation of morals and legislation," only makes sense, they say, in that context. Thus, a modern-day American utilitarian might well conclude that an act that contributes to the greatest happiness (including security) of the greatest number of Americans can be justified for American actors.

Second, many critics point out that utilitarianism fails to recognize any overriding constraints on the application of its principles, such as human rights, justice, international laws, and equality. As a result, they believe the rights of minorities and less powerful nations can be justifiably violated. Radical utilitarians concede that, in extreme cases, violations of widely accepted international norms could create such a generalized loss of trust, fear, and uncertainty in the world that the net "harm" would outweigh the "good." But, in their opinion, such cases are rare, and, in general, the end *does* justify the means, as long as the end maximizes happiness for the greatest number in the group, society, or nation.

Veritatis Splendor

Pope John Paul II (1920–2005) attempted to destroy decisively what he saw as a growing tendency toward moral relativism in the world in his encyclical *Veritatis Splendor* (The Splendor of Truth), released in 1993. He starts off by stating in very simple terms the issue he intends to address:

> No one can escape from the fundamental questions: What must I do? How do I distinguish good from evil? (Section 2)

Veritatis Splendor is a no-nonsense reaffirmation of the moral absolutist position. John Paul II rejects the concept that there can be an "ethical order, which would be human in origin and of value for this world alone" (37), and which would take precedence over the immutable natural law or, as he puts it, "the universal and objective norm of morality" (60). He makes clear that

> . . . human activity cannot be judged as morally good merely because it is a means for attaining one or another of its goals, or simply because the subject's intention is good. (72)

He specifically condemns the utilitarian or pragmatic concept that "behavior would be right or wrong according to whether or not it is capable of producing a better state of affairs for all concerned" or of "maximizing goods and minimizing evils" (74).

Veritatis Splendor categorically rejects "utilitarianism," "consequentialism," and "proportionalism," which is the belief that the morality of an action depends on a calculation of its foreseeable consequences and on a weighing of the proportional good or bad effects of that action. Such a standard, according to John Paul II, would make it impossible to prohibit universally any specific action and would instead make morality dependent on cultural, societal, and even individual values. In other words, circumstances might legitimize even grossly immoral choices, because there would be no such thing as "exceptionless" moral evils. These theories, he continues, are in error because they attempt "to justify, as morally good, deliberate choices of kinds of behavior contrary to the commandments of the divine and natural law" (76).

Just to make certain that this point is hammered home, the encyclical emphasizes that there are certain actions that are "intrinsically evil" and never morally acceptable. It cites numerous examples, such as homicide, genocide, theft, physical and mental torture, "attempts to coerce the spirit," arbitrary imprisonment, prostitution, and treating people as ends, not as human beings deserving of dignity (80). The encyclical refers to the observation of St. Thomas Aquinas that it would be morally wrong to steal food in order to feed the poor, because "no evil done with a good intention can be excused" (80). The same prohibition is included in the 1992 *Catechism of the Catholic Church*, Section 1761:

> There are concrete acts that it is always wrong to choose, because their choice entails a disorder of the will, i.e., a moral evil. One may not do evil so that good may result from it.

Two other authorities, Saint Augustine and the Apostle Paul, are used to buttress this point:

> As for acts which are themselves sins, like theft, fornication, and blasphemy, who would dare affirm that, by doing them for good motives, they would no longer be sins, or, what is even more absurd, that they would be sins that are justified? (Saint Augustine, *Contra Mendacium*, VII, 18)

> Why not say, then, "Let us do evil so that good may come?" Some people, indeed, have insulted me by accusing me of saying this very thing! They will be condemned, as they should be. (Rom. 3:8)

Veritatis Splendor, without question, is a blanket condemnation of the deception, manipulation, and coercion that are the staples of espionage and covert action. U.S. national security, according to the papal encyclical, would clearly be insufficient justification for such inherently immoral acts.

Critics of *Veritatis Splendor* find it to be stark, unyielding, and unrealistic. Even Saint Thomas Aquinas, they point out, seems to acknowledge proportionality and a "greater good" justification in his Just War Doctrine. For the "proportionalists," in particular, Pope John Paul II's encyclical seems to be an oversimplification. They contend that it does not adequately address the kinds of difficult moral decisions that *have* to be made in today's world, where questions of good and evil are not conveniently black and white.

U.S. ATTITUDES TOWARD SPYING

Covert action should not be confused with missionary work.
—HENRY KISSINGER

The life of the nation is secure only while the nation is honest,
truthful, and virtuous.
—FREDERICK DOUGLASS

America has always had a love-hate relationship with intelligence. For most of U.S. history, in fact, Americans have had an aversion to spying. That aversion was reflected in the fact that the United States did not have a truly professional civilian intelligence service until the establishment of the Office of Strategic Services in 1942. Even today, many Americans believe the CIA, the FBI, the NSA, and other U.S. government intelligence agencies are more likely to pervert American values and freedoms than to protect them. As recently as the 1990s, Senator Daniel Patrick Moynihan, a former vice chairman of the Senate Select Committee on Intelligence, argued publicly that the CIA should be dissolved and its functions taken over by the State Department.

What is the proper role of intelligence gathering in a democratic society? Can spying and democracy ever be reconciled? Isn't there something inherently un-American about sneaking around, stealing other countries' secrets, interfering in other countries' affairs, lying, manipulating, and deceiving? America has struggled with these questions.

It might be instructive to go back to early American history. In September 1776, colonial forces under General George Washington had just suffered a disastrous defeat by the British at the Battle of Long Island. Washington's troops had barely managed to retreat back across the East River to Manhattan. The British, under the command of General William Howe, were threatening an invasion of Manhattan, and the attack could come at any time.

Washington's problem was compounded by the fact that he knew practically nothing about the size of Howe's invasion force, its armaments, or its intentions. He desperately needed intelligence. Several of Washington's officers were briefed on the situation and on the urgent need for one of them to volunteer to put on civilian clothing, to sneak behind British lines on Long Island, to gather intelligence on the British, and to deliver it back to Washington. This was obviously a high-risk operation with only a slight chance that the spy would come back alive. At first no one volunteered. There were several reasons for this. Fear was clearly one factor. No one wanted to die. It was also true that the Americans had no experience in spying and therefore lacked the training for such a mission. There was no time or expertise to give the spy a professional backstopped cover. He would likewise have no communications or support while he was on his spying mission. All of these were valid reasons not to volunteer.

But these were not the real reasons no one stepped forward. The real reason was that spying was not considered *honorable*. Because of the cultural norms of the time, no officer or gentleman would engage in such an under-handed activity. No one respected a contemptible spy. Nevertheless, one of the American officers was tempted, twenty-one-year-old Nathan Hale from Connecticut. Hale spent an agonizing night debating with his friends whether he should accept the mission. One of his fellow officers told him that the mission was deceitful and improper and would result in his ignominious death. "No one," he said, "respects the character of a spy." Still, Hale persisted, and he finally told his friend that he had decided to accept the mission because, as he was quoted later by his friend, "any kind of service necessary to the public good becomes honorable by being necessary."

The next day, as we know from our history, Nathan Hale volunteered for the spy mission. After about a week behind the enemy's lines, he was captured by the British. As a spy, he was ordered to be hanged without a trial. He was denied even the basic comforts of a bible or a clergyman, which he had requested, because spies, being despicable, were entitled to no privileges of any kind.

Nathan Hale's statue stands before the entrance of CIA headquarters at Langley, Virginia. For all of us who have chosen intelligence as a profession, he is a role model of courage and honor and a great source of inspiration. And his rationale for spying—"any kind of service necessary to the public good becomes honorable by being necessary"—has been one of the moral and ethical foundations of U.S. intelligence.

But, in a democracy, is spying so necessary that it becomes moral and ethical? That is still an open question. One thing is clear, however. Spying, as practiced by the United States of America, is illegal. Espionage is a crime in every country, and the United States practices it in almost every country.

Covert action, defined as intervening secretly in the affairs of foreign countries, is a blatant violation of international law. But the CIA, with the approval of the National Security Council and the president of the United States, has conducted dozens of covert action operations around the world, some known, others still classified. We Americans live in an interventionist nation. We have frequently invaded other countries militarily; we have even more frequently invaded other countries secretly. Since the CIA's founding in 1947, a partial list of countries in which the United States has conducted CIA covert action interventions would include Italy, Iran, Guatemala, Indonesia, Vietnam, Laos, Congo, the Dominican Republic, Cuba, Chile, Angola, ████████████████, Nicaragua, ████, Afghanistan, and ████. There are many others.

United States espionage and covert action activities overseas *are* legal under U.S. law (with some notable exceptions, such as Iran-Contra), but they flout foreign and international law. Do the American people care about that? Isn't it at least ironic that the United States, the self-proclaimed champion of freedom and self-determination, has attempted on so many occasions to impose its will covertly on foreign countries and, in some cases, to overthrow their democratically elected governments? Or does necessity trump all? National security exists to ensure the survival of a state, and a state that neglects national security can perish. It is not surprising, then, that many Americans consider intelligence a necessary component of national security and are willing to accept a little "ruthlessness" on the part of their intelligence services in protecting their security.

America was the last major country in the world to establish a professional intelligence service. The British, French, Russians, Chinese, Poles, Koreans, Germans, Austrians, and even the Vatican already had long traditions of effective—and ruthless, when necessary—intelligence services to protect their security interests. Until World War II, the rest of the world must have looked on the United States as an intelligence babe in the woods, as unbelievably naïve, and as a strange kind of would-be world power.

There was some military intelligence in our early history, but it was almost exclusively low-level, tactical, and ineffective. It is hard to find anything worthy of being called U.S. intelligence in the War of 1812, the Mexican War, the Civil War, the Spanish-American War, or World War I. The great powers of Europe were conducting stunningly sophisticated and successful intelligence operations on a grand scale. But not the United States. We seemed hopelessly behind, and no one seemed concerned about it.

President Woodrow Wilson was an idealist who was putting all his hope after World War I in the creation of a League of Nations and the dawn of a brave new world of open diplomacy, a world in which espionage would have no place. Perhaps Wilson was not fully aware that a young genius in the U.S. War Department, Herbert Yardley, was quietly bringing the United States into the modern world of spying. Yardley and his cipher unit represented the first faint sign that America was finally awakening to the need for intelligence. The giant was slowly rousing. By 1920, Yardley and his Black Chamber, as he called it, had broken four Japanese codes, two German codes, and even some British codes. During the critical Washington Conference on the Limitation of Armaments in 1921, thanks to Yardley, U.S. negotiators could read virtually all the encrypted communications between Tokyo and the Japanese delegation in Washington, giving the American government a decisive advantage. In the next eight years, the Black Chamber produced over 10,000 decryptions of diplomatic communications. U.S. intelligence was finally catching up with its European counterparts. But not for long.

In 1929, the highly moralistic Henry Stimson became secretary of state. When he learned that the United States was actually reading Japanese diplomatic traffic, his reaction was shock and outrage. He considered the activities of the Black Chamber unethical, and he ordered the operation to be shut down. As Stimson so famously and, I believe, fatuously put it, "Gentlemen do not read each other's mail." Moral nicety had triumphed over national security. America would stay true to its democratic ideals and anchor itself in the moral high ground. America, at least for the time being, would not engage in SIGINT (signals intelligence), HUMINT (human intelligence), IMINT (imagery intelligence), or covert action.[1]

It really took World War II to change things. The atrocities of the Germans and the Japanese and the threat they represented to our security finally removed much of America's squeamishness about the dirty business of spying. It was not easy, though. President Roosevelt initially resisted creating a wartime civilian intelligence service. It was not until 1942 that Roosevelt, in response to the pleading of our British allies and the exigencies of the war, created the Office of Strategic Services (OSS). The OSS was given responsibility not only for intelligence collection, but also for sabotage, subversion, guerilla warfare, propaganda, and the other black arts of the intelligence profession.

And wonder of wonders! The United States turned out to be really good at it. Traditional American values of fair play took a back seat to winning the war, and the OSS proved to be a world-class player in deviousness. There can be no doubt that the operations of the OSS in Europe, Asia, and Africa contributed greatly to the Allied victory in World War II. One might have thought, then, that America's historic reluctance to engage in espionage and covert action had been overcome once and for all. But that was not the case.

An early glimmer of the resurgence of the antispying mindset occurred in late 1944, when the OSS was able to purchase some Soviet cipher material from the Finns. The OSS, of course, hoped to be able to use the material to begin breaking the Soviet codes. But when Edward Stettinius, the new secretary of state, found out what was going on, he protested strenuously to President Roosevelt that it would be unethical to read the Russians' codes because they were our ally in the war against Germany. Roosevelt ordered the OSS to give the code books back to the Russians, to inform them exactly what had happened, and to assure them no improper use had been made of the material.

William Donovan, the head of the OSS, was pressing hard in 1944 and 1945 for the establishment of an OSS-like intelligence service after the war. He foresaw the coming confrontation between the United States and the USSR and thought the United States needed the best intelligence possible to protect its interests. When Donovan made this case to new president Harry Truman in mid-1945, he got nowhere. Truman knew nothing about intelligence when he took office and seemed to view the whole idea of spying with distaste. He made several references during this period about not wanting to create an "American Gestapo." In September 1945, just a few days after V-J Day, Truman disbanded the OSS and rejected Donovan's proposal to establish a new peacetime intelligence service on the OSS model.

The looming Soviet threat soon convinced Truman that he did, in fact, need some kind of intelligence service, but he was not sure what he wanted. The postwar intelligence organization that he approved in 1946, the Central Intelligence Group, was a weak coordination body for analysis, with very little espionage or covert action capability. Truman had developed an appreciation for SIGINT in the final months of World War II, particularly the Japanese intercepts, but he was certainly no fan of the nastier hands-on world of HUMINT and covert action. Still, Truman could not ignore the spread of Communism across Eastern Europe and the danger of further Soviet expansionism. He realized he needed to do something more. He created the Central Intelligence Agency in 1947 as part of the National Security Act, and the new organization was in place and operating by September 1947. About one-third of the first employees of the CIA were OSS veterans, and the spirit and ethic of the OSS clearly infused the new agency.

Truman quickly had to come to grips with the question of what kind of creature he had created. The Italian elections were to take place in April 1948, and the Communists appeared well positioned to win. All of Truman's advisers told him a Communist victory in Italy would be disastrous for the United States. In a move that was probably contrary to his instincts, Truman approved a major CIA covert action campaign in Italy to prevent the

Communists from winning. The brand new CIA secretly funneled money to
the Italian Christian Democrats, arranged for anti-Communist articles to
appear in the press, conducted propaganda operations, and carried out mis-
cellaneous dirty tricks. The American journalist Howard K. Smith called the
effort a "CIA tidal wave." It is impossible to measure the effect of the CIA's
operation, but the Christian Democrats, contrary to all earlier predictions,
won in a landslide. Truman privately thanked the CIA for a job well done.

Truman always downplayed his role in the Italian operation and did not
like to talk about it. The truth, though, is that he was an active participant
and, perhaps grudgingly, had concluded that the external threat in this case
would have to countermand his scruples. He would later turn down other
CIA covert action proposals, most significantly in Iran, but in Italy in 1948
Harry Truman entered the spy world and got his hands dirty. He was the
first president to exercise what Robert McFarlane, President Ronald Reagan's
national security adviser, would later call the "intermediate option" between
going to war and doing nothing.

In a 1963 interview with the *Washington Post*, Truman tried to set the
record straight. It is apparent that he did not want his legacy tarnished by any
intimation that he approved or supported the darker side of CIA operations:

> For some time I have been disturbed by the way the CIA has been
> diverted from its original assignment . . . I never had any thought when
> I set up the CIA that it would be injected into peacetime cloak-and-
> dagger operations . . . (T)his quiet intelligence arm of the President
> has been so removed from its intended role that it is being interpreted
> as a symbol of sinister and mysterious foreign intrigue and a subject
> of cold war enemy propaganda.

President Dwight D. Eisenhower had no such qualms. By the time he
took office in 1953, the mood of the country had changed. The Cold War
was in full force. China had fallen to the Communists. The Soviets had
detonated an atomic bomb. The United States had fought a bloody war
against the Communists in Korea. This was the period of the Rosenbergs,
Alger Hiss, Joseph McCarthy, NSC 68, and the Red Scare. Eisenhower liked
intelligence and intended to use it aggressively to fight Communism. He
could not have had two better implementers of his take-it-to-the-enemy
policy than John Foster Dulles, his secretary of state, and Allen Dulles, the
director of the CIA. In short order, Eisenhower and the Dulles brothers
carried out CIA covert action operations to overthrow Mohammed
Mossadegh in Iran in 1953 and Jacobo Arbenz in Guatemala in 1954.
Mossadegh and Arbenz were both guilty of the same sins in the eyes of

John Foster Dulles: they tolerated Communists in their governments; they were suspiciously cozy with the Soviets; and they did not respect private property. They simply had to go. During this period, in fact, anything that was perceived as helping to stop Communism seemed acceptable. Eisenhower approved CIA assassination attempts against Communist leaders Patrice Lumumba in the Congo and Fidel Castro in Cuba. It is also hard to believe that Eisenhower was unaware that the planning for the Guatemalan coup in 1954 included large-scale assassinations of Communists and Communist sympathizers. No CIA assassinations actually took place, but not for lack of will or approval. The CIA was on a roll, and Eisenhower liked what he saw.

In July 1954, Eisenhower tasked World War II hero General James Doolittle to look into how the CIA's covert operations could be made even more effective. Doolittle's secret report, now declassified, was delivered to Eisenhower in September 1954. It strongly reinforced Eisenhower's already hard-line inclinations.

It is now clear that we are facing an implacable enemy whose avowed objective is world domination by whatever means and at whatever cost. There are no rules in such a game. If the United States is to survive, long-standing American concepts of "fair play" must be reconsidered. We must develop effective espionage and counterespionage services and must learn to subvert, sabotage and destroy our enemies by more clever, more sophisticated and more effective methods than those used against us. It may become necessary that the American people be made acquainted with, understand and support this fundamentally repugnant philosophy.

Eisenhower would later call intelligence a "distasteful but vital necessity." We hear this same argument repeatedly: *necessity*, in terms of national survival, may require the acceptance of "distasteful" and "repugnant" intelligence practices. It is true that throughout history, in times of fear, whether realistic or not, Americans *have* been willing to tolerate intelligence activities they might otherwise abhor in ordinary times. If a poll had been taken of the American people during the Eisenhower years, I think they would have agreed by a large majority that "long-standing American concepts of 'fair play' must be reconsidered."

An ideal democratic society would be open and transparent. It would not operate in secret. It would not infringe on the rights and freedoms of its citizens. And it would not use abroad techniques that it would eschew at home. But, as we have seen, American attitudes toward spying have varied widely over the years. When we felt safe within our borders, protected by two oceans and with friendly neighbors to the north and south, we could afford the luxury of moral purity and absolutism. We could reject spying as unethical and un-American. In periods of peril, however, we have turned to our intelligence agencies to protect us—and we have not always been fastidious about the techniques they have used.

U.S. government officials have not been bashful about the morally ambiguous nature of intelligence work. "There are few archbishops in espionage," said Allen Dulles. And Richard Helms, director of the CIA from 1966 to 1973, added succinctly, "We're not in the Boy Scouts." This attitude is fine when it is simply an acknowledgement of the reality of intelligence work—in other words, that it unavoidably encompasses unsavory elements. The trouble arises when intelligence practitioners seek out the unsavory for its own sake—and relish in it. Kent Pekel in his excellent article "Integrity, Ethics, and the CIA" in the spring 1998 issue of *Studies in Intelligence* quotes a senior CIA officer on this subject: "In this business, you start to get soiled when you *want* to do the 'dirty' part of espionage rather than feeling that you *must* do it to achieve noble goals."

Official U.S. attitudes toward spying reflect on occasion what I refer to as the very dangerous "righteousness trap." Defending our country against "fiendish foes" becomes an obsession, and zealotry easily seeps in. The threat appears to be so great and the enemy so evil that anything goes. The legal and moral constraints that govern the conduct of ordinary people do not apply to these self-proclaimed "champions and defenders" of our republic. This attitude was particularly prevalent in the heat of the Cold War in the 1950s, 1960s, and early 1970s, but there have been other examples of the "righteousness trap" since then. The conviction that "my cause is so just that I am above the rules" (*cf.* Cicero's adage "In time of war, the laws fall silent.") has led to some incredible errors in judgment, human rights abuses, and violations of the law.

It is not a pretty litany. It was this attitude that led to MKULTRA, the CIA's notorious drug research program from 1953 to 1963 that included administering mind-altering drugs to unwitting American subjects. It was this attitude that led to SHAMROCK, NSA's illegal interception of Americans' communications from the end of World War II until 1975. It was this attitude that led to COINTELPRO, the FBI's illegal program from 1956 to 1971 to surveil, disrupt, and "neutralize" political dissidence in the United States, including anti-war protesters, Communists, Black Nationalists, civil rights leaders, native American organizations, and others. At the CIA, James Jesus Angleton launched a series of illegal operations to ferret out what he thought was Communist treachery everywhere. HTLINGUAL was the CIA's illegal opening of mail to and from U.S. citizens. HONETOL was a frenzied mole hunt inside the CIA, a vicious campaign that destroyed many careers and lives. MHCHAOS was the CIA's illegal surveillance of U.S. antiwar activists during the Vietnam War. And it was this "righteous" mindset that led to perhaps the most egregiously illegal pseudo-intelligence operations in U.S. history: Watergate and Iran-Contra. The righteousness trap is seductive, and many otherwise dedicated and honest public servants have succumbed to it. It is an occupational hazard for national security professionals.

I want to dispel the notion that this phenomenon is in any way political. Although Democratic presidents have tended to be slightly more averse to espionage and covert action than Republicans, this has not always been the case. John F. Kennedy approved the Bay of Pigs operation, initiated the CIA's secret war in Laos, encouraged the murder of Ngo Dinh Diem in Vietnam, and pushed the CIA hard to assassinate Fidel Castro. Such a stalwart Democratic moralist as Jimmy Carter had become a strong supporter of covert action by the end of his term. *Every* U.S. president, in fact, from Truman to the present, has used covert action to accomplish what he wanted overseas without (if all goes well) showing the American hand or paying a political price.

It has been a roller coaster. I lived through the attacks on the CIA and FBI by the Church and Pike committees.[2] I have seen the CIA, FBI, NSA, and other U.S. intelligence agencies vilified in the press and elsewhere. I have heard numerous calls from U.S. politicians for the reform, break-up, or elimination of the CIA. I am aware that many universities in our country, including some today, have refused to allow CIA recruiters on campus. The U.S. intelligence community has its advocates and champions, to be sure, but large segments of the American population distrust it, want no part of it, and condemn its methods. They have seen the abuses of the past and are highly skeptical of intelligence operations in general. As a group, they are deeply concerned about infringements on civil liberties in the United States and human-rights violations abroad. Their voices deserve to be heard.

The final Church Committee report of 1976 is a good place to start:

> The Committee finds that covert action programs have been used to disrupt the lawful political activities of individual Americans and groups to discredit them, using dangerous and degrading tactics which are abhorrent in a free and decent society.

Philip Agee, a CIA case officer for twelve years, resigned from the Agency in 1969 to protest what he considered to be CIA violations of human rights in Latin America. He became a professional anti-CIA activist and agitator, moving around Europe for many years and eventually ending up in Cuba, where he lives today. His exposé *Inside the Company: CIA Diary*, was published in 1975. It includes this comment:

> In the CIA we justified our penetration, disruption, and sabotage of the left in Latin America—around the world for that matter—because we felt morality changed on crossing national frontiers. Little would we have considered applying these methods inside our own country.

Another CIA dissident, Ralph McGehee, who served as a CIA case officer for twenty-five years in Vietnam, Japan, Taiwan, Thailand, and the Philippines, had this to say in an interview with *Harper's Magazine* in September 1984:

> I believe that CIA covert operations, whether paramilitary or not, have helped destroy democracy around the world. By means of these operations, the CIA has replaced popular governments with brutal, murderous, U.S.-controlled military dictatorships that torture and kill their own citizens. Whether they involve paramilitary actions, political interventions, propaganda campaigns, or other kinds of deception, covert operations are all designed to benefit U.S.-based multinational corporations that expropriate the national resources of so-called target countries. These operations hurt the indigenous peoples and eventually Americans themselves . . .
>
> The United States cannot continue to destroy freedom throughout the world by means of covert operations without ultimately destroying it at home. Covert operations violate the rights of all Americans: they allow the president to take actions abroad that the American people would never support. By imposing strict rules of secrecy, the president threatens the constitutionally guaranteed freedoms of the American people. CIA covert operations are an immediate threat both to the peoples of other nations and to our own way of life.

There are many supporters of McGehee's point of view. Lots of Americans, however, disagree. They are grateful for what the U.S. intelligence community is doing and believe its actions are necessary for the protection of our country. The primary threat today is terrorism, not Soviet expansionism, but the reaction is similar: a willingness to tolerate extraordinary measures to counter what they perceive to be a threat to our survival—even at the cost of some of our values and liberties. They are willing to push the envelope. Their view is that we can remain faithful to our democratic principles and still fight terrorism with all the techniques at our disposal, both fair and foul. They do not think this is a time for what they would consider to be misplaced scrupulosity.

I will concede that spying is a dirty business. But my question is this: what's the alternative? No intelligence? Should we abstain from lying, cheating, deceiving, and manipulating and do without the intelligence they produce? Should we unilaterally discontinue espionage and covert action operations overseas? Should we put all our trust in overt sources of information, diplomacy, and the peaceful arts—and hope our enemies will not take advantage of us? Is that the real world? Would that be safe?

Probably not, but the debate still goes on. I think most of the debate today centers on *when*, not *if*, heavy-handed activities are justifiable. It is much easier to see the United States taking the gloves off against al Qaida than against less critical targets. Assassinating Osama bin Laden would be relatively uncontroversial. Assassinating Hugo Chavez, on the other hand, would most likely be considered criminal. There seems to be general agreement in the U.S. public that we live in perilous times and must work together to find a path toward peace and security. A basis for compromise therefore exists. Isn't there then some way to reconcile these two opposing views of the morality of spying? Can't we work together to draw a line acceptable to both sides? Can't the United States find a reasonable middle ground between fair and foul?

──SCENARIOS──

"Well, that was war, and only fools thought it could be waged with kid gloves on."
—Ashenden, British intelligence officer in Somerset Maugham's
The Hairless Mexican (1928)

"Non faciat malum, ut inde veniat bonum."
(You are not to do evil that good may come of it.)
— Juvenal

We are now going to enter a world that few Americans ever see or even know exists. The fifty scenarios that follow are taken from the real world of espionage and covert action. ████████████████████ ██ ████████████████████████████████████ All of the scenarios are fictionalized, and no conclusions about actual operations, past, present, or future, should be drawn from the names, places, or specific operational details presented in the scenarios. However, all of the scenarios raise moral issues that U.S. intelligence practitioners currently face or could conceivably face in the future.

For each of the fifty scenarios, I have asked a wide range of "commentators" to respond whether they consider the specified course of action morally acceptable or morally unacceptable. The commentators represent different political views, religions, professions, and ages. Many of them told me how much they struggled in making their decisions. Their responses show that serious, well educated, scrupulous, and patriotic Americans can and often do disagree on these issues. This is understandable, because these are not easy questions. But it does not mean we should simply throw up our hands and refuse to take a stand. The moral issues raised here or variations of them are debated by the media almost every day. I have been struck by how misinformed much of the discussion on these topics in the public arena has been. My hope is that this section of the book will encourage a debate on these important moral issues and eventually lead to clearer guidelines for U.S. intelligence personnel. Brief biographies of the commentators are included at the end of the book.

I encourage the reader to reach his or her own conclusion—yea or nay—after each scenario, before reading the opinions of the commentators. Then see if your opinion changes after reading their arguments. Some of the moral issues discussed are close calls, but please try to respond instinctively as you would if you were a senior policy maker or intelligence officer and had to approve or disapprove the operation. This is real life. Situations like these are occurring every day, and decision-makers in the field don't have the luxury of abstaining.

SCENARIO NO. 1:
HOMOSEXUAL BLACKMAIL

Rolando Montemayor is a Cuban Dirección General de Inteligencia (DGI)[1] officer under cover as second secretary at the Cuban mission to the United Nations in New York. He previously served in the Cuban embassy in Madrid, Spain, where the CIA successfully ran a double agent operation against him. The double agent, a young Spanish Communist journalist, reported to his CIA case officer that he strongly suspected that Montemayor was homosexual.

When Montemayor moves to New York, the CIA passes its information on him to the FBI. The FBI and CIA agree to conduct a joint operation against Montemayor in New York in an effort to recruit him as a penetration of the DGI. The FBI surveillance of Montemayor indicates that he frequents gay bars in New York and engages in promiscuous homosexual sex. Using telephone taps and infrared photography, the FBI acquires incontrovertible evidence of Montemayor's homosexual activities. Homosexuality[2] is grounds for dismissal from the DGI, and Montemayor has carefully concealed his sexual orientation from his family, friends, and colleagues.

———

Would it be morally acceptable for the CIA and FBI to attempt to recruit Montemayor by blackmailing him on the basis of his homosexuality?

Professor Richard Graving of the South Texas College of Law:
Yes. The circumstances and particular facts make this an easy case. Montemayor is himself a participant in the Great Game. Presumably it is a vocation he has willingly chosen. He may have tried to conceal his sexual orientation in Madrid, but his conduct in New York indicates a certain indifference, or at least carelessness. Montemayor has assumed the risks of his calling as well as the risks of his only semiprivate lifestyle.

Graduate student Roxana Botea of the Maxwell School at Syracuse University:

Yes. It is morally acceptable for the CIA and FBI to attempt to recruit Montemayor. While blackmail may be illegal and unethical domestically, there is no international prohibition against it. There are no established norms in international affairs that deal with blackmail on the basis of homosexuality. Given that Cuba is a long-time adversary of the United States, I see no problem in using these means to get information. I do, however, wonder whether Montemayor's fear that his superiors will discover his sexual orientation is greater than his loyalty to his country. I am not entirely convinced that negative incentives such as blackmail are effective long-term.

Former middle-school and high-school teacher Barbara Ziesche:

No. Montemayor's sexual preference should not be an issue in the CIA's recruitment endeavor. The fact that he did not reveal his homosexuality to the Cuban government should not give the CIA leverage to use it against him and to exploit him. Threats work, but is that how one wants to operate? Humanism, respect, cultural understanding, and truthfulness are some of the elements that make for a progressive and open-minded society. Too many times we go the other way and sell our soul for whatever the price will bear—a Faustian concept—but in the end, it will come back to get us. As a "mensch," I cannot condone this.

Former CIA officer Louise Corbin:

No. I have a close relative who is gay. I am sensitive to the repercussions of "outing" a homosexual; he is subject to ostracism by friends, family, and society in general—and to depression and suicidal ideation at a rate much higher than the general population. Under the best of circumstances, blackmail is repugnant. In this instance it is punitive, with potentially serious unforeseen ramifications. I cannot help feeling that my reactions are different today from what they would have been if I were still working at the Agency. By that I mean to say that, while working, it was easier to get caught up in the enthusiasm and to remain focused on one's mission, rather than looking critically at the ethical issues involved in the work. I am not suggesting that I was lacking a moral compass back then, just that my reactions to the scenarios today are much stronger and less influenced by the world of operations. I find now that I judge the cases first in an ethical context and only secondarily for their intelligence potential.

Former CIA officer Mary Lee Lieser:

Yes. If I reviewed a written proposal to blackmail Montemayor with the evidence at hand, I would approve it.

Dr. Geoffrey Tumlin, assistant director of the Center for Ethical Leadership at the Lyndon B. Johnson School of Public Affairs at the University of Texas:

Yes. Presumably Montemayor could provide useful information and approaching him about his homosexuality is morally acceptable. If he balks, the CIA can decide to escalate the threat to go public if that will compel him to cooperate. Of course, if the information is made public, Montemayor will likely be fired and hence made useless as a source.

Ph.D. student Margaretta Mathis:

No. Dirty politics.

Ph.D. student Margaret Meacham:

No. People cannot be controlled. If blackmail were used, Montemayor would simply bide his time, act cooperative, and then sabotage the operation as he is able. The issue of using a private matter to leverage Montemayor's cooperation is unacceptable, whether he is gay, straight, or bisexual. Ethically, it is wrong.

Former CIA officer John Hedley:

Yes, but counterproductive. Although this case, as labeled, is about blackmail pure and simple, I find myself troubled more by practicality than morality. Short of violence, it may not be morally unacceptable to try to elicit cooperation by threatening to reveal something that would cause extreme embarrassment or be career-threatening, if disclosed—be it sexual orientation, an extramarital affair, past criminal record, or whatever. But this is, in effect, a ransom demand: pay up in information or else. As a practical matter, the use of coercion to secure cooperation seems unlikely to be effective. An agent who hates and fears his case officer is not likely to be reliable or helpful.

U.S. Army Lieutenant Colonel Tony Pfaff:

Yes, though in this day and age it is a shame that anyone would care. Intelligence officers have an obligation to behave in such a way that they are not vulnerable to counterintelligence operations. However, this does not mean that other agencies cannot take advantage when they do. If a player on a sports team makes a mistake, we do not expect the other team not to take advantage of it. It may be chivalrous not to do so, but this is not required. This kind of blackmail would be impermissible if a nonintelligence person were involved.

Writer, poet, and teacher Burke Gerstenschlager:

No. It would be morally unacceptable to blackmail Montemayor for any reason. In the current socio-political climate, homosexuality is such a controversial topic that more "mundane" ethical issues are subject to being ignored or massaged in light of the current furor. Those who believe homosexuality is immoral may, in Montemayor's case, condone blackmail on the theory that the former is more immoral than the latter, and his homosexuality invalidates any moral protection. Blackmail, therefore, can be inverted and transformed into a "just" retributive act. Such a claim of "just desert" is sanctimonious. Declaring blackmail to be morally acceptable as the lesser of two evils creates a slippery slope upon which it is difficult to establish any solid ethical foundation. Montemayor's homosexuality should have no bearing whatsoever on the decision to recruit him. Blackmail, regardless of what he sought to hide, would be morally unacceptable because it would objectify him in such a way that he would become wholly dehumanized and transformed into a mere instrument and means for the CIA and the FBI. The only wage the CIA and FBI would pay Montemayor would be the promise to keep his secret. He would be faced with the situation of losing universal freedom in order to sustain his right to privacy. Privacy is never privacy when it is under the duress of extortion. This kind of extortion is tantamount to slavery and slavery is always morally unacceptable.

Author's comment:

CIA case officers are taught during their training that blackmail rarely works and therefore should generally be avoided. This rationale, however, is more practical than moral. As pointed out by Hedley and Meacham, a bitter and recalcitrant agent would probably produce unreliable intelligence and could be a control problem. A good case officer–agent relationship depends heavily on trust and respect. An argument could be made, however, that in the case of a hostile intelligence officer, like Montemayor, a long-term cooperative relationship would not be necessary. The blackmail pitch could be formulated as a demand for a one-time dump of information: "Identify all the Cuban intelligence officers in New York and tell us everything you know about Americans who have been recruited by the DGI. If you lie or hold back, we will know—and will use our information and photos against you." An approach like this might remove the practical obstacle, but would it pass the moral test?

SCENARIO NO. 2:
TROJAN HORSE

The Chinese foreign intelligence service, the Ministry for State Security

(MSS),[3] has as one of its primary operational objectives to steal defense-related technology from the United States. The Cox Report,[4] released in 1999, documented for the first time the extent of such technology theft by the MSS and analyzed the implications for U.S. national security.

The MSS uses a variety of illegal mechanisms and cutouts (clandestine intermediaries) to acquire embargoed U.S. technology. The CIA learns from a sensitive intelligence source that the MSS is using a French aerospace company as a front for illegal acquisitions. The French company purchases the items from a trading company in Long Beach, California, and then secretly transfers them to the Chinese. The same CIA source indicates that the MSS has just tasked its French cutout to acquire on its behalf an extremely sensitive U.S.–manufactured radar tracking system. The heart of the radar tracking system is a U.S. high-performance computer. This system has several different military applications and, as a result, cannot legally be sold to China. It also has a variety of legitimate uses in civilian aviation.

The CIA, using sensitive intelligence assets, has the capability of inserting a "doctored" or sabotaged computer into the illegal MSS technology acquisition channel—through Long Beach, to France, and then on to China. The sabotaged computer can be programmed so that the radar tracking system will fail at a critical moment of high usage. The false information could cause an accident for the military users, or, if the system is assigned by China to one of its major airports, could result in a civilian aircraft disaster. The CIA has no way of knowing the identity of the ultimate end user of the sabotaged computer.

———

Would it be morally acceptable for the CIA to sabotage the computer system for the radar tracking system without knowing whether the ultimate Chinese end user is military or civilian?

Practicing attorney Christopher Scherer:
No. Since the system is designed to fail, the act is morally unacceptable. The modified computer is a weapon that is utilized without reasonable knowledge of the likely victim. In that case, one cannot balance the moral import of the lives of the victims against that which is to be gained by their loss. This is morally unjustifiable by definition.

Ph.D. student Margaretta Mathis:
No. There are more direct means of stopping the technology transfer.

Ph.D. student Margaret Meacham:
No. The U.S. goal should be to shut down the Chinese efforts to ac-

quire our technology. With that said, the United States should not engage in sabotaging a computer when it could result in deaths. However, it is morally acceptable to give them a sabotaged computer with our spyware in it or re-engineered software that does not work at all. In other words, it is O.K. to sell them a lemon.

Professor Michael Porter of the University of Missouri:

No. It seems inconceivable that such a plan could ever be approved, primarily because doing so could cause harm to others. Those who would be hurt were not responsible for the situation that set up this draconian response.

Dr. Geoffrey Tumlin, assistant director of the Center for Ethical Leadership at the Lyndon B. Johnson School of Public Affairs at the University of Texas:

No. This civilian aircraft disaster is a risk that cannot be taken. An alternative would be to blow the cover of the French company.

Graduate student Russell Rodriguez of the George Bush School of Government and Public Service at Texas A&M University:

No. No matter the end user, there is a strong possibility that injury or death to innocents could result. A morally acceptable alternative would be to design the computer so that it catastrophically fails as soon as the system is assembled and powered up for the first time. This way, the Chinese would lose the time, money, and effort expended in acquiring the radar, but no human lives would be put at risk.

Professor Howard Prince, director of the Center for Ethical Leadership at the Lyndon B. Johnson School of Public Affairs at the University of Texas:

It depends. This would only be acceptable if we had a high degree of certainty that the computer was going to be used exclusively in military application—and then only if hostilities were imminent.

Former CIA officer Robert Mills:

It depends. What it would depend upon is the state of the military and political relationship between the United States and China at the time the scenario took place. If relations are improving and we feel China is less of a threat, we might not want to risk the chance that the computer failure would cause a civilian aircraft disaster. However, if there is a worsening of relations precipitated by something like a Chinese invasion of Taiwan, the risk of downing a civilian aircraft might become more acceptable. If there were to be hostilities between the United States and China, the possibility of a civilian airliner disaster would not be a moral issue given the fact that recent and future conflicts assume a certain number of collateral civilian casualties.

Author's comment:

These so-called Trojan Horse operations had their proponents throughout the Cold War, especially during the tenure of William Casey as director of the CIA. The Soviet KGB systematically stole U.S. computers, software, radars, aerospace technology, semiconductors, machine tools, and other technology to help the USSR keep pace militarily with the United States during the Cold War. The CIA learned in the early 1980s that the KGB was desperately trying to acquire illegally a sophisticated U.S. computer system to operate its vitally important Trans-Siberian gas pipeline. After sabotaging the computer so that it would alter the valve settings in the pipeline to a dangerously high level, the CIA allowed the "Trojan Horse" to be "stolen" by the KGB. As a result, the pipeline experienced a massive pressure buildup and exploded in the Siberian wilderness. There were no known casualties, but there easily could have been. This amazing story has been told for the first time in Thomas Reed's excellent book *At the Abyss: An Insider's History of the Cold War*, published in 2004. The purpose of this and similar operations was to create doubt in the minds of the Soviets about the reliability of illegally acquired U.S. technology, possibly deterring them from their thievery. A potential variation on the sabotage operations would be to insert secret software into computers illegally acquired by our adversaries, so that U.S. intelligence would have unlimited and undetected access to all the information in those computers.

SCENARIO NO. 3:
FALSE FLAG

Ali-Reza Rahami is a twenty-six-year-old official in the Iranian Ministry of Defense. He has personally observed the torture, imprisonment, and other ill treatment of students, journalists, and political dissidents by the Iranian security authorities. He is secretly opposed to such treatment as a matter of conscience, but he is afraid to express his views openly because of his fear of reprisals.

Robert Ericsson is a thirty-five-year-old Swedish-American dual citizen who has been recruited by the CIA as a nonofficial cover (NOC) officer in Iran. He works in Tehran under cover as an automotive parts dealer.

Ericsson meets Rahami at an automobile fair in Tehran and the two develop a friendship. As their trust deepens, Rahami confides in Ericsson that he is unhappy with the oppressive nature of the Iranian government. Rahami considers himself a loyal Iranian citizen but would welcome a transition to a gentler and more humane regime. After obtaining approval from CIA headquarters, NOC officer Ericsson attempts to recruit Rahami using a "false flag" approach.

The CIA would very much like to recruit Rahami as a penetration of the Iranian Ministry of Defense. Ericsson assesses Rahami as vulnerable to recruitment on the basis of his ideological aversion to torture and other oppressive activities by his government. He also knows that Rahami hates the United States. Ericsson, therefore, stresses his Swedish nationality and tells Rahami (falsely) that he secretly reports to the international organization Amnesty International. He says that Rahami can become a valuable confidential source for Amnesty International by providing inside information on exactly what is going on in the Iranian military and security services.

Would it be morally acceptable for the CIA to use Amnesty International as a "false flag" to recruit Rahami as an agent?

Former CIA officer Haviland Smith:

Yes. I have absolutely no moral problem with this. The key here is that Rahami clearly wants and is ready to do something about what he perceives to be injustices committed by his own government, even knowing it would be dangerous. In that respect, we are helping him while he helps us—a perfect symbiotic relationship. He is not being coerced, blackmailed or in any sense inveigled into telling us things he should not. If he were, this would not wash for me. Rahami is a perfect volunteer and our job with volunteers is to set the table so they can accomplish whatever goals they have on their minds. As long as those goals are consistent with ours, we are on solid ground. The only problem here, and it is a practical one, is that this is unlikely ever to turn into a stable operation. It is being conducted in a hostile environment with a young and probably immature agent who will find himself under increasingly heavy pressure. For that reason, we would have to consider the possibility that the operation might blow and that Amnesty International would be mentioned as the ostensible recipient of the information. I do not know if Rahami is in a position to give us information worth the risk of conducting the operation. If he is, or proves to be, we should stick with it. If not, we should let it die.

P.S. I hope Robert Ericsson is one hell of a savvy and experienced case officer, because this is likely to turn out to be a very difficult case.

Former CIA officer Burton Gerber:

No. A false flag recruitment of Rahami using Amnesty International as the ostensible sponsor fails my ethics test. While espionage against the Iranian Ministry of Defense is merited and false flag recruitment in certain circumstances is justified, the use of Amnesty International, an important international human rights organization, is not ethical. There are other means to be explored and implemented without bringing possible grievous harm to Amnesty International. For instance, Ericsson could represent a special group of individuals concerned with human rights violations, anxious to bring them to the world's attention. This so-called group would be without the international standing of Amnesty International, but an effective recruiter should be able to convince Rahami that this private group has the money and influence to inform other nations' leaders (Germany, France, etc.) of the true human rights situation in Iran and thereby help to alleviate it. An additional fact, not ethically based but operational, is that a flap involving CIA's use of Amnesty International would be very damaging to the Agency and to the United States.

Former CIA officer Gena Mills:

Yes. Given the importance of this target, this is a case where the end justifies the means. There would appear to be limited risk of this deception becoming unraveled (Amnesty International probably has its own stable of assets reporting to it secretly on a variety of subjects of interest). Once the recruitment has been finalized and Rahami is beginning to report, Ericsson could "clarify" that while he has no "official" association with Amnesty International, he does secretly pass information to it and it, in turn, may at times request clarification or additional information.

Former State Department officer John Salazar:

It depends. This would be morally acceptable only if Amnesty International provided its approval, which is unlikely. It would be preferable to ask the Swedes to recruit Rahami for us and to obtain the information through them.

Author Ralph Peters:

Yes, but foolish. It is too easy to check up on the employment credentials of someone who claims to work for a high-profile organization such as Amnesty International. I say morally acceptable, because Amnesty International, sad to say, takes politically driven positions. Thus, it counts as a player in the game, not an impartial benefactor.

Former CIA officer John Hedley:

Yes, but risky. It is not immoral to pretend to be someone you are not. This is what a NOC—or anyone under cover—does all the time. But practicality is the determining factor for me. The information the United States seeks about Iran would surely exceed the kind of limited information of interest to Amnesty International. Suspicion is bound to be aroused by tasking that goes beyond regime treatment of those apprehended by the Iranian security authorities. Thus, the risk of using this kind of cover outweighs the prospective gain.

Retired U.S. Navy Captain Richard Life:

Yes. If such a fabrication convinces Rahami to provide unique information not otherwise available to the CIA, then the goals of both the United States government and Amnesty International are likely to be achieved. Hopefully, over time the president's national security team and select allies will use the intelligence to pressure Iran into dramatically changing its policies and practices regarding human rights.

Professor Abraham Clearfield:

No. Amnesty International is the moral conscience of the world. It is totally impartial and fair in its assessments of oppressive treatment by governments of their citizens. If the CIA uses Amnesty International as a front for intelligence gathering, the oppressive governments will have an excuse to dismiss the judgments against them, citing Amnesty International as a tool of the CIA. It is unlikely that the information provided by Rahami could be used by the CIA to lighten the suffering of the dissidents, but actions by Amnesty International could bring world pressure to bear on the Iranians and perhaps result in some easing of the torture of the prisoners.

Author's comment:

False flag approaches definitely have a role to play in espionage operations. The CIA on occasion targets a foreigner for recruitment but knows that the potential agent would never knowingly work for the CIA or cooperate willingly with the U.S. government. This individual, for example, might be vehemently anti-American. For that reason, the CIA might decide on a "false flag" recruitment approach, whereby the agent never knows that he or she is actually being recruited by the United States and the CIA. The CIA officer making the recruitment pitch poses as a representative of the false flag country or organization. These are very delicate operations requiring excellent linguistic skills, cultural awareness, and acting ability. It might be the case, for example, that an African official would never work for the

Americans but might work for the French. A Brazilian leftist might never work for the CIA, but might be willing to work for the Cuban DGI. A CIA officer uses a variation on false flag operations when he or she poses as a representative of an international organization, a think tank, or a commercial firm. The agent might be induced to provide useful information on that basis, but would never knowingly provide information to the CIA. Both the CIA and the FBI are very adept at false flag operations.

The FBI has on several occasions made successful use of false flag operations for counterintelligence purposes. In the early 1990s, the FBI developed fragmentary information that a former NSA (National Security Agency) employee, Robert Lipka, had worked for the Soviet KGB from 1964 to 1974. This information was insufficient for prosecution, and there seemed to be little likelihood that the FBI could obtain additional evidence of Lipka's espionage. In a brilliant false flag operation, an FBI counterintelligence expert, posing as a Russian intelligence officer, made contact with Lipka, now a coin dealer and heavy gambler, and lured him into discussing his past work on behalf of the KGB. On the basis of these admissions, Lipka was arrested in 1996, convicted of espionage, and sentenced to eighteen years in prison. In what I think is a hilarious footnote to this operation, the Russian intelligence service, the SVRR,[5] actually had the chutzpah to complain about the FBI's false flag tactics against Lipka. An SVRR spokeswoman said this in 1996:

> Intelligence services maintaining partner-like relations should invariably observe the unwritten rules of honor, including that of not recruiting people under an alien flag . . . the FBI broke these rules.

That's a noble sentiment, but I can easily come up with dozens of examples of how the Russians themselves violated the "unwritten rules of honor" in their operations against the United States.

In 1989, the disaffected former CIA officer Philip Agee was used by the Cuban DGI in a false flag operation against a CIA employee stationed in Mexico City. Agee posed as a member of the CIA's Inspector General's office and told the CIA employee that he was conducting a sensitive investigation of alleged wrongdoing in the CIA office. He asked for the employee's help and began to question her about CIA personnel and the activities of the Mexico City office. This cleverly designed and executed operation was foiled when the CIA employee became suspicious and confided in two of her colleagues. Agee, who now lives in Havana, denies any involvement in the operation.

SCENARIO NO. 4:
HIT TEAM

The Federal Bureau of Investigation Building at 935 Pennsylvania Avenue in Washington, D.C., is severely damaged by a truck bomb. More than 700 FBI employees are killed in the attack and 1,000 are injured. Highly reliable intelligence sources, including SIGINT, provide incontrovertible proof that the bombing was the work of Dr. Abdullah Ali Rahman, a senior operative of al Qaida and a disciple of Osama bin Laden. Rahman is in hiding in Sudan, where he is being protected by Islamic fundamentalist supporters. The CIA finds out from intelligence sources exactly where Rahman is and has the capability of inserting a hit team into Sudan. Other options, such as kidnapping Rahman or appealing to the Sudanese authorities for assistance in his capture and extradition, are excluded for operational and political reasons.

———

Would it be morally acceptable for the CIA hit team to assassinate Rahman inside Sudan?

Pastor Tom Nelson of Denton Bible Church in Denton, Texas:
Yes. This is warfare. Rahman is a soldier. Take him out as you would any enemy soldier.

Former FBI senior official Oliver "Buck" Revell:
Yes. If we are truly at war against terrorism (actually the war is against radical Islam, usually termed Jihadist, since terrorism is but a tactic used by this element) and we have knowledge that an active leader, who has blood on his hands, is only reachable by a "hit team," then I would deem this action necessary and "morally acceptable." I would call this unit a "special operations team," as its actions would be legal in time of war, and not a "hit team," which connotes criminal activity.

Former CIA officer Richard Corbin:
Yes. While in general I oppose extrajudicial punishment, I believe it would be morally justified in this case because judicial punishment is not an option. Assassination such as this should, however, be a last resort. Since Rahman is a disciple of Osama bin Laden, we could reasonably expect him to strike again. The assassination operation must not kill innocent people.

Graduate student Sarah Forbey of the George Bush School of Government and Public Service at Texas A&M University:

No. First and foremost, assassination undermines law and order. It leads to the abandonment of the peaceful system of conflict resolution the United States wishes to model and encourage. In dire need, as to stave off violence, an assassination is tenable, but based on U.S. executive authority alone it becomes vigilante justice. An independent, knee-jerk assassination of Rahman would be interpreted as tit-for-tat, demeaning the legitimacy of our government and telegraphing that our methods are no more founded on law and the democratic will of the people than those of the terrorists. In keeping with Kant's Categorical Imperative, if all states engaged in assassinations, world order would be gravely threatened.

Professor Harry Mason of the Patterson School at the University of Kentucky:

Yes (class vote). I discussed this scenario with my graduate class on National Intelligence at the Patterson School and asked the students to vote. The students are well traveled, speak several languages, and in most cases have lived abroad. Two are in the military and just returned from combat in Iraq. I try to steer clear of politics, but I do know that one student was very active in the Gore campaign and another works in the local office of Democratic Representative Ben Chandler. In general, I would say a conservative to moderate political view accounts for half to two-thirds of the class. The class voted 17-0 to authorize the CIA hit team to assassinate Rahman in Sudan. Due to the severity of the attack on the FBI facility there was little dissent.

Dr. Randy Everett, M.D., from Fort Collins, Colorado:

Yes. The incontrovertible nature of the intelligence makes this easier to decide. In the absence of a nation-state, the United States has declared war on Islamic fundamentalist terrorists. These terrorists have again attacked Americans on American soil and the United States has put them on notice. Al Qaida, other terrorists, and the countries harboring them have opened themselves up to attack from the United States. The current lawlessness in the Sudan and the international condemnation, however toothless, of the genocide there should make such a CIA operation more palatable to our allies and the international community. International "approval," however, is not necessary for moral acceptability.

Former FBI special agent Stanley Pimentel:

Yes. Ideally, we would kidnap Rahman from Sudan and return him to the United States to face prosecution. The U.S. Supreme Court has ruled such a kidnapping constitutional. In this scenario, however, this objective cannot be carried out successfully due to operational and political reasons.

Therefore, to realize justice for all those killed and wounded in the attack and to send a message to the terrorists that their actions will not be tolerated, assassination is the only viable option. If we fail to assassinate this individual, we send a message that we are powerless to prevent an attack against us and unable to exact retribution for terrorist acts. We must retaliate, just as the Israelis have done over the years.

Professor Terry H. Anderson of Texas A&M University:

Yes, but incontrovertible proof is the key. The world, with only a few exceptions, supported the U.S. invasion of Afghanistan to capture or kill Osama bin Laden. Iraq is an entirely different issue—and immoral.

Archbishop J. Michael Miller, C.S.B., secretary of Catholic education at the Vatican in Rome:

No. I find your scenario interesting—but disturbing. It confronts the question of using evil for good. On this point, of course, the Catholic moral tradition has a clear response: we can never do evil, even for a good purpose. The end does not justify the means. Please see the encyclical of Pope John Paul II on this point, *Veritatis Splendor*.

Author's comment:

The above results are consistent with what I have heard in discussions with numerous groups around the country. The 17-0 vote at the University of Kentucky is extreme, but probably not surprising. The majority, perhaps a large majority, of the American people do not object to the idea of assassinating terrorists who have conducted terrorist attacks against the United States. A *Newsweek* poll in December 2001 showed that 65 percent of Americans favored giving U.S. military and intelligence personnel the authority to assassinate terrorists in the Middle East, and there were majorities in the poll for carrying out such assassinations in Asia, Africa, and Europe as well. I doubt that American public opinion has shifted much since then.

When the United States used a Predator drone armed with a Hellfire missile to assassinate six suspected terrorists in Yemen in November 2002, there was virtually no media or public protest. The primary target of that operation, Qaed Salim Sinan al-Harethi, was suspected of being behind the terrorist attack on the U.S.S. *Cole* in October 2000. The five other victims in the car incinerated by the CIA missile included a U.S. citizen suspected of involvement in a terrorist cell in Buffalo, New York. No one seemed to mind that he and the other suspected terrorists were killed.

The "Use of Force" Resolution that Congress passed on September 14, 2001, probably did not apply. That resolution specifically limited the use of force to the U.S. armed forces and only against "nations, organizations, or persons" the president had determined "planned, authorized, committed, or aided the terrorist attacks that occurred on September 11, 2001, or harbored such organizations or persons." There were allegations that al-Harethi had coordinated communications for the 9/11 attacks, but they were unsubstantiated and the United States was never pressed to provide a legal justification for the attack.

The same was true when another U.S. Predator Hellfire was used to assassinate the senior al Qaida operative Haithem al-Yemeni in Pakistan in May 2005. The American public seemed to take that assassination in stride, with no perceptible debate on whether the U.S. action was legal, let alone moral.

The U.S. government has been no stranger to assassinations. The CIA covert action operation to overthrow the leftist government of Jacobo Arbenz in Guatemala in 1954 initially included widespread assassinations of Guatemalan leftists (to be carried out by Guatemalan hit teams) as part of the plan. This aspect of the operation was eventually canceled and no assassinations took place, but the Eisenhower administration did not balk when the idea was first proposed. Eisenhower also approved a plan to assassinate the Congolese leader Patrice Lumumba in 1960. This plan, too, was scrapped before being carried out, and a senate committee later found there was no proof the CIA had been involved in the actual assassination of Lumumba in 1961.

The Kennedy brothers ordered the CIA to assassinate Fidel Castro, and several assassination plans, mostly harebrained, were put in motion. Attorney General Robert Kennedy, in particular, seemed to have no legal or moral qualms about using the CIA to murder the Cuban leader.

Operation Phoenix in Vietnam in the 1970s is alleged to have included massive assassinations of Viet Cong cadres as a key part of the plan. There certainly were abuses, including summary executions in the field, but the true nature of Operation Phoenix is still being debated. The most compelling book on the subject is Mark Moyar's *Phoenix and the Birds of Prey*.

Disclosure of CIA wrongdoing by the Church Committee in 1975, including the many attempts by the CIA to assassinate Fidel Castro, led to President Gerald Ford's Executive Order 11905 of 1976, which stated that "no employee of the United States Government shall engage in, or conspire to engage in, political assassination." President Ronald Reagan extended this ban on assassination in 1981 with Executive Order 12333, which is still the guiding authority today:

2.11 Prohibition on Assassination. No person employed by or acting on behalf of the United States Government shall engage in, or conspire to engage in, assassination.

How is it then that the U.S. bombing of Libya in 1986 was not a violation of Executive Order 12333? U.S. bombers attacked several nonmilitary targets where Libyan leader Moammar Gadhafi was thought to be present, killing his fifteen-month-old adopted daughter in the process. President Reagan ordered the attack in retaliation for Gadhafi's role in the bombing of La Belle Disco in Berlin, a nightclub frequented by American servicemen.

How is it that the missile attacks on Saddam Hussein's bunkers and residences in Iraq in 1991 and 1993 were not violations of Executive Order 12333? Or the Predator attacks in Yemen and Pakistan in 2002 and 2005? And what about the assassination of Dr. Rahman in Sudan, as posited above? Wouldn't that be a violation of Executive Order 12333? The law, whatever it is and however it is being interpreted, can easily be changed. The question is whether assassinating Rahman would be *moral*.

The morality of using hit teams to assassinate terrorists was the focus of Steven Spielberg's movie *Munich*, released in December 2005. In response to the massacre of eleven Israeli athletes and managers at the Munich Olympics of 1972 by the terrorist group Black September, Israel's Mossad formed a special hit team to track down and assassinate eleven Palestinians who either participated in or helped to plan the murders. Spielberg, who calls his movie a "prayer for peace," takes the point of view that retaliatory assassinations are counterproductive and engender even more violence. I enjoyed parts of *Munich* as a thriller, but was put off by the heavy moralizing and many inaccuracies. In particular, I found Spielberg's insinuation that the CIA paid off Black September to buy protection from terrorist attacks on Americans to be not only absurd, but insulting. It's not surprising that Spielberg gets so many things wrong, because he based his movie on George Jonas's sensationalized and error-ridden book *Vengeance*, published in 1984. Fortunately, readers interested in learning the real facts of the Munich massacre and the Israeli hit team can read Aaron Klein's fine book *Striking Back*, published in 2005.

SCENARIO NO. 5:
TORTURE

In a cave in the Tora Bora region of eastern Afghanistan, U.S. forces capture Muhammad Azam Iqbal, the mastermind of several terrorist attacks against U.S. military and diplomatic installations in Afghanistan and Pakistan. Intelligence sources confirm that Iqbal was personally involved in the planning and funding of terrorist operations against Americans, including the recent bombing of the U.S. consulate in Lahore. Eighteen Americans and twenty-two local Pakistani consulate employees died in that attack alone. The capture of Iqbal is a coup for U.S. intelligence. There is little doubt that he has extensive information on terrorist communications, financing, planning for future attacks, and the identities of other terrorists. Iqbal is delivered by the U.S. military to a CIA detention center for interrogation.

Efforts to elicit useful intelligence from Iqbal using normal interrogation techniques are unsuccessful. He is administered sodium pentothal and sodium amytal against his will, but these drugs also fail to produce the desired results. If Iqbal's information is to be actionable, it must be extracted from him quickly. Torture seems to be the only option. The following torture techniques are available to make him talk:

1) Forcing him to stand in bare feet on bricks or stones for long periods.
2) Shaking him abruptly back and forth.
3) Kicking or beating him with fists and clubs.
4) Forcing him to watch the torture of other prisoners.
5) Dislocating his joints.
6) Feigning drowning by forcing him under water.
7) Burning him with cigarettes, lighters, or torches.
8) Poking him with an electric cattle prod.
9) Attaching electrodes to his body, especially his genitals, and shocking him.

———

Would it be morally acceptable to use full-fledged torture, including beatings and electric shock, to obtain Iqbal's information on terrorist plans, funding, and personnel?

Rabbi Peter Tarlow:

It depends. The term torture covers at least three different and separate concepts: the use of cruel behavior for sadistic pleasure; the use of cruel behavior to force a confession (past event); and the use of extreme force or induced pain to prevent a tragedy from occurring (future event). Our concern here is with the third form of torture. I will classify the aggressive physical or psychological questioning used solely for the purpose of saving non-combatant lives by the Biblical term *inui* (from the root *ayin, nun, heh*, meaning "to induce an answer").

There is an inherent issue of validity. How do we know that the person to whom *inui* is applied can produce the needed information? The question of validity is of major importance because the historical record reveals that often people placed in situations of intense physical and mental pressure will produce invalid answers simply to stop the pain. In such cases, no information would be more valuable than false information.

In the case of Iqbal, I will assume the following: (1) those administering the "medicine" are doing so for purposes of *inui* only and are people who do so for the highest ethical and moral reasons; (2) the policy has a high degree of reliability and consistency of action; and (3) there is an expected high degree of validity in the information to be obtained.

Even with all the above conditions, my heart tells me that any form of pain used to force an answer is wrong. I also realize, however, that war is not an action of the heart but of the mind. It is counter-productive for me to take a position that may cost the lives of hundreds or thousands of innocents.

Rabbinic Judaism recognizes this division between the head and the mind by classifying war into three categories: Milchemet Malchut, Milchemet Mitzvah, and Milchemet Chovah. The first category, Milchemet Malchut, is war for the aggrandizement of the government. In such a war no form of torture or *inui* is permitted. Milchemet Mitzvah is a war fought for G'd. Since the only Milchemet Mitzvah permitted in Judaism is against pure Amalekites and the last pure Amalekite died during the reign of King Saul, this type of war is no longer an issue. This means that the only form of war to be considered here is Milchemet Chovah, a war of obligation to save one's life. I will assume that the decision to torture Iqbal comes under Milchemet Chovah and is therefore open to ethical and moral discussion.

In such a war, the following principles apply:

- The principle of Pikuah Nefesh (saving of life). This principle states that under the assumption of a good inclination and only for the purpose of saving lives religious laws may be broken to save lives.

- Equality of blood. We may not shed another's blood simply to save our own. This second principle appears to contradict the first, but it does not. From the perspective of war, the issue is the saving of noncombatants' lives. It is not a question of whether U.S. blood is "redder" than someone else's blood, but rather of whether we can save innocent life.

- A life saved is preferable to two lives lost. Thus, we do everything possible to save as many lives as possible, without losing sight of the fact that the enemy is also made *b'tzelem Elokim*, in the image of G'd. We seek to protect the innocent while at the same time recognizing the common humanity that unites us to our enemy.

In summary, therefore, the following questions need to be asked with respect to the torture of Iqbal:

(1) Will the intelligence gained directly save lives or will it be of secondary importance?

(2) Is the action for reasons of Milchemet Chovah and not Milchemet Malchut?

(3) Will the torture be purely *inui*, that is, the minimal amount of pain applied for the purpose of saving lives?

If the answer to all three is yes, then some form of *inui* would be permitted.

Ph.D. student Margaret Meacham:

No. The use of drugs, hypnosis, and psychological methods are acceptable. However, it is always unacceptable for the United States to use physical torture when it thinks it is expedient to do so but denounces all other countries that use the same tactics. We have fought several wars in the past and will fight other wars in the future. Let us not set a precedent for such immoral treatment, nor be hypocritical by saying one thing in public and doing another thing in private.

Professor Howard Prince, director of the Center for Ethical Leadership at the Lyndon B. Johnson School of Public Affairs at the University of Texas:

Yes. This appears to be a case where graduated torture would be justified. Iqbal has a history of killing and is at the heart of a terrorist network of destruction. It is likely that he has future attacks in various stages of planning, and if these could be aborted many lives might be saved.

Pastor Tom Nelson of Denton Bible Church in Denton, Texas:

No. That means to that end lowers a nation. We should see ourselves as above torture.

Former CIA officer William Lieser:

Yes, but with great misgivings. While I find torture morally reprehensible in most situations, I find myself torn in this case by the prospect of a significant loss of lives if information is not obtained from this murderous source. I would find it difficult to face the families or colleagues of any person killed or maimed in such a terrorist act if I had not done everything in my power to prevent it. I would probably authorize escalating forms of coercion against Iqbal in the hope of getting from him the information we need to save lives.

Ph.D. student Margaretta Mathis:

No. Perhaps because I knew a former POW who was tortured during the Vietnam War I do not think any form of torture is morally acceptable.

Professor Mark Moyar of the U.S. Marine Corps University:
Yes, but not directly. The United States should not engage in torture as a general rule, but in the case of a foreign national who has committed heinous acts against the United States and refuses to speak with interrogators, the United States would be justified in allowing its Pakistani and Afghan allies to use whatever methods they chose. Iqbal was not fighting overtly, so he is not a prisoner of war and is not protected by the Geneva Convention. The human lives that could be spared through Iqbal's interrogation outweigh any concerns about his well-being.

Dr. Geoffrey Tumlin, assistant director of the Center for Ethical Leadership at the Lyndon B. Johnson School of Public Affairs at the University of Texas:
It depends. This is a tough case. Ultimately, I would have to be quite certain that "full-fledged torture" would extract actionable intelligence that would most likely prevent the future loss of life. If I could make that determination, I would authorize torture.

Author's comment:
I find it interesting that there seems to be a greater revulsion on the part of Americans to torturing terrorists than to killing them. My informal surveys around the country have been consistent on this point. Tracking down and killing terrorists is generally accepted, whereas any hint of torture by the U.S. military or the CIA overseas produces a firestorm of criticism and demands for accountability. It is remarkable, therefore, that such a renowned legal expert and civil libertarian as Alan Dershowitz in his book *Why Terrorism Works* argues that the torture of terrorists in certain "ticking bomb" cases can be morally justified in the interests of saving lives. Many of our closest allies have resorted to torture in times of great national stress and peril: the French in Algeria, the British[6] in Northern Ireland, and the Israelis in the Middle East. The U.S. has struggled in its efforts to define what constitutes torture and when, if ever, it might be justified. In a now-notorious 2002 memo to the White House, the U.S. Department of Justice advised that the torture of terrorists could be justified in certain extreme cases. The memo stated that "necessity and self defense" could legitimize torture if American lives were at stake. The definition of torture in the memo was vague, leaving a great deal of ambiguity about how the guidelines would actually be implemented in the field. The Bush administration quickly backed away from the memo when it was publicly disclosed and has consistently

stated that it abides by international conventions and treats all prisoners humanely.

Nevertheless, President Bush initially resisted efforts by Senator John McCain in 2005 to introduce legislation that would ban "cruel, inhuman, or degrading" treatment of foreign detainees. The White House argued that it was duty-bound to protect American citizens from terrorist attacks and should not have its hands tied by restrictive legislation. Various administration officials, including Vice President Richard Cheney, National Security Adviser Stephen Hadley, and CIA Director Porter Goss, repeated earlier statements that the United States does not engage in "torture," but defended the administration's practice of using "innovative" and "enhanced" interrogation techniques. They claimed that these techniques work and have been responsible for obtaining valuable information from terrorist suspects. A member of the Senate Intelligence Committee was quoted as saying that "enhanced interrogation techniques" had been successful in the questioning of Khalid Sheikh Mohammed, the principal mastermind of the 9/11 attack, and in obtaining from him information that thwarted future terrorist attacks against Americans.

Since much of the debate revolved around semantics, the CIA was pressed to clarify exactly what it meant by "enhanced interrogation techniques." According to press reports, the CIA maintained a secret network of detention centers in various countries around the world where terrorist suspects were held and interrogated. Goss told the press in November 2005, "We use lawful capabilities to collect vital information, and we do it in a variety of unique and innovative ways, all of which are legal and none of which are torture." CIA officials stated that the then-permissible techniques included shaking and striking the prisoners, forcing them to stand while handcuffed and shackled for up to forty hours, holding them naked in a "cold cell" at 50 degrees and periodically dousing them with cold water, and "waterboarding" them. Waterboarding consists of attaching a prisoner to an inclined board, covering his face with plastic wrap, and pouring water over him, creating in him instant panic and an overwhelming sensation of drowning. Reportedly, it was waterboarding that broke Khalid Sheikh Mohammed.

According to a public opinion poll released by *Newsweek* magazine in November 2005, 58 percent of Americans would approve of the use of torture to prevent a future terrorist attack. Nevertheless, President Bush, facing a strongly negative bipartisan political reaction and scathing editorials, announced in December 2005 that he would no longer object to Senator McCain's antitorture legislation. He said his support of the legislation would "make it clear to the world that this government does not torture and that we adhere to the international convention of torture, whether it be here at home or abroad."

SCENARIO NO. 6:
KIDNAPPING AND TORTURE BY SURROGATES

Egyptian citizen Khalid Nabeel El Kadir is a leading member of the violent terrorist group Egyptian Jihad. El Kadir runs a large cell of this organization in Sofia, Bulgaria, a cell that U.S. intelligence officials consider one of the most dangerous terrorist operations in Europe. One day, as El Kadir is walking down the street in downtown Sofia, Bulgarian security agents sneak up behind him, slip a burlap bag over his head, immobilize him with chloroform, and throw him into the back of a nearby van. Watching and supervising this operation from a short distance away are officers of the U.S. CIA.

El Kadir is taken to a safehouse[7] outside Sofia, where he is subjected to two days of interrogation by CIA officers and beatings by his Bulgarian guards. Next, he is put aboard a CIA-chartered plane and flown to Cairo, where the CIA's good friends in Egyptian intelligence are keenly interested in meeting with this senior member of the Egyptian Jihad. In Cairo, El Kadir is subjected to more beatings and torture by the Egyptian authorities. CIA officers do not participate directly in the beatings and torture.

The interrogation of El Kadir and the military trial that follows produce lengthy confession transcripts on the activities of the Egyptian Jihad around Europe. Although El Kadir's confession is coerced, it is consistent with other information and soon leads to putting the Sofia terrorist cell out of business. El Kadir is executed.

————

Was it morally acceptable for the CIA to plan, supervise, and fund the kidnapping of El Kadir and to turn him over to Egyptian security authorities for torture and interrogation?

Former CIA officer Eugene Culbertson:
Yes. It was morally acceptable because El Kadir was an Egyptian citizen. To contemplate the morality of his treatment by his own people would be to define their cultural concept of "torture" and to judge it in comparison with our own. The CIA cannot impose American mores and laws on a counterpart intelligence service of a sovereign nation with respect to the policies and laws governing that nation's own citizenry.

Undergraduate student Aaron Tatyrek of Texas A&M University:
Yes. El Kadir is a threat to American interests abroad and could harm

the interests of our allies as well. Having the CIA organize this process while abstaining from the torture and execution aspects of this mission is justifiable. It allows us to take out a significant threat while at the same time preserving our public face of operating ethically.

Former United States Information Agency (USIA) officer John Williams:

It depends. On the one hand, it is not the business of the United States to campaign for the elimination of interrogation methods we deem distasteful and even morally repugnant. After all, such practices have continued for thousands of years in many parts of the world and would not in any case be amenable to alteration simply because the United States is against them. On the other hand, we stand as an international champion of human rights and so cannot be indifferent to practices we find questionable. On a more practical level, in the world that now exists, extreme methods or the threat of their use may be justifiable in the hands of third parties when these measures could be critical to saving lives. In the case of El Kadir, I believe that justification for the operation described lies in the question of whether U.S. lives and property were in extreme and immediate danger. If the Sofia cell had a history of operating against European or other non–U.S. assets, I believe any such operation should have been the responsibility of those under the most immediate threat. If, however, there was evidence of a plot against the United States, this action was defensible. All this is quite apart from the question of whether extreme methods can be relied upon to consistently yield useful, actionable results. As we are aware, a considerable body of evidence suggests that torture, or the threat of its use, is often counterproductive. In this scenario, however, it seems to have served its purpose.

Former CIA polygrapher John Sullivan:

It depends. In my career, I never tortured or even witnessed the torture of anyone, but I have certainly tested people who have been tortured. During Iran-Contra, I was in Latin America when a CIA case officer told me that the "locals" would stick a soldering iron up their suspects' asses and turn it on. The case officer was genuinely disgusted by this, but did not see what he could do about it. The line between moral and immoral can sometimes get blurred. If crossing that line can save lives, is it justified? My tendency is to say no, yet I know that if doing so would save my sons' lives, I would probably do it.

Graduate student Russell Rodriguez of the George Bush School of Government and Public Service at Texas A&M University:

Yes. El Kadir is a terrorist and a murderer. If he had been captured unilaterally by the Bulgarians, the chances are his fate would have been the same, that is, transfer to Egypt. All the CIA is doing is speeding up the process. The many lives that can be saved justify this action. I do not agree with torture in principle, but, in this case, El Kadir is subject to the laws and procedures of Bulgaria (where he is captured) and of Egypt (where he is interrogated and tried).

Professor Terry H. Anderson of Texas A&M University:

It depends on what national and international laws El Kadir has broken, which is not clear. I do not think the current practice of the Bush administration of capturing "suspected terrorists" and evading U.S. law by handing them over to other nations for beating and torture is moral.

Author's comment:

The practice of sending individuals like El Kadir to third countries for interrogation and trial is known as rendition. Renditions have been extremely controversial. Critics contend that they are used by the U.S. government to outsource torture and are a violation of human rights. Defenders of the practice argue that renditions are necessary to get terrorists off the streets, to obtain intelligence, and to ensure that justice is done in cases where a trial in the United States is not feasible for lack of evidence or other reasons. Renditions are quicker, quieter, and easier than formal legal extraditions, which can be protracted, uncertain, and politically charged. Exact numbers are hard to come by, but it is clear the United States has been involved in dozens of renditions since September 11, 2001. At a press conference in April 2005, President Bush was asked about renditions and gave the following answer: "We operate within the law and we send people to countries where they say they're not going to torture the people." The truth, however, is that the United States has regularly sent suspected terrorists to places like Egypt, Jordan, Saudi Arabia, Pakistan, and Syria, where allegations of torture have been commonplace. Most intelligence officials are well aware of this and recognize the dirty underside of renditions but still believe, in some cases, that they are an essential tool in the war on terrorism.

A subsidiary question is whether it is moral to accept and to use intelligence known or suspected of having been acquired by a friendly country through torture. Should the U.S. as a matter of principle reject intelligence that its allies obtained from terrorist suspects by torturing them? Would it be morally acceptable, in cases like that, for the U.S. simply to take the intelligence, but not to ask too many questions about how it was obtained? Other countries face the same issue. In late 2005, former British diplomat Craig

Murray charged that Britain accepted and used intelligence from Uzbekistan that it knew had been obtained by torture. A legal adviser to the British government, quoted in the *New York Times*, said it was "not illegal to obtain and to use intelligence acquired by torture." He added that information acquired by torture would not be admissible in a British legal proceeding but could still be used by the government for intelligence purposes.

SCENARIO NO. 7:
TRUTH SERUM

Ismael Aziz, a high-ranking member of al Qaida, is arrested as he is trying to enter the U.S. illegally from Canada. A search of his belongings provides overwhelming evidence that Aziz is part of a major new terrorist attack being planned against the United States. The FBI has strong reason to believe that he knows when and where the attack is to take place and who else is involved, but he refuses to talk.

Would it be morally acceptable for the FBI to use drugs on Aziz against his will in an effort to elicit information from him on the planned attack?

Former FBI senior executive John Guido:

Yes. The keys here are "overwhelming evidence," "major new terrorist attack," and "strong reason to believe that he knows when and where." Preventing such an attack could save many lives, which would justify use of some extraordinary techniques, such as drugs, to obtain the necessary information. The justification would be even stronger if there was an indication that the attack was imminent. In this instance, the goal is to prevent loss of life, and there is no permanent physical harm to Aziz. The information should be used only to prevent the attack, not to prosecute Aziz for a crime.

Former CIA polygrapher John Sullivan:

Yes. Although I have some problem with truth serum in terms of efficacy, I have none, at least in the case of Aziz, on moral or ethical grounds. The consequences of not getting the information are such that anything, excluding torture, is on the table. If the information has to be obtained, this is probably the most humane way to try to extract it. In my thirty-one years in the CIA, I had no experience at all with sodium pentothal or any other type of truth serum, but I know we considered it unreliable. In this case, the possibility of saving thousands of lives outweighs any pangs of conscience I might have.

Former CIA and Army officer Jack Bosley:

Yes. In my view, when traditional moral issues and defense of the nation are in conflict, defense of the nation prevails. In the case of Aziz, our reasons are not to find out whether he was true to his wife or fudged on his accountings, but to defend the realm. The use of truth serum is a standard technique of many foreign investigative services. Examples are France, Britain, Germany, Russia, India, and Israel. The fact that other nations use this method does not justify similar action by the U.S. government, but it will soften the PR impact when the circumstances become public knowledge.

Former FBI special agent Stanley Pimentel:

Yes. The most important factor is the prevention of a catastrophic event that could take the lives of dozens of persons and cause major destruction of property. If obtaining the information from Aziz is the only way to prevent this attack, then injecting him with a truth serum would be morally acceptable. Current conventions, treaties, laws, and regulations prohibit the administering of drugs to suspects to elicit confessions or information. To get around these restrictions and to be in a position to administer truth serum to an unwilling subject like Aziz, a presidential executive order or laws enacted by Congress would be required. The overall good of the majority of people would dictate a change in the current restrictions.

Professor Terry H. Anderson of Texas A&M University:

Yes. There is overwhelming evidence of an attack to kill innocent civilians.

Former CIA officer John Hedley:

Yes. Routine police arrests in the U.S. often require restraint against the detainee's will, well before guilt or innocence can be established. The restraint required to administer truth serum does not involve torture. It is therefore a morally acceptable way of seeking to elicit cooperation and information, and one that is far more likely to yield useful information than torture. The former chief of CIA operations in Afghanistan, Milt Bearden, has been quoted as saying any time you merely threaten to torture a foreign national he'll sign anything and admit to anything. "You don't get intelligence worth squat as a result."

Author's comment:

The most common of the so-called truth serum drugs are thiopental sodium (marketed as sodium pentothal) and sodium amytal. These drugs are sedatives and anesthetics that, at least in theory, reduce a subject's resistance and inhibitions. They have no harmful side effects. The U.S. Office of

Strategic Services experimented with truth drugs during World War II, but the results were inconclusive. Most intelligence and security professionals today regard the use of drugs in interrogations as unreliable. The practice, moreover, is a clear violation of the U.S. Fifth Amendment prohibition against self-incrimination, and it has been interpreted under international law as an outlawed form of torture. U.S. courts, however, have shown an inclination to consider public safety exceptions to constitutional rights and might be open to such an argument in the case of using truth serum in terrorist interrogations, particularly if the threat is imminent. Former CIA and FBI director William Webster, widely respected for his moral probity, caused a stir in 2002 when he suggested publicly that the United States should use truth drugs against terrorist detainees.

SCENARIO NO. 8:
JOURNALISM COVER

The CIA has recruited thirty-two-year-old Brian Gunter for the Clandestine Service Training Program. Gunter is a graduate of the University of Missouri's School of Journalism and worked for seven years as a journalist for the Associated Press before joining the CIA. He speaks fluent French and Swahili. Gunter is motivated by patriotism and feels privileged to have the opportunity to serve his country in the CIA.

Gunter excels in his operational training at the Farm. Shortly before he graduates, he is approached by the CIA's Africa Division[8] with a proposal that he serve in Africa under cover as a journalist. The CIA has a close relationship with the publisher of *World News Weekly*, a respected international affairs magazine based in Tampa, Florida. The publisher offers to hire Gunter as the magazine's African correspondent and to allow him to use this cover for his intelligence activities overseas. No one else on the magazine's staff will be aware that Gunter is actually a CIA officer.

On the basis of his education and experience, Gunter is well qualified for this cover. He will roam the continent of Africa from his base in Nairobi and will send in regular factual reporting to *World News Weekly* on events in Africa. The CIA will not influence the content of his reporting in any way.

In addition to doing his full-time cover job as a journalist, Gunter will spot, assess, develop, and handle intelligence assets for the CIA. He will also use his journalistic credentials to gain access to places and targets that would not normally be accessible to U.S. government officials.

———————

Would it be morally acceptable for the CIA to send Gunter to Africa under cover as a journalist for *World News Weekly*?

Professor Bruce Gronbeck of the University of Iowa:

No. For almost a century, U.S. journalistic institutions have preached that freedom of the press brings with it obligations. As the journalist's code of ethics took shape through the early and, especially, the middle parts of the twentieth century, it sought to instill a code of behavior that would purify and protect public information. Both John Dewey and Walter Lippmann preached that guarded public information was necessary for the democratic process. Lippmann worried about "the pictures in our heads" that bad journalism could construct, and Dewey was concerned about the eclipse of the public that would follow when institutions (including journalism) ran roughshod over the public's right to know. I would argue that the same worries have to be brought to international journalism. Indeed, the CIA itself after World War II steadily beat on the world's totalitarian press—especially Russian—through its work with Radio Free Europe and Radio Liberty. To ask a journalist explicitly to do something other than to gather and report information independently of other goals is morally unacceptable.

Former CIA officer Haviland Smith:

Yes, but unwise. I do not see the issue of journalistic cover as a moral dilemma. To me, it is simply a practical issue. If I were in the chain of command, I would like to be very confident that the publisher is aware of the risks he is taking when he lets one of his "employees" wander about as a case officer for the CIA. Where the issue falls apart for me is that Gunter will be reporting to his magazine as its African correspondent. I think the Agency is really asking for trouble because of the likely allegations that would be made on the heels of the ever-possible revelation that Gunter is a CIA officer. We get on very dangerous ground when it is possible to allege that the CIA, through reporting of this nature, is trying to influence U.S. public opinion and policy on Africa. Why not give him cover as a car salesman? Or set him up with a fabricated journalism cover?

Author Thomas Powers:

Yes, but foolish. I do not think it would be morally wrong to give Gunter journalism cover, but I do think it would be foolish. This respected international affairs magazine, *World News Weekly*, is respected because it does serious quality work. We can assume it helps Americans, including policy makers, to understand the world. Gunter's secret role, when discovered, will threaten the magazine's credibility, endanger other American journalists, and serve to isolate America in the world. What's the gain? In addition, if Gunter is going to recruit and handle intelligence assets, he is going to become known to local services eventually, if not immediately, with the result that

WNW will soon have a ripe odor among intelligence services everywhere. I'm against it.

Los Angeles Times journalist Bob Drogin:

No. This scenario is morally unacceptable. An American journalist operates with a unique franchise: he represents the public trust. Our Founding Fathers enshrined this franchise in law by adopting the First Amendment specifically to protect an independent press. Thus, reporters must be free to act as a watchdog on government actions and abuses, including those of the CIA. Using an American reporter and news magazine as cover for covert U.S. government operations, including spying and handling intelligence assets for the CIA, is a betrayal of that trust. It also endangers other U.S. journalists, who often are accused of spying by autocratic regimes in Africa and elsewhere (I know, because I worked as a reporter there for four years). Their only defense is that the U.S. government has publicly forsworn such activity.

Professor Harry Mason of the Patterson School at the University of Kentucky:

Yes (class vote). The vote in favor of journalism cover in my graduate class was 16-1. Those approving were influenced by the merits of the position and the fact that Gunter's reporting would not be controlled by the CIA. The one no vote was based on the possibility that the use of the media for cover could place American journalists overseas at more risk of foreign terrorism.

Professor David S. Allen of the University of Wisconsin–Milwaukee:

No. This is problematic both for the press and ultimately for the CIA. Gunter's greatest loyalty ought to be to the public. By entering into a monetary relationship with the CIA, he is at the very least raising questions about where his greatest loyalty lies. By engaging in this arrangement, Gunter is severely damaging the legitimacy and credibility of two institutions in American society. The press's independence will be called into question, both in the national and international communities, and the CIA loses one of the institutions that can effectively serve as a watchdog on its activities. Whether the CIA will attempt to influence Gunter's reporting does not really matter. Once word leaks out that the press has entered into this type of agreement with the CIA—and word will leak out at some point—damage to both institutions will be done. Historically, we know these types of relationships have existed in the past and might very well exist today. The point is not whether the press and CIA can get away with it. The question ought to go directly to understanding what the fundamental purpose of each institution in American society is and whether this practice helps advance that mission. Journalism cover does not help to advance the legitimacy and independence of either institution.

Ambassador Henry Grunwald, former editor-in-chief of Time, Inc.:

Yes. I have no great problem with allowing Gunter to use journalism cover. If we are going to have a spy service, then our spies obviously have to work under cover. The question then comes down to whether using a press cover is somehow more reprehensible than a business, law, or medical cover. A case can be made for this, but not a very strong case, especially after 9/11. I believe that morality cannot be judged entirely apart from circumstances and, while twenty or thirty years ago I might have insisted on absolute purity for journalists, I can no longer feel that way.

Professor Robert Jensen of the University of Texas:

No. The primary role of journalists in a democratic society is to provide information, analysis, and opinion that is independent of the major centers of power in the society. To do that, journalists must remain truly independent of those powers. There is a strong presumption against journalists collaborating with any outside agencies, and an even stronger presumption when those agencies are involved in fundamentally immoral projects. The CIA is a fundamentally immoral institution, with a fundamentally immoral mission.

Author's comment:

In strictly operational terms, journalism is excellent cover. Most of the major intelligence services of the world have used press cover extensively, and many still do. Journalism is good cover because journalists do the same thing for reporting purposes that spies try to do for espionage purposes, namely to move around, meet lots of people, ask questions, and collect information. The Senate Select Committee on Intelligence, chaired by Senator Frank Church of Idaho, in 1976 documented more than fifty cases of the use of journalism cover by the CIA since its founding in 1947. There was widespread condemnation of the practice at that time, and the country was led to believe the CIA had renounced all use of journalism cover. That was not exactly true. In testimony before the Senate intelligence oversight committee in 1996, the then-director of central intelligence, John Deutch, admitted that the guidelines established by the CIA after the Church Committee hearings had allowed exceptions to be made in the interests of national security. Deutch argued that this exception should be preserved to give the DCI all available options in extreme crisis situations. He cited hostage-taking incidents and threats of imminent attack against Americans by weapons of mass destruction as examples of times when a DCI might need to exercise the option of using journalists for intelligence purposes. Stansfield Turner, the DCI under President Jimmy Carter, acknowledged in an interview that he had in fact authorized journalism cover on three occasions during his tenure.

The American press was apoplectic. It pointed out that American journalists overseas were often accused of being spies, and the admission that the CIA actually used journalists as spies, even exceptionally, would add fuel to the fire. American journalists everywhere, said these critics, would be in increased jeopardy.

Ted Koppel of ABC News spoke for many members of the press when he told the same committee, "I am opposed to the CIA having the legal option of using journalistic cover. The CIA has broken laws. It will again. Many governments assume that journalists are working for the CIA, because they use journalists. How often the waiver is actually used is irrelevant. It is how it is assumed to be used."

Former hostage and Associated Press correspondent Terry Anderson testified in the same vein, "Journalists are in danger. In much of the world the CIA is held in great disfavor. Journalists begin with a presumption of involvement. I was accused of being a spy. I was on a list of CIA agents put out by fundamentalist Shiites. When we make rules, it depends if people have been disrespectful of rules, if they have been stretching the rules. There is sufficient evidence in the history of the CIA to put it in this category."

The Intelligence Authorization Act for Fiscal Year 1997 stated that it was the policy of the United States that no element of U.S. intelligence could use any individual for intelligence collecting purposes who "(1) is authorized by contract or by the issuance of press credentials to represent himself or herself, either in the United States, or abroad, as a correspondent of a United States news media organization; or (2) is officially recognized by a foreign government as a representative of a United States media organization." The Act in the next section provided, however, that this policy could be waived by the president of the United States if necessary "to address the overriding national security interest of the United States."

This debate is still very much alive today. Many Americans, especially journalists, argue that the prohibition of the use of journalism cover by the CIA should be total, without exceptions. Others contend that the international threats to America's security are so severe today that the CIA needs greater flexibility in choosing covers, including journalism cover.

SCENARIO NO. 9:
OPERATIONAL USE OF JOURNALISTS

Relations between the U.S. and the Palestinians have deteriorated in the face of increased U.S. political and military support for Israel. The National Security Council tasks the CIA to expand its intelligence collection capabilities against Palestinian and pro-Palestinian groups in the region.

The CIA approaches Sylvie Selman, a Middle East correspondent for CNN, and recruits her as an intelligence source. Selman is a Lebanese-born American citizen who has worked for CNN for ten years. She speaks native Arabic. Selman has excellent contacts with the Palestinian National Authority, the Islamic Resistance Movement, the Popular Front for the Liberation of Palestine, and other pro-Palestinian groups in the Middle East. In return for a CIA salary of $250,000 a year, she agrees to provide the CIA with everything she learns from her sources. She will not slant her reporting in any way, but she will accept intelligence requirements from the CIA and will seek out contact with specific individuals at CIA direction. The CIA is confident that this arrangement will be very helpful in obtaining information and insights on the Middle East that would not otherwise be available to the U.S. government. The U.S. national security adviser and the director of the CIA approve the operation.

Would it be morally acceptable for the CIA to recruit Sylvie Selman under these circumstances and to use her as a source of intelligence on the Middle East?

Former USIA officer Philip Brown:

No. I have no doubt that the CIA has and continues to buy journalists, both American and non-American, but I have no hesitation in describing this practice as morally unacceptable. Mind you, I hear the other side, "What if it turns out that the journalist could have provided information that would have prevented 9/11; are you really so squeamish that you can't spend a little dirty money to save lives?" Answer: It is morally unacceptable. I also think it would be just plain stupid. I can't imagine that the activity would remain secret forever and when it or a similar case became public the price to be paid in lost credibility for the individual, the news organization, and the U.S. (if it had any credibility left in the Middle East) would be enormous. If we are so bad off that Sylvie Selman can get information that we cannot get on our own with all our enormous resources, the answer is not to buy her but to train our own Arabic-speaking intelligence officers.

Former USIA officer John Williams:

Yes. The key here is that Ms. Selman's reporting would in no way be tainted or slanted by her association with the CIA. In fact, her insight might be deepened by her contact with some of the people described. I recognize that many who jealously guard the prerogatives of the Fourth Estate will take issue with this, saying that inevitably her reporting will reflect her additional responsibilities and that, by definition, such an arrangement would make her less than unbiased. But I believe it is the responsibility of any professional journalist to maintain a clear distinction between the reporting function and personal feelings and views. Simply being asked to seek out individuals whom she might not include in her reporting otherwise does not, in my view, do violence to her responsibilities as a journalist.

Former CIA officer David Edger:

Yes. It would be morally acceptable to recruit Ms. Selman, but maybe not wise. Traditionally, intelligence services have pressed journalists into service as observers and as action agents. Early in my career, I handled a stringer for a major news organization in precisely such a role, namely, as an observer of revolutionary groups. This source never took journalistic direction from me, nor did he in any way slant his stories or "go easy" on the U.S. government. Still, if his cooperation with the CIA had been revealed, it would have created a firestorm of controversy. I am sure all of his written work would have been subjected to the most intense textual analysis in an effort to find proof that he was influenced by his work with the CIA. It would have been fairly easy to find pieces where he seemed to be slanting our way. He was, after all, on our side.

Rules prohibiting the use of journalists as sources and preventing the use of journalistic cover by staff officers have been enacted by more than one service. The reasons given are to protect the integrity of journalism, to keep suspicion off real journalists, who are in harm's way, and to make certain that intelligence services are not propagandizing their own citizens. Other services, including some from well-known democracies, do not accept this argument. They regularly field journalists as sources. Their decision to do so is based on the fact that all cooperation is purely voluntary and no attempt is made to slant what the journalists write.

It is easy to justify the use of journalists in cases where great human risk is at stake. If a journalist could meet with a group preparing a "dirty bomb," practically anyone would approve his or her use. Equally, if hostages are involved, a journalist might well be asked to describe where the hostages are being held. In the case of Ms. Selman, the coverage is directed against a long-standing, intractable problem. It might be argued that the risk to public perception overrides the value of using her as a source, but such a decision is a political one, not a moral one.

Author Thomas Powers:

No. As a CNN correspondent, Sylvie is in search of sound bites for television. She needs punchy copy to make the evening news. If she starts asking probing questions about Palestinian National Authority gossiping and feuding with Syria, it will be clear in a minute that this is not what is going on the air. Besides, what is the PNA going to tell Sylvie that it would not tell the *New York Times*? I am also concerned that Sylvie's growing dependence on the quarter million a year could encourage her to fabricate items of interest to keep the paychecks coming. CNN is going to start wondering what is taking Sylvie so long to get a thirty-second clip of Mahmoud Abbas when she's off trying to find out who was behind the latest suicide bombing. Sylvie is going to be threatened personally and professionally . . . and the CIA is not going to learn much. I'm against it.

***Los Angeles Times* journalist Bob Drogin:**

No—but a close call. I can imagine cases where an American journalist could obtain information in the course of reporting on Palestinian groups that might prove critical to preventing a terrorist attack or other crises. In those cases, a U.S. journalist would have an obligation to share that information with government authorities, as any citizen would. This is not that kind of life-or-death situation, however. Indeed, Selman is going much farther across the line here. She is secretly accepting a great deal of money from the CIA to actively spy on routine intelligence issues while using her CNN job as cover. This violates her contract with CNN, betrays CNN viewers, who expect news from an independent source, and endangers other journalists.

Ambassador Henry Grunwald, former editor-in-chief of Time, Inc.:

Yes. I have no great problem with this.

Professor David S. Allen of the University of Wisconsin–Milwaukee:

No. My reason for finding this morally unacceptable is related directly to the mission and purpose of the press as an institution. As a Middle East correspondent for CNN, Selman has the job of telling people what is happening in that area of the world. By accepting a salary from the CIA and agreeing to be "tasked," she has effectively surrendered her legitimacy to cover the CIA as a news story. It is true that much of what she discovers in her job as a CIA operative will also have news value, but it is unlikely that her job as a journalist will allow her to cover the CIA as a news story. And the CIA is part of the story. This is directly related to what a journalist ought to do and how that duty differs from what a CIA operative does.

Author's comment:

The cases of Brian Gunter of *World News Weekly* in the previous scenario and Sylvie Selman of CNN here raise similar issues but are distinct. Gunter is a trained professional CIA staff officer who is given press cover for the purpose of carrying out espionage duties. His primary responsibilities and loyalties are with the CIA. Selman is a legitimate journalist, who is being coopted by the CIA to assist in the collection of information. Her tasking by the CIA is secondary and incidental to her primary duties for CNN. The Gunter case is a relatively straightforward moral issue and usually evokes a quick yea or nay reaction from commentators. The Selman case, however, is a bit more complicated.

U.S. correspondents overseas tend to be very savvy and well connected to the local scene. They frequently rub shoulders with U.S. personnel in their countries of assignment, including, whether they realize it or not (and they often do), CIA officers. It is not unusual for U.S. foreign correspondents to develop information or contacts they know would be of value to U.S. intelligence. Should they be absolutely prohibited from sharing that information with the CIA or other U.S. agencies? Say, for example, a U.S. journalist was allowed access to locations inside North Korea that were previously closed to Americans and was also granted a lengthy private interview with Kim Jong-il. Would it be inappropriate for that journalist to sit down privately with the CIA's North Korean analysts after his return to the U.S. to share his observations and impressions? What if an Iranian diplomat in Paris developed a friendly relationship with a U.S. journalist and offered to give her a packet of secret documents for passage to the CIA? Should she refuse? Another example would be if a Chinese intelligence officer serving in the United States under New China News Agency cover wanted to defect to the U.S. and asked a trusted American journalist contact to be his intermediary to the FBI. Would that be permissible? The U.S. Intelligence Authorization Act for Fiscal Year 1997, which attempted to establish U.S. policy guidelines in these matters, actually left the question wide open by refusing to prohibit "the voluntary cooperation of any person who is aware that the cooperation is being provided to an element of the United States Intelligence Community." So, apparently, voluntary and witting cooperation by an American journalist with the CIA is not contrary to U.S. government policy.

The worlds of journalism and spying intersect in many permutations of the above scenarios. Nicholas Daniloff, the Moscow correspondent of

U.S. News & World Report, was arrested by the KGB in 1986 and accused of being a CIA spy. KGB major Stanislav Levchenko was working in Tokyo under cover as a Soviet journalist when he defected to the United States in 1979. Kim Philby worked for MI6 in Beirut under journalistic cover. Soviet master spy Richard Sorge had cover as a German journalist in Japan during World War II. Most overseas correspondents of the New China News Agency are MSS officers.

SCENARIO NO. 10:
HUMAN RIGHTS VIOLATORS

The Maoist terrorist group Sendero Luminoso has reemerged as a serious threat in Peru. In addition to making numerous attacks against Peruvian officials and installations, it has kidnapped and murdered several American businessmen and diplomats. Just recently, it bombed the U.S. Embassy in Lima, killing eight more Americans. The CIA secretly provides equipment, training, and intelligence to the Peruvian National Police and the Peruvian military to help them fight terrorism.[9] As a result, the Sendero Luminoso attacks against Americans in Peru have decreased significantly.

We learn, however, that on some occasions, when the Peruvian National Police and military capture known Sendero Luminoso terrorists in the field, they do not always bring them in for trial because such high-profile trials tend to be dangerous and the members of the judiciary are often corrupt. Instead, in their frustration, they summarily execute these terrorists on the spot in what is clearly a human rights violation.

Would it be morally acceptable for the CIA to continue equipping, training, and providing intelligence to the Peruvian National Police and military for counterterrorism operations knowing, as it does now, that they sometimes commit human rights violations?

Former CIA polygrapher John Sullivan:
It depends. This one is difficult for me. My main reservation is about whom the Peruvians are killing. Are those they are killing known to be members of Sendero Luminoso? I do see ghosts of William Colby's Phoenix Program in Vietnam, but I am one who saw some merit in that program. In any event, if it became known that the Peruvians were indiscriminately killing innocent people, I would cut off aid.

Professor Peter Feaver of Duke University:
[The views expressed by Professor Feaver are personal and are not in-

tended to reflect those of any particular group, institution, or organization.]

It depends. It would not be morally acceptable for the CIA to continue with business as usual. But steps short of a complete curtailment of activities would be acceptable, especially if there is evidence that our aid is strengthening the elements in Peru that oppose these human rights violations.

Former State Department officer John Salazar:

It depends. This would be morally acceptable only if an honest effort were made by the U.S. to reform the Peruvian military and police forces and to reform the Peruvian judicial system.

Rabbi Peter Tarlow:

No. The answer is clearly no, and the U.S. should set its conditions for aid. In this case, there is simply no justification for the human rights violations, and aid should be terminated.

Former CIA officer Burton Gerber:

This scenario is posited as an either/or situation. I believe that a different course recognizing all the factors can lead to efforts to achieve an ethical solution. First, from an ethical standpoint, the CIA cannot tolerate by inaction the murder of persons taken prisoner by the Peruvian government authorities. CIA personnel in contact with the Peruvian National Police and the Peruvian military have clear access to senior officials, perhaps also to field operators. They also have the means and weapons the Peruvians need to accomplish their mission. (Even with the American deaths, Sendero Luminoso is a much more serious threat to Peru than to the U.S. government). So, the CIA ought to be able to use its leverage to prevent or reduce human rights violations. For instance, the Agency should have a training program for those who are likely to be the first on the scene to capture SL terrorists. That program should emphasize the intelligence value of keeping prisoners alive for interrogation (not torture!) so that the Peruvian authorities get better leads to destroy SL. At the same time, the CIA officials should be making this case with the Peruvian senior authorities in Lima and in provincial capitals and discussing how Peru may be able to address the inadequate or corrupt judicial system. In other words, there are positive steps the CIA officials can take which will be designed to prevent or reduce the human rights violations and at the same time improve the anti-SL campaign.

Admiral Bobby R. Inman, former director of the National Security Agency and deputy director of central intelligence:

Yes, but with an added focus on human rights. We should urge the Peruvians to end their policy of executing terrorists who have surrendered. The overall threat to the lives of U.S. citizens assigned to work in Peru justifies our continued efforts to eliminate the threat.

Lt. Col. Tom Ruby, USAF, Department of Joint Warfare Studies, Air Command and Staff College:

[The views expressed are those of Lt. Col. Ruby and do not necessarily reflect the official policy or position of the United States Air Force, the Department of Defense, or the U.S. government.]

No. It would be morally unacceptable for the CIA to continue providing aid to the Peruvians if the CIA were certain that some of the police and military were engaged in clear human rights violations. This would violate the doctrine of double effect and would furthermore make the U.S. a party to violations of international conventions to which the U.S. is a signatory. Murder is always objectively wrong. There are no situations that allow for murder or summary execution. If the Peruvian government made a good faith effort to oversee its operations to ensure that no further human rights violations were committed, then the support could continue. Otherwise, no.

Ambassador Joseph E. Lake:

It depends. The moral acceptability of continuing aid depends on how the relationship is managed. Only if the following conditions were met would I see the program as morally acceptable:

1) the CIA made clear the U.S. government's commitment to human rights, including legal due process;
2) the CIA insisted that as part of its training program the military and police officials receive briefings on human rights and due process; and
3) the U.S. government supported an assistance program to train other Peruvian officials, including the judiciary, in human rights issues.

Not only would the U.S. be addressing a real terrorist threat, but it would also be addressing some of the root causes of terrorism, as well as specific human rights issues. Without U.S. government involvement and support for human rights, the situation is unlikely to change.

Anonymous active duty U.S. military officer No. 1:

Yes. It is morally acceptable for the CIA to continue to provide support and training. Although the Peruvian National Police is committing human rights violations, the CIA is not. The training and intelligence provided by the CIA are for the greater good.

Anonymous active duty U.S. military officer No. 2:
Yes. The bottom line here is that we are fighting bad guys and some-times you have to get dirty. Americans are being killed and the Peruvians are fighting the people who are responsible. While this may not be ideal, at least something is getting done. To do nothing would be an even bigger mistake.

Author's comment:
The Peruvian scenario raises an extremely important question: To what extent can U.S. intelligence agencies associate with human rights violators and other criminals in carrying out their responsibilities? The CIA received intense criticism for having maintained a paid-agent relationship with Pana-manian dictator Manuel Noriega. The CIA has had close working relation-ships over the years with foreign intelligence services that do not adhere to American moral and human rights standards. A frequently cited example is the CIA's cooperation in Iran with the Shah's oppressive SAVAK. There are numerous other examples in Latin America. The CIA, in its unsuccessful efforts to assassinate Fidel Castro, at one point made contact with the Ma-fia. All of us who have served as CIA case officers have handled agents who would not be welcome in polite society. It is clear the CIA has gained con-siderable benefit from many of these relationships, but the question, of course, is at what moral cost?

This issue came to a head at the CIA in 1995. In reaction to the murder of the Guatemalan husband of an American citizen by an individual with ties to the CIA, the then-DCI John Deutch decided that the CIA's Director-ate of Operations would have to clean up its act. Specifically, a new regula-tion was promulgated (I remember it well) that established strict procedures for the recruitment or retention of any intelligence assets with known or suspected involvement in human rights violations or other significant crimi-nal activity. Each such case would have to be reviewed by the CIA's Office of General Counsel and, in some cases, approved personally by the DCI. In fairness, the intent of the regulation was simply to conduct a salutary scrub of the CIA's foreign agents to eliminate those of marginal value and with particularly egregious backgrounds. That would have been fine. The unin-tended effect on the morale and risk-taking of the CIA's overseas stations,[10] however, was devastating. The situation was made worse when popular and respected CIA officers were held personally accountable for what had hap-pened in Guatemala and received harsh disciplinary treatment. The message was clear. Do not take risks. Do not deal with unsavory characters. Do not put yourself through the hassle of all that paperwork. The appalled reac-tions of many experienced DO officers were not surprising. Their question was: How do you expect us to penetrate terrorist groups, narcotics trafficking organizations, and organized crime if we can only recruit choir boys? As former CIA officer Dewey Clarridge told the BBC in 2000, "We sometimes dealt with people who had blood on their hands because, unfortunately, they tend to know more about what terrorists are up to than do the Mother Teresas of the world."

After 9/11, the regulation was revised. The CIA's overseas stations were still required to pay close attention to the moral uprightness of their recruited assets, but the standards and procedures were less stringent. Most DO officers saw this as more forward-leaning than the previous policy, but others detected lingering risk aversion on the part of field officers.

SCENARIO NO. 11:
TORTURE TRAINING

The Jordanian General Intelligence Department (GID) cooperates closely with the CIA in the war on terrorism and has helped the United States thwart several terrorist attacks against Americans. The GID asks the CIA to train its personnel in effective interrogation techniques, including torture, to use against terrorists. The GID has in its custody dozens of terrorist suspects who, it believes, have valuable and actionable information on terrorist operations and personnel throughout the Middle East, including attacks against U.S. civilian and military personnel. The GID believes it can be much more successful in extracting this information if it uses more sophisticated and effective interrogation methods.

Would it be morally acceptable for the CIA to provide the Jordanian GID with training in sophisticated interrogation techniques, including torture, to use against terrorist suspects?

Former FBI senior executive John Guido:
No. First, what does the CIA know about torture techniques? Teaching sophisticated interrogation techniques such as depriving physical comforts, providing false information, and using drugs to put the subject at a psychological disadvantage would be morally acceptable, even though some people would call this torture. Teaching actual physical torture techniques would not be acceptable. The CIA should not teach techniques that the CIA itself is not allowed to use.

Graduate student Russell Rodriguez of the George Bush School of Government and Public Service at Texas A&M University:
No. We, as Americans, hold ourselves to a higher standard. We do not

torture people. If, however, the Jordanians can find someone else to help them, that is their business.

Professor Harry Mason of the Patterson School at the University of Kentucky:

No (class vote). My graduate intelligence class voted 2-15 against providing torture training to the Jordanians. The major factor was the unfavorable publicity that would fall on the CIA if the training were revealed. In addition, the class believed that the Jordanians were already sufficiently adept at "interrogation" techniques.

Professor Richard Graving of the South Texas College of Law:

No. While there surely are cases where the ends justify the means, this cannot be said of "sophisticated" torture of mere "suspects," especially by those not subject to U.S. government and media vigilance. By performing the training, the U.S. is more than complicit. It is directly responsible. This is not a case of interrogating a proven terrorist about a ticking nuclear bomb he credibly claims he has planted somewhere in Manhattan.

Michael Bohn, former director of the White House Situation Room:

No. We should have nothing to do with any treatment of foreign prisoners that we would find unacceptable if U.S. citizens were subject to the same handling.

Author's comment:

The CIA unfortunately has expertise on torture because so many of its officers and other U.S. government officials have been subjected to it. Drug Enforcement Administration (DEA) special agent Enrique "Kiki" Camarena was viciously tortured and then murdered by Mexican drug dealers in Guadalajara in 1985. I am reminded also of the valiant men of the U.S.S. *Pueblo* and their eleven-month captivity and torture at the hands of the North Koreans in 1969. The commanding officer of the *Pueblo*, U.S. Navy Commander Lloyd "Pete" Bucher, and his wife Rose were the honored guests of the George Bush School of Government and Public Service at a conference on North Korea in 1999. The Buchers received a standing ovation from the participants. The American hero Pete Bucher, a victim of severe torture at the hands of the North Koreans, died in California in 2004.

An equally heinous example was the torture of CIA officer William Buckley. Buckley was the CIA's chief of station in Beirut in 1984 when he was kidnapped by a pro-Iranian terrorist group calling itself Islamic Holy War. Despite repeated efforts by the U.S. government to secure Buckley's release, he was held captive for fifteen months and brutally tortured by the terrorists before being executed. His decomposed body was dumped in southern Beirut in 1991. His remains were returned to the U.S. for burial at Arlington National Cemetery.

When former President George Bush does guest lectures on intelligence at the Bush School, my students frequently ask him about William Buckley. I have seen this happen several times and on every occasion, when President Bush begins to speak of Buckley, he visibly tears up.

SCENARIO NO. 12:
HUMANITARIAN AID WORKER COVER

The terrorist group Hamas has started targeting Americans in addition to its usual attacks against Israelis. A van carrying four American students working in Israel is the latest victim of a Hamas suicide bombing. All four Americans are killed.

The CIA desperately needs to recruit penetrations of Hamas to prevent future terrorist attacks. It is severely hampered in this effort, however, by its poor access to Palestinians in the Gaza Strip and on the West Bank.

Michael Harrington is a twenty-eight-year-old graduate of Columbia University, where he earned a Ph.D. in Middle Eastern Studies. He grew up in Lebanon, where his parents were faculty members at the American University of Beirut. He speaks fluent Arabic. The CIA recruits Harrington and assigns him to the Near East Division of the Directorate of Operations. Harrington's recruitment and training have been completely covert; he has revealed to no one that he is in the CIA.[11]

At the direction of the CIA, Harrington responds to an employment vacancy notice for the United Nations Relief and Works Agency for Palestinian Refugees in the Near East (UNRWA). He is the best qualified of the many applicants and is hired as a program manager for UNRWA's office in the Gaza Strip. This position will give him regular access to Palestinian refugee camps. Harrington's CIA assignment will be to monitor the activities of Palestinian militants in the camps and to spot and assess candidates for recruitment. Those who are recruited and fully vetted will be instructed to do everything they can to join Hamas so they can pass information to the CIA from inside that organization.

———

Would it be morally acceptable for the CIA to use UNRWA humanitarian aid worker cover for Harrington in the Gaza Strip in an effort to penetrate Hamas?

Former FBI senior official Oliver "Buck" Revell:

Yes. In war, the ability to penetrate the enemy camp is absolutely essential and can shorten the conflict, prevent surprise attacks, and save lives. I find it morally acceptable to use any cover that would allow such a penetration, especially against an enemy that recognizes no law or standards in its conduct of aggression and terror.

Professor Bruce Gronbeck of the University of Iowa:

It depends. It depends on whether Harrington is in fact carrying out the humanitarian goals of UNRWA as fully as possible. Assuming that he is, then I would see no moral conflict in his covert activities. In a sense, he is empowering Palestinians to work in particular ways within their own culture, and so long as they are not coerced in some way to do that, I see no particularly difficult moral problems.

Ambassador Joseph E. Lake:

It depends. Whether the CIA's use of UNRWA humanitarian aid worker cover is morally acceptable or not depends on the role of the individual involved. If Harrington's role is recruitment and monitoring, I find it morally acceptable. If he is going to engage in covert action (subversion, sabotage, propaganda, etc.), I would find his work morally unacceptable.

Writer, poet, and teacher Burke Gerstenschlager:

No. It would be morally unacceptable for the CIA to use UNRWA cover to penetrate Hamas. Using an international relief organization for intelligence purposes not only puts individuals and organizations at risk, but also threatens to derail the peace process in the Middle East. If Harrington were ever discovered to be a CIA officer, he would jeopardize further U.S. efforts to infiltrate Hamas and would also compromise the work of the UN as a humanitarian organization. Moreover, this course of action would be morally unacceptable even if Harrington were never discovered. His undercover work would be contrary to the spirit and goals of UNRWA. Harrington has much to offer UNRWA, apart from spying. Wouldn't it better for him to provide a good example of American service and goodwill toward the Palestinians through nonclandestine activities? He could help to dismantle the stereotypes and to dispel the animosity toward Americans in the region. He could inculcate positive feelings toward Americans among the people in the camps, people whom Hamas actively recruits for attacks upon Americans. Thus, Harrington could add legitimacy to our humanitarian efforts in the Middle East and further protect American lives.

Practicing attorney Christopher Scherer:

Yes. In an age of Machiavellian *realpolitik*, the Palestinians would be naïve to assume that international relief organizations and NGOs are not being manipulated for unforeseen ends. There is no reasonable expectation of privacy on the part of the refugees in the camp that would constrain Harrington from monitoring and recruiting them.

Professor Abraham Clearfield:

Yes. UNRWA has been providing aid to Palestinian refugees for decades. Hundreds, if not thousands, of Palestinians are employed by UNRWA to service the refugees. Harrington's CIA role, if discovered, would not permanently damage UNRWA because its aid is needed and essential. But Harrington, if successful in his CIA work, would gain information that might prevent future attacks—not only attacks against Americans but also suicide bombings against Israel. Peace in Palestine will only be possible when the militants are reined in, and Harrington's work is a small step in that direction.

Professor Peter Feaver of Duke University:

[The views expressed by Professor Feaver are personal and are not intended to reflect those of any particular group, institution, or organization.]

Yes. Morally acceptable, but politically risky.

Former CIA officer Eugene Culbertson:

Yes. In a risk versus gain analysis, this type of passive spotting and assessment by Harrington would be expedient and morally acceptable. In addition, the expertise for which UNRWA hired him would allow him to render valuable humanitarian service. If, however, his clandestine role were ever exposed, the potential political fallout would be enormous and far-reaching. Every base must be covered with extraordinary care. This would include strict compartmentation[12] and clearances at least as high as the director of the CIA, possibly even up to the national security adviser, the congressional oversight committee chairpersons, and the president. Special precautionary measures would have to be taken to safeguard the CIA's asset and operation.

Author's comment:

The United States has often been accused of using humanitarian aid organizations as cover for intelligence operations. I can recall hearing allegations of this kind at various times concerning the Peace Corps, the Agency for International Development, the Organization for Security and Cooperation in Europe, the International Committee of the Red Cross, AmeriCares, and others. The CIA regulation signed by DCI Stansfield Turner in 1977 prohibited the CIA from using journalists, the clergy, or Peace Corps volunteers for intelligence purposes. As acknowledged by DCI John Deutch in 1996, however, there was a provision in the regulation for exceptions, and some were made, although not many. The existence of this "loophole" infuriated many members of the affected groups, who demanded an outright ban on such activity.

The exception provision has been retained, but as a matter of policy the U.S. intelligence community has been extremely reluctant to enter into these sensitive areas. Peace Corps volunteers are definitely hands off. ■

██

██

████████████████████████████The Peace Corps, for its part, rejects any applicant who has had any connection with a U.S. intelligence organization, either personally or through a close family member. When my son Joshua left the Navy in 2004, he submitted an application to the Peace Corps, not knowing about the prohibition. Josh has an excellent academic record, is well traveled, and speaks fluent Spanish. Everything seemed to be going smoothly in his Peace Corps interview until his examiner asked him the fateful question. Have you or any member of your family ever had any association with a U.S. intelligence organization? Since Meredith and I were by then out from under cover, Josh answered truthfully that both his mother and father had been CIA officers. His interview with the Peace Corps ended abruptly.

The CIA is required by Executive Order 12333 to collect intelligence "in a vigorous, innovative and responsible manner that is consistent with the Constitution and applicable law and respectful of the principles upon which the United States was founded." Today, there is extraordinary pressure on the CIA to penetrate terrorist groups and to thwart future attacks against America. There is no denying that cover as humanitarian aid workers could give CIA officers access to refugee camps, disenfranchised neighborhoods, and other breeding grounds of terrorism that would not otherwise be accessible to them. But the question is whether using such groups is worth the political risk and consistent with "the principles upon which the United States was founded."

SCENARIO NO. 13:
MISSIONARY COVER

The FBI has successfully recruited a Chinese diplomat serving in the Chinese Embassy in Washington. He has proved to be an extremely valuable and reliable source, providing intelligence on political developments in China, the Chinese Communist Party, Chinese positions at the United Nations, negotiations between the U.S. and China, and a variety of other subjects. The FBI assigns the codename High Sierra to this important agent. High Sierra reports to his FBI handlers that in six months he will be transferred back to China, where he will occupy a senior position in the Yunnan provincial government in Kunming. He will also have a high-ranking position in the local Chinese Communist Party.

High Sierra wants to continue working for U.S. intelligence inside China. He says he will have excellent access to political and economic intelligence while he is there. More importantly, he believes that after two or three years in Kunming he will be transferred to Beijing, where his value to U.S. intelligence will be even greater. High Sierra insists on personal handling[13] in Kunming.

The FBI briefs the CIA on the operation and asks if it is interested in handling High Sierra after his return to China. The CIA agrees.[14] A CIA officer is introduced into the case during the final months in Washington to help prepare High Sierra for inside handling. High Sierra quickly learns the essentials of surveillance detection and "denied area" tradecraft.[15]

The U.S. government has no official presence in Kunming. The CIA's options for placing a case officer there under nonofficial cover are extremely limited. There is, however, one cover opportunity that presents itself. Theresa Emmit is a thirty-three-year-old Chinese speaking case officer with a strong Christian background. She can arrange to have herself hired as a missionary working for the U.S.–based Divine Word Outreach in Kunming.

———————

Would it be morally acceptable for the CIA to place Theresa Emmit in Kunming under Christian missionary cover to handle High Sierra?

Pastor Tom Nelson of Denton Bible Church in Denton, Texas:
No. The church has a special sanctuary to operate that should not be violated. One should never use the church, the Red Cross, or any other compassionate group for intelligence purposes.

Graduate student Sarah Forbey of the Bush School of Government and Public Service at Texas A&M University:
Yes. This operation contributes to our country's mission and is in harmony with the tenets of our moral foundation. While extremely risky, the two professions (missionary and spy) are not irreconcilable.

Former CIA officer Mary Lee Lieser:

No. Theresa Emmit's background appears perfect to handle High Sierra inside China, but for her to do so under missionary cover would be totally unacceptable.

Rabbi Peter Tarlow:

Yes. Since we are permitted to break the laws of *marit-ayin* (appearances) to save lives, there is no moral objection to planting CIA case officer Emmit among the missionaries. The positive outweighs the negative. Furthermore, we have no way of knowing what damage the missionaries are doing to the people among whom they are working, or if they are intent on creating a pattern of cultural genocide.

Undergraduate student Laura Zandstra of Texas A&M University:

It depends. I could go either way. On the one hand, all religions promote peace. Hinduism, Christianity, Islam, and Buddhism all seek different aspects of peace. So, using religion as cover to further America's objectives of peace and freedom would be moral. On the other hand, by allowing Theresa Emmit to affiliate herself with Divine Word Outreach we endanger all its employees. If Emmit is compromised and her cover is blown, her CIA role could cost the lives of innocent missionaries. The pursuit of freedom should never endanger the lives of unknowing, innocent civilians.

Author's comment:

In his testimony before the Senate Intelligence Committee in 1996, DCI John Deutch stated that he strongly believed "in the division between government and the church." He added that he had no intention of using the clergy for intelligence purposes and had seen no situations during his time at the CIA that would cause him to reconsider that position. He reaffirmed his strong support for the 1977 CIA regulation that had outlawed any operational use of clergy. As he had done in the case of journalists, however, he argued forcefully that a procedure for waivers in extreme cases should continue to be allowed for missionaries and clergy. He said the criteria for such waivers would be strict and he envisaged the actual granting of waivers would be "extremely rare."

In cold operational terms, religious cover can offer certain advantages. Missionaries, for example, often frequent difficult-to-reach areas and generally benefit from a presumption of honesty and trustworthiness. They often win the trust of the local people and are invited into their confidences. Foreign governments are sometimes (but not always) hesitant to interfere in their work for fear of international criticism. Still, many Americans are very uncomfortable with the idea of mixing religion and spying. For them, using God's servants for crass intelligence purposes would be tantamount to sacrilege. I wonder, though, if the same reservations would apply if the CIA proposed to recruit a militant Shia cleric in Iran.

There are no publicly available figures on how many clergy waivers, if any, have been granted by the CIA. The fact that waivers can ever be granted is sharply criticized by many U.S. religious leaders. The National Association of Evangelicals, for example, issued a strong condemnation of the practice in 1996.

Other countries have not been so reticent. U.S. Army Colonel George Trofimoff, who was convicted in 2001 of spying for the Soviet Union, was recruited by a Russian Orthodox priest working for the KGB. Former East German intelligence chief Markus Wolf[16] claimed that his organization had a German Benedictine monk active as a source inside the Vatican. In 2005, a Polish priest was accused of spying on Pope John Paul II for Polish intelligence during the Communist era. There have been several press reports that ███ ██████████████████████████████ in the 1980s ███████████████ ████████████████████████ in support of Solidarity in Poland, including the use of Roman Catholic priests and nuns. (The definitive book on that subject remains to be written.)

SCENARIO NO. 14:
OPERATIONAL USE OF ACADEMICS

The military regime in Burma has resisted heavy U.S. pressures to introduce democratic reforms, to release political prisoners, and to hold free elections. In fact, the Burmese government has clamped down even more heavily than before on political opposition.

William Doerfler is a professor of mechanical engineering at the University of Wisconsin. Two years ago he accepted a visiting professorship at the University of Rangoon to teach engineering courses there. He is enjoying his time in Burma and recently extended his teaching contract for two more years. Professor Doerfler, under the terms of his contract, is strictly forbidden to engage in political activity at the University of Rangoon. He has violated this provision of his contract, however, by maintaining discreet regular contact with supporters of the opposition National League for Democracy (NLD). His friends in the NLD have grown to trust him and have increasingly confided in him about their underground activities against the military government.

At the Fourth of July reception at the U.S. Embassy in Rangoon, Doerfler has a lengthy conversation about Burmese politics with a political officer from the embassy. He reveals to this officer his unauthorized involvement with the NLD and offers to report on his contacts with the NLD to the

CIA. He asks the political officer to arrange a meeting for him with a CIA officer in the embassy so he can volunteer his services to the CIA as a reporting source on the NLD. He says he is willing to insinuate himself even further into opposition groups, if that would be helpful, and to elicit information from his contacts in response to CIA tasking. Doerfler makes clear that he seeks no compensation from the CIA for his cooperation but simply wishes to be of service.

————

Would it be morally acceptable for the CIA to recruit Professor Doerfler as an intelligence source on opposition political groups in Burma?

Former CIA officer Robert Mills:
Yes. To me this is a very clear-cut case where the recruitment would be morally acceptable.

Professor Peter Feaver of Duke University:
[The views expressed by Professor Feaver are personal and are not intended to reflect those of any particular group, institution, or organization.]

Yes, especially since Doerfler initiated the contact and volunteered. Any unwelcome approach to Doerfler by the CIA would be morally suspect, but framed this way, it is O.K. On pragmatic grounds, however, I have reservations. This kind of activity compromises academics more generally and, as in the case of journalists, there are significant benefits to be gained from the legions of "pure" academics—who would come under unwarranted suspicion if this ever came out.

Colonel Cindy R. Jebb of the United States Military Academy:
[The opinions expressed by Colonel Jebb are her own and do not necessarily reflect the views of the United States Military Academy, the Department of the Army, or the Department of Defense.]

It depends. If the purpose of the CIA is to discover information that could help the U.S. better influence the ruling regime toward democratic reform, then yes, it is morally acceptable. The risk with this action, however, is that the CIA's exploitation of academics may ruin the ongoing academic exchange program between the two countries. What would be the impact of that? Would it damage U.S. national security? Another question presents itself: If Doerfler is found out, what will be the fate of the members of the opposition groups who are identified with him? If, after examining all these considerations, it is still judged that recruiting Doerfler will enhance U.S. national security, then it is morally acceptable.

Professor Michael Porter of the University of Missouri:

Yes. To be honest, I was a bit surprised that I agreed that this deceit could be acceptable behavior. My primary rationale is that no one will be hurt by it. The American government will have a way to gain valuable information that it can use to undermine those opposed to democracy in Burma. Doerfler seeks no compensation. It is assumed that there may be some risk to him of getting caught in the deception, as he is not a professional operative of the CIA. Nonetheless, if he is informed of the potential dangers and agrees to do it anyway—for the sake of worldwide peace—Godspeed.

Writer, poet, and teacher Burke Gerstenschlager:

It depends. The Burmese regime is so oppressive against its own people and neighbors that it invalidates itself as a legitimate institution of power and authority. Thus, there is no moral problem in Professor Doerfler's violating his teaching contract with the Burmese government. The CIA has a convoluted history regarding the instigation and promotion of regime change in a number of sovereign states. Thus, any infiltration of opposition groups or contact or cooperation with them must be carefully scrutinized. The ideal opposition group would promote democratic principles in a manner consistent with the customs and belief systems of the country's various subcultures. Its goal should be to preserve and sustain human dignity and freedom for perpetuity. However, just because an opposition group is against the Burmese government does not mean that its intentions are democratic and well meaning. The NLD has gained international recognition as a legitimate opposition group, so working with it would not be a moral problem per se. But it would be morally unacceptable for the CIA to recruit Professor Doerfler unless there is an open agreement between the NLD and the CIA that he would be an intelligence source. Only in this way could real democratic principles be validated and encouraged. Granted, this would probably restrict the amount of information that Professor Doerfler would obtain, but such open cooperation in good faith would protect NLD as an independent and legitimate opposition group and promote healthy diplomatic ties with the United States in the future.

Professor Richard Graving of the South Texas College of Law:

It depends. It may not be expedient. It is Doerfler who has breached his contract and offers to breach it even more seriously. His motive may be important in predicting his future behavior. The CIA's motive, too, is important. Is it to influence? If so, how? If exposure of the amateur Doerfler occurs, how will this affect U.S. policy or international reputation? How will it affect the utility of other U.S. academics overseas? If Doerfler acts *ultra vires* (in an unauthorized manner), will this impact the CIA and the U.S. (compare the Diem case in Vietnam and the Schneider case in Chile). This is more than an "operational" problem.

Graduate student Roxana Botea of the Maxwell School at Syracuse University:

Yes. Burma is not a U.S. ally and therefore this activity does not violate international norms. Given that the professor's work is voluntary, I see no moral dilemma in having the CIA work with him. My only hesitation comes from the difficulty in deciding whether this is truly a matter of national security, and therefore within the purview of the CIA, or whether it is mainly a humanitarian endeavor, more suitable for the State Department. However, I still lean toward CIA involvement. Since democracies are less likely to go to war with one another, it is worthwhile here to covertly monitor and encourage pro-democratic elements in Burma.

Author's comment:

The Church Committee Report of 1976 disclosed extensive involvement of the CIA with the U.S. academic community:

> The Central Intelligence Agency is now using several hundred American academics ("academics" includes administrators, faculty members and graduate students engaged in teaching), who in addition to providing leads and, on occasion, making introductions for intelligence purposes, occasionally write books and other material to be used for propaganda purposes abroad. Beyond these, an additional few score are used in an unwitting manner for minor activities.
>
> These academics are located in over 100 American colleges, universities, and related institutes. At the majority of institutions, no one other than the individual concerned is aware of the CIA link. At the others, at least one university official is aware of the operational use made of academics on his campus. In addition, there are several American academics abroad who serve operational purposes, primarily the collection of intelligence.

The partnership between the U.S. intelligence community and academia goes back to OSS days and is alive and well today. There are currently numerous forms of interaction, including research contracts, scholarly exchanges, jointly sponsored conferences, speeches, job fairs, officers-in-residence, and scholarships. Most of these activities are overt, in keeping with policies of greater openness at the CIA, FBI, NSA, and elsewhere, but some individual relationships remain classified.

Many American academics believe that secrecy, which is a way of life at the CIA, is totally incompatible with the free and open exchange of ideas that characterizes academia. They want no part of anything having to do with the CIA. They do not like the FBI, NSA, or other U.S. intelligence agencies much better. They are outraged when they learn of existing or proposed CIA collaborations with schools like the Rochester Institute of Technology, Michigan State, Rutgers, Harvard, MIT, or other universities. They oppose the National Security Education Program and the Pat Roberts Intelligence Scholars Program, both of which award college scholarships to students interested in intelligence careers. CIA officers-in-residence would not be welcome at many universities, and CIA recruiters find a decidedly cold reception at some campuses around the country. Other American academics, usually quietly, are happy to do what they can to help.

SCENARIO NO. 15:
P-SOURCES

The CIA is considering establishing discreet relationships with university professors around the country for help in spotting and assessing candidates for recruitment. Within the CIA, these cooperating academics will be known as "P-sources," with the P standing for "professor."

Cynthia Abernathy is an associate professor in the Department of Asian Languages and Literature at the University of Washington. She also serves as a graduate student adviser. The CIA is urgently seeking qualified applicants with knowledge of Chinese, Korean, Japanese, Urdu, and Hindi. In an unofficial conversation with a CIA friend, Dr. Abernathy indicates she is willing to assist the CIA on campus. Specifically, she says she can be on the lookout for American citizen graduate students at the University of Washington who have a special gift for Asian languages and who also possess the patriotism, integrity, sense of adventure, and other qualities the CIA finds attractive in prospective employees. She will pass the names of these students to the CIA, which can then make cold recruitment approaches to them, never disclosing that Dr. Abernathy provided the lead. Neither the CIA nor Dr. Abernathy will ever reveal to anyone that they have a cooperative relationship. Dr. Abernathy will be unpaid.

Allen Johnson is a professor of political science at Florida A&M University, a historically black college in Tallahassee, Florida. The CIA, in an effort to encourage more African-American students to apply for employment, seeks a special confidential relationship with Dr. Johnson. Under the terms of this agreement, Dr. Johnson will subtly make positive references to the CIA in his classes. Whenever possible, he will encourage interested students to apply. In addition, he will spot and assess other Florida A&M students for cold non-attributable recruitment approaches by the CIA. The CIA will pay Dr. Johnson a secret salary of $1,000 a month for his services.

Yang Zhilin, a Chinese-American, is an assistant professor in the Department of Electrical Engineering and Computer Sciences (EECS) at the University of California, Berkeley. Dr. Zhilin volunteers to work for the FBI as an informant on foreign graduate students studying in the EECS Department at Berkeley, particularly the Chinese students. The FBI is trying to recruit Chinese students who will return to China to work in sensitive defense areas. If these students are recruited while they are in the United States, they will be turned over to the CIA for handling as intelligence sources inside China. Dr. Zhilin's assignment for the FBI will be to befriend the Chinese students, report on their personalities and activities, and assess their vulnerability for recruitment. He will not be directly involved in the recruitment pitches and the FBI will make every effort to conceal Dr. Zhilin's role in spotting and assessing. Dr. Zhilin will be unpaid.

————

Would it be morally acceptable for the CIA to recruit professors Abernathy and Johnson as P-sources and for the FBI to recruit Professor Zhilin as a campus reporting source?

Former middle-school and high-school teacher Barbara Ziesche:
No. Having a professor make subtle hints in class about the CIA is morally unacceptable. Usually professors have office hours during which students visit, and it is there that the professor could give the information to the student. The CIA could put ads in the campus newspapers, but to have a professor actively assist in the recruitment of students is not morally acceptable.

Professor Harry Mason of the Patterson School at the University of Kentucky:
Yes (class vote). P-sources were endorsed by the students in my graduate course on intelligence by a vote of 13-4. The no votes were due largely to the secret salary paid to Dr. Johnson.

Former FBI senior executive John Guido:
Yes, but with reservations. The relationship with Abernathy is clearly acceptable in that she has voluntarily agreed to be of assistance to the government in furtherance of national security goals and is not providing any confidential information. The relationship with Johnson is not as clearly

acceptable. While he is not violating any laws or providing any confidential information, his acceptance of payment for services brings his motivation into question. Is he doing this to be helpful to the government or for financial gain? While his motivation may be immaterial to the CIA, would disclosure of this financial arrangement be detrimental to the Agency's reputation? While not illegal or immoral, this relationship might not meet the test of "daylight." The relationship with Zhilin differs in that he is voluntarily providing information, and while some of the information may be sensitive, it pertains to foreign students, not U.S. citizens. Public disclosure of this relationship might generate concern in some limited academic circles, but it would not cause concern in the general population.

Former CIA officer Robert Mills:

Yes. The described actions are in the national interest and do not appear to have a strong moral component. I find them all morally acceptable.

Professor Bruce Gronbeck of the University of Iowa:

It depends. I really worry about the second case in the scenario, the case of Allen Johnson. Professor Johnson is being asked to alter what is being taught to U.S. citizens in an effort to affect recruiting. Furthermore, the fact that he is being paid means—regardless of how little comparatively he is being paid—that he has economic allegiance as well as moral-political allegiance to CIA goals. Given that CIA operations are necessarily covert, Professor Johnson cannot reveal in his classroom the basis for his evaluations. Educationally, economically, and morally, then, he is violating some of the ethical underpinnings of public education. In the other two cases, there appear to be no elements that distort education, provide an economic basis for Agency-student contacts, or even affect what Professors Abernathy and Zhilin say about the CIA. Neither of them seems to be distorting the institutional integrity of public educational bodies.

Michael Bohn, former director of the White House Situation Room:

Yes, for Abernathy. It is standard practice for U.S. intelligence agencies to employ talent scouts.

No, for Johnson. Paying him to make subtle references to the CIA is repugnant. Johnson is different from Abernathy because of his pay and his positive actions, rather than passive observations.

Yes, for Zhilin. This is a common recruitment tactic practiced by many countries.

Professor Terry H. Anderson of Texas A&M University:

Yes, for Abernathy. Her behavior is acceptable. She is not recruiting and is unpaid. The student will decide if he or she wants to work for the CIA.

No, for Johnson. It is not moral for a professor to accept a secret salary to recruit for any agency or company.

No, for Zhilin. His job is to educate, not to report on students.

Author's comment:

P-sources were widely used in the early days of the CIA, but are used less often now. ██ ██ ████████████████████████████████ CIA recruitment is much more open today. CIA recruiters make regular visits to college campuses (where they are welcome), participate in job fairs, and advertise in campus publications. Strong emphasis is placed on increasing the number of minority applicants. The most common source of applications today is via the CIA website.

Many American colleges and universities are opposed to any FBI or CIA presence on their campuses. That makes it difficult for the FBI to carry out its national security responsibilities in the higher education arena. It is no secret, for example, that the intelligence services of Russia, China, and other countries make extensive use of graduate student cover at American universities to insert their officers. How can the FBI effectively monitor this activity without some level of support from university administrators and professors? Terrorists, also, have discovered that student visas are a relatively easy way to gain entry into the United States—and they know as well that there is virtually no follow-up by U.S. authorities to monitor their academic status once they are in the country. A large number of U.S. schools resist providing information to the FBI or other U.S. government agencies about their students, including their foreign students. They are concerned about their students' privacy, of course, and want to prevent them from being targeted for any reason by U.S. law enforcement and intelligence agencies.

The case of Dr. Zhilin above raises the extremely sensitive issue of whether the FBI and CIA should be allowed to target foreign students in the United States for recruitment as intelligence sources. From a purely intelligence standpoint, there are many attractive targets in this population. How many of these Chinese, Iranian, Pakistani, Indian, and other students who are working toward advanced degrees in nuclear engineering, electrical engineering, aeronautical engineering, computer engineering, physics, and chemistry at U.S. universities will be going back to sensitive military-related jobs in their own countries? A sizeable number. Should U.S. college campuses be recruitment-free zones for them while they are here? Or should they be fair game?

SCENARIO NO. 16:
PROSTITUTE FOR TERRORIST

The CIA has had a major intelligence success. It has recruited a penetration of an important al Qaida cell in Hamburg, Germany. This new source, encrypted FZOBSTACLE, is providing the CIA with extremely valuable intelligence on terrorist activities and personnel, not only in Germany but also throughout Europe. His information has proven to be accurate and reliable. On the basis of FZOBSTACLE's reporting, two al Qaida operatives have recently been arrested in Madrid. Also, thanks in large part to his intelligence, an al Qaida terrorist attack against the U.S. Embassy in Stockholm was prevented.

At a secret meeting in a safehouse in Hamburg, FZOBSTACLE asks his CIA case officer to provide him with a prostitute. He says it would be dangerous for him to frequent red-light districts in Hamburg, because he knows the German police patrol there heavily, and he is concerned about the risk of disease. FZOBSTACLE therefore asks the CIA to arrange a discreet rendezvous for him with a medically cleared call girl. He adds that if the CIA does not comply with his request he will break off contact, and the CIA will lose him as an intelligence source.

Would it be morally acceptable for the CIA to procure a prostitute for FZOBSTACLE?

Former FBI senior official Oliver "Buck" Revell:

Yes. The control and care of valuable intelligence sources is both delicate and difficult. I would certainly authorize providing a prostitute to FZOBSTACLE to preserve the vital intelligence he is supplying. The same action would be more difficult in the United States since it would violate U.S. law. However, if a source in the United States were providing information that preempted acts of terrorism and saved lives, I would authorize this accommodation as an "otherwise illegal act" justified by urgent necessity and therefore "morally acceptable."

Retired U.S. Navy Captain Richard Life:

Yes. I have no moral problem with the procurement of sexual favors as long as the prostitute has chosen her profession, was not forced into it by a white slaver, is independent and not controlled by a pimp, and is at least in her mid-20s.

Former CIA officer Richard Corbin:

Yes. Prostitution in this case would be between consenting adults and would be without a victim. I find it morally acceptable.

Professor Terry H. Anderson of Texas A&M University:
Yes. He is saving lives.

Former FBI special agent Stanley Pimentel:
Yes. I believe it would be morally acceptable to provide FZOBSTACLE with a medically cleared call girl. His threat to cut off his relationship with the CIA if the Agency does not provide the prostitute is sufficient grounds to grant him his wish. Of course, this could continue for some time and could cost the CIA a lot of money. Is it morally wrong? Yes. However, in light of the information FZOBSTACLE is providing it is morally acceptable. Such penetrations of the al Qaida network are rare and are worthy of exploitation by almost any means.

Author's comment:
The FBI and CIA faced a similar moral dilemma in the case of Arkady Shevchenko in the 1970s. Shevchenko was the highest-ranking Soviet at the United Nations in New York when he decided to defect to the United States in 1975. He was in an unhappy marriage and was disillusioned with the Soviet system. After his initial discussions with the CIA and FBI, Shevchenko agreed, somewhat reluctantly, "to stay in place," that is, to continue working as the U.N. under secretary general while secretly spying for the United States.[17] His position at the U.N. gave him high-level access to Soviet foreign policy information and negotiating positions, particularly with regard to arms control talks. Shevchenko turned out to be an intelligence gold mine for the United States.

Shevchenko met with his CIA and FBI handlers in safehouses in New York City. It was quickly apparent to the CIA and FBI that Shevchenko was a sad and lonely man. He complained to his case officers, in fact, how depressed he was and how desperately he wanted a woman in his life. He asked the FBI to provide him with the services of a call girl.

The proposal to use U.S. taxpayer dollars to procure a prostitute for Shevchenko was such a serious moral issue that it had to go all the way to the highest levels of the U.S. government for decision. (I would love to have been a fly on the wall when President Jimmy Carter was briefed.) The great fear was that if the U.S. government refused Shevchenko's request he might do something reckless on his own. He was a highly visible and well-known senior diplomat, and the KGB watched all Soviet personnel closely. Shevchenko might be observed while frequenting prostitutes. He might be the victim of a crime. He might contract a disease. The United States ran the risk of losing a very valuable intelligence source if Shevchenko ended up doing something foolish. For reasons of national security, therefore, the FBI provided Shevchenko with a prostitute.

Her name was Judy Chavez. Shevchenko worked in place for the FBI and CIA for three years, and Judy became a fixture in the case. It did not take her long to figure out what was going on. And, even worse, Arkady fell in love with her.

Shevchenko defected in 1978, when Soviet suspicions of a leak started focusing on him. He was generously compensated for his work for the CIA and FBI and was assisted in his resettlement in the United States. Sadly, though, Judy was not true. Her tawdry tell-all book, *Defector's Mistress: The Judy Chavez Story*, appeared in 1979. Poor Arkady was brokenhearted.

Shevchenko's own best-selling book, *Breaking with Moscow*, was published in 1985. It is possibly the best book ever written by a Soviet defector. It is not only a powerful indictment of the Soviet Communist system, but also a thrilling human story of espionage. Shevchenko died in Bethesda, Maryland, in 1998.

SCENARIO NO. 17:
CHILD PROSTITUTE

There is a serious threat of war with North Korea. The North Koreans have massed troops on the border with South Korea and have engaged in increasingly belligerent rhetoric. They have at least ten nuclear warheads in their arsenal and have stockpiled 5,000 tons of chemical warfare agents. Last fall, the North Koreans successfully tested the latest version of their Taepo-Dong missile, which the CIA now believes is capable of reaching targets as far away as the U.S. Midwest. In response, the U.S. has increased its military presence in South Korea to nearly 80,000 troops.

The CIA has recruited an outstanding North Korean source, encrypted DBMIRROR. DBMIRROR is a senior North Korean official who travels outside the country regularly on official business. He has a universal contact plan[18] so he can initiate contact with the CIA wherever he shows up. His intelligence reports on the North Korean military threat, leadership politics, and secret negotiations with the Chinese have received the highest evaluations. He is the CIA's only high-level HUMINT source on North Korea.

DBMIRROR is corrupt and venal. He was originally recruited in Copenhagen while serving there as the North Korean ambassador. At that time, he asked for and received from the CIA a recruitment bonus of $500,000 in cash. Since then, he has been paid a monthly salary of $50,000, which is deposited into a secret Swiss bank account.

DBMIRROR is in Bangkok to represent North Korea in sensitive discussions with regional officials. When he can break away from his duties and colleagues, he meets secretly with his CIA case officer in an alias-rented hotel room. He is providing extremely valuable intelligence on the crisis on the Korean peninsula.

At one of these meetings, DBMIRROR asks the CIA to provide him with the services of a pre-pubescent girl for his carnal pleasure. He says that if the CIA does not comply, he will break off the relationship. He insists he is too high profile to take the risk of procuring a young girl on his own. Child prostitutes of this kind are readily available in Bangkok.

———

Would it be morally acceptable for the CIA to provide DBMIRROR with a child prostitute? If not, and if DBMIRROR quits as a result, would it be morally acceptable for the CIA to burn him (expose him as a spy) to the North Koreans?

Former CIA officer Mary Lee Lieser:
No. It would be morally unacceptable to provide him with a child prostitute. I would have no problem in threatening to burn him to the North Koreans. If he chose to ignore the threat and did actually break contact, I would proceed and consider it morally acceptable to do so.

Pastor Tom Nelson of the Denton Bible Church in Denton, Texas:
No. Child prostitution is as great an evil as the evil we hope to prevent. This is an unacceptable means.

Former CIA Information Management Officer Ray Brewer:
No. No matter how valuable DBMIRROR is, there are lines we cannot cross, and child prostitution is one of them.

Author Ralph Peters:
No, but this is a very personal view. I am repelled by any exploitation or abuse of children. Someone with a less emotional reaction might well deem this acceptable for "the greater good." I would not hesitate to burn him. He is not only a traitor and a thug, but also a child abuser.

Former CIA officer David Edger:
No. A government official involved in procuring the services of such a prostitute, who is obviously to some degree in sexual slavery, would be

violating his own moral code and abetting a practice that is universally condemned. This demand is similar to demands made by spies throughout the years and must be deflected by reason or simply refused. The source will probably not quit. He will be angry, but he will get over his miff. Realistically, we cannot prevent him from finding a child as a sexual partner, and we probably should not try to keep him from making his own arrangements, but we should not assist him.

It would not be morally acceptable to burn him for his sexual proclivities. It would also be stupid. DBMIRROR might quit, but then recontact us the next time he is abroad. He has been useful to us and lived up to his end of the bargain. There is no reason we should not do the same by maintaining his security.

Author's comment:

████████████████████████████████████
████████████████████████████████████
████████████████████████ The agent sputtered a lot and repeated his threats, but did not quit. The money was too good.

CIA case officers are often forced to deal with some highly unsavory characters. Most of the agents I worked with in my career were people I admired and respected. I think particularly of several Russians and East Europeans I handled who put their lives in my hands to help fight their Communist regimes. We called them "ideological" spies. Many of them refused any form of compensation. Conversely, some of the agents and developmentals I worked with in my career would make DBMIRROR look good. As Meredith so accurately put it one night after we had just finished wining and dining an unusually sleazy character we were developing, "The things we do for our country!"

SCENARIO NO. 18:
TERRORIST ACT FOR BONA FIDES

The CIA in Jakarta has recruited a young member of the Indonesian terrorist group Jemaah Islamiyah (JI). The agent has been encrypted ZTACCORDEON. JI exploded a bomb inside the Jakarta Hilton hotel two months ago, killing forty-five people, including seven Americans. JI is also known to have been responsible for the bombing of the U.S. Embassy in Bangkok one year ago and for other terrorist attacks against U.S., Indonesian, British, Australian, Israeli, and Dutch interests in the region. It has been well established that JI has close ties to al Qaida.

ZTACCORDEON has been trained by JI in bomb building, using RDX and other high explosives. He has not yet, however, been fully admitted into the inner planning councils of JI. He reports that JI does not trust its new recruits until they have proven their loyalty and ardor by committing a terrorist act themselves.

ZTACCORDEON has been ordered by JI to build a car bomb and to place it under the car of an Indonesian police official who incurred the wrath of JI by tracking down and arresting two of its members. If he refuses, he will be considered suspect by the group and will be expelled from any involvement in its activities.

At a car pickup meeting[19] in Jakarta, ZTACCORDEON asks his CIA case officer for approval to carry out the bombing.

Would it be morally acceptable for the CIA to approve the car bombing for the purpose of preserving ZTACCORDEON as a penetration of Jemaah Islamiyah and enhancing his access within the group?

Ambassador Joseph E. Lake:

It depends. Whether it would be morally acceptable depends on how the action is handled. If the Indonesian police official can be clandestinely warned so that he is not injured and the bombing is "arranged" for a location where others are unlikely to be injured, then the action is acceptable. If it is impossible to arrange the bombing in this manner, then approval of the action is morally unacceptable.

Former CIA officer Haviland Smith:

No. When I had the Counterterrorism Staff back in the 70s, this was already a problem and for very good reason. If you are running a terrorist organization, the absolute best way to prove a potential recruit's bona fides is to get him or her to kill someone on your behalf. I think we all know that when we go into counterterrorism operations. If I were running a terrorist organization, I would seriously think about running just such a "volunteer" into the CIA. If the terrorists played it smart, they might end up with a bulletproof assassin! Rejection of this kind of proposal is a cultural imperative in the U.S. If we ever get to the point where we can go ahead with it, then we are no longer the society we think we are—certainly not the one the founding fathers had in mind. We would become terrorists ourselves. There is an important follow-on to this issue: What do you do with the agent after he refuses to kill the terrorist target? If we tell him not to do it, what moral responsibility do we have to him in the event his refusal to carry out the act is viewed by the terrorists as an indication that he is working against them? Can we just disregard the fact we have put this man's life in danger?

Professor Abraham Clearfield:

It depends. It is a terrible dilemma to ask someone to commit murder in the hope of preventing further mayhem and destruction. Jemaah Islamiyah is a terrible organization that will certainly attempt additional acts of terror. On the other hand, murdering the police official may deter the Indonesian police from pursuing other JI militants. This poses a dilemma for the CIA case officer. He should weigh the potential benefits of this car bombing against how likely it is that lives will be saved by penetrating the JI organization. He may wish to study similar cases from the past to determine if one evil of this kind will be compensated by continuing positive outcomes in the future.

Professor Mark Moyar of the U.S. Marine Corps University:

No. Under no circumstances should the United States contribute to the killing of innocent people in neutral or friendly countries for the purpose of gaining intelligence. There are certain humanitarian principles that should never be violated, and this scenario covers one of them. In addition to being unacceptable from a moral standpoint, this action would end up hurting the United States more than it helped, for when the word of the act eventually came out, as it usually does, the United States would suffer a loss in moral prestige among foreign governments. It is questionable, moreover, whether sanctioning the killing would actually result in the collection of critical intelligence, since we cannot predict what the agent's future access might be.

Former CIA officer David Edger:

No. It is not morally acceptable to allow ZTACCORDEON to kill the police officer to enhance his bona fides. While it is tempting to do so, and one can argue that we are sacrificing one life to protect many more, it is wrong to approve even a small terrorist act to attempt to prevent future terrorist acts, as yet undetermined. If the requirement were to murder another terrorist, a drug dealer, or some other "bad guy," it might be easier to justify, but it would still not pass the morality test. On the other hand, there is no moral objection to using a person who might have committed terrorist acts in the past as a source. Any terrorist penetration we are likely to have has probably been guilty of such acts. While we do not condone them, there is no moral requirement to deny ourselves the services of this source just because he has committed terrorist acts in the past.

Former CIA officer Burton Gerber:

No. It is my firm position, and I believe it is also the legal position of the United States, that we may not participate in or sponsor an act of terrorism, even if it should help our agent to establish his/her bona fides. This is admittedly a crisis point in these kinds of operations. What do you do when your asset is being tested in a way that violates our ethics and laws? I believe we cannot compromise this important point. There are several things the case officer can consider. One would be for the agent to look into the matter: casing, determining what kinds of materials to assemble, where to fabricate the bomb, etc., and then for some reason prove to be either inept or lazy. This happens in real life and, in itself, if not repeated over a period of time, should not be cause for suspicion. In the meantime, of course, the case officer must exploit the source for as much information as possible in order to confound, compromise, or eliminate the terrorist organization. The agent is already in contact with some people in Jemaah Islamiyah. He already knows some names, phone numbers, safe areas, and such. And these data, even if not the center of the organization, will be helpful in reducing its effectiveness, maybe even leading to other potential sources with more information.

Author's comment:

The CIA and FBI have often been criticized for not having enough penetrations of terrorist organizations. The above scenario points out one of the major reasons this is true. Terrorists test one another by blood. No terrorist is fully trusted by the rest of the group until he or she has been directly involved in the planning or execution of a deadly terrorist attack. When U.S. intelligence agencies have successfully recruited low-level terrorist assets, sooner or later this problem has become a stumbling block. Terrorists who do not kill do not reach the inner planning councils of their organizations. Until they do so, their access to important information is strictly limited.

U.S. law enforcement officials face a similar problem. How long can the FBI keep an informant inside the Mafia in place without allowing him to commit criminal acts? Can DEA let one of its penetrations of a Mexican drug cartel participate in a small-scale shipment of heroin into Miami in expectation of a huge bust later on? The Mafia and the drug cartels are not stupid. If their operations are rolled up, they are very good at finding the leaks in their organizations. Terrorists are just as smart.

There are other reasons why human penetrations of terrorist organizations have been and will probably always be rare. Terrorist organizations operate in small close-knit groups. Many of their members come from the same villages and have known one another for years. They operate in tightly compartmented cells. They have excellent tradecraft and are suspicious of outsiders. They are fanatically loyal to their cause and cannot be bought. They are also invisible, so they are virtually impossible to find, let alone to spot, assess, develop, and pitch.

I hear frequently that the CIA must train more case officers to speak Arabic, Farsi, Pashto, Dari, etc., and must also come up with better covers for them. That's certainly true, but until the inherent drawbacks in recruiting terrorists, discussed above, are solved, HUMINT is never going to be the answer to preventing future terrorist attacks against Americans.

SCENARIO NO. 19:
ELECTION TAMPERING

The president of Venezuela, Vicente Garrido, has moved his country to the far left and has severely strained relations with the United States. Earlier this year, he expelled all U.S. military personnel from Venezuela and cut the staff of the U.S. Embassy in Caracas in half. He maintains close ties with Communist Cuba and appointed a Cuban-trained officer to head his security service. Several international human rights groups have expressed concern about the flagrant human rights violations in the country. Garrido has publicly announced his sympathy for the Colombian terrorist group FARC and has provided the Colombian guerillas with training bases and safe havens inside Venezuela. U.S. intelligence recently confirmed that Garrido and his Cuban allies are supplying FARC with weapons and other support.

DEA and CIA reporting has established conclusively that Garrido is allowing the Middle Eastern terrorist groups Hezbollah and Hamas to engage in widespread drug trafficking and money laundering operations in Venezuela, with profits exceeding $100 million a year.

The Organization of American States (OAS) condemned Venezuela last month for its human rights violations, support of terrorism, drug trafficking, and undemocratic government.

Although Garrido has tried to stifle all political opposition in Venezuela, he has reluctantly agreed to a recall referendum early next year in the face of intense international pressure. The Venezuelan opposition is weak and poorly funded.

The U.S. National Security Council has directed the CIA to develop a plan for aggressive covert action to prevent a victory by Garrido in the referendum. The U.S. president signed the necessary finding[20] to authorize the covert action in Venezuela.

The CIA operation to oust Garrido from power is encrypted PDPLAYBOOK. The major elements of the plan are the following:

1) secret funding of the Venezuelan opposition;
2) smear tactics against Garrido and his supporters, including forged documents and letters;
3) disruption of Garrido's campaign speeches and rallies;

4) efforts to foment unrest and anti-Garrido sentiment in the military and in prodemocracy labor unions;

5) use of local media assets recruited by the CIA to plant stories critical of Garrido;

6) stuffing of ballot boxes;

7) bribery of election officials to report results favorable to the opposition.

———————

Would it be morally acceptable for the CIA to implement Operation PDPLAYBOOK, as described above, to defeat Vicente Garrido in the recall referendum?

Professor Mark Moyar of the U.S. Marine Corps University:

Yes. I would normally have reservations about tampering with a fair election, but based on the allegations of human rights violations in this instance, it is likely that Garrido himself plans to tamper with the elections, depriving the elections of moral value. Venezuela as a whole would likely be better off without him, so the United States would be acting in the best interests of that country. In addition, Garrido's facilitation of terrorist and drug operations that harm the United States makes this case an issue of self-defense. Previous efforts of this type, most notably in Europe in the late 1940s, seem to have been effective without harming the moral prestige of the United States.

Former CIA officer Louise Corbin:

No. Operation PDPLAYBOOK, as outlined, is morally unacceptable to me, most particularly when it comes to items six and seven. We are a democracy that supports free and democratic elections. What kind of moral authority would we have if we became engaged in the bribery of election officials and ballot box stuffing? What our country stands for should be the guideline for conduct in our government as well.

Professor Harry Mason of the Patterson School at the University of Kentucky:

Yes (class vote), but narrowly. The students in my graduate course on intelligence found the election tampering scenario morally acceptable by a close vote of 9 to 8. Those who voted no were mostly troubled by the ballot box stuffing.

Former USIA officer John Williams:

No. As distasteful as Garrido and his modus operandi might be to the

U.S., he does not appear to pose a direct and dire national security threat. Further, the United States, as the region's most powerful and oldest democracy, must continue to lead by example and principle. Most fundamentally, it cannot credibly uphold standards of freedom of choice and freedom from coercion and political fear if it actively undermines these—for however justifiable a cause—in the hemisphere. If the operation only included action item number one, secret funding of the Venezuelan opposition, I believe it would have been morally acceptable. After all, Garrido's opposition is weak, fragmented, and timid because of his political brutality. The democratic process in the country would be considerably advanced by not only funding the opposition but also by carrying out a series of actions to strengthen its cohesion and impact in the days before the referendum. Garrido's acquiescence to the referendum resulted from intense international pressure. A regional effort should be made to bring further pressure to bear on Garrido to cease his political bullying. Measures up to and including a regional boycott of Venezuelan oil should be considered. Finally, international monitoring of the referendum should be implemented. If the opposition still comes up short, the OAS and individual American states should make it clear that they expect to see Garrido's political adversaries represented fairly in any new government, proportionally based on referendum results.

Former USIA officer Philip Brown:

Yes. If President Garrido is as bad as described or, more importantly, as much of a threat to U.S. interests as would seem to be the case, I would not veto Operation PDPLAYBOOK on moral grounds. But I fully expect to read some ten or twenty years later that we were sold a bill of goods, that the United States government lied to us, and that, in fact, we overthrew a decent man.

Professor Robert Jensen of the University of Texas:

No. For more than fifty years, the CIA has been not just an intelligence-gathering agency, but also a tool of U.S. policymakers to extend and deepen U.S. domination of the world. It has carried out covert operations involving coups, economic warfare, rigged elections, and assassinations as part of the U.S. project of empire building. That project is motivated not by concerns for people in other countries but by the iron law of post–World War II U.S. foreign policy. Development in the Third World that is independent of the United States must be derailed whenever possible. This project is fundamentally immoral. Any collaboration with this project is immoral. The obligations of citizenship require that we seek to end projects like this and to eliminate the institutions that carry them out.

Author's comment:

In 1948 President Harry Truman ordered the then–brand new CIA to do everything possible to prevent the Italian Communist Party from winning the April 1948 elections in Italy. The Communists had taken over most of Eastern Europe by then, and the U.S. considered it strategically imperative to ensure that a pro-Soviet government did not take power in Italy. The CIA responded with an elaborate, extensive, and ultimately successful covert action campaign, its first major operation of this type. The pro-Western Christian Democrats won in a landslide.

It is well documented that the CIA conducted large-scale covert action operations in Chile in an effort to influence the results of the presidential elections there in 1964 and 1970.

SCENARIO NO. 20:
SEDUCTION AND COMPROMISE

Erin Pendleton is a twenty-seven-year-old CIA case officer serving under cover in Rome. To expand her spotting opportunities, she joins the S.G. Roma tennis club in the heart of the city. She knows that this club is frequented by foreign diplomats, including several from countries of interest to the CIA. Pendleton is an excellent tennis player and has no trouble arranging matches with potential targets who belong to the club. She also works out in the club's fitness center and occasionally stops for a drink in the club bar. She has found the S.G. Roma club to be an excellent spotting venue.

One afternoon Pendleton notices a player alone on a court practicing his serve. She approaches him and asks if he would be interested in a quick set or two. He agrees.

The player is Hossein Sadegh, the forty-two-year-old deputy chief of mission in the Iranian Embassy. After an hour of tennis, Sadegh invites Erin to have a cool drink with him in the bar. They agree to meet at the club the following Thursday for another game of tennis.

The CIA is delighted that Pendleton has made contact with such a high-priority target. The chief encourages her to continue the assessment and development[21] of Sadegh in an effort to move him toward full recruitment as a penetration of the Iranian government. As deputy chief of mission, Sadegh would have access to all the classified traffic in the embassy, the ambassador's office, and the code room. The CIA is in desperate need of HUMINT on Iran. Acquisition of the Iranian diplomatic codes, moreover, would be an intelligence bonanza for CIA and NSA.

Pendleton and Sadegh quickly become regular tennis and lunch partners. After two months it is obvious to Pendleton that Sadegh is smitten with her and that his primary interest in her is romantic. He has never been married. Pendleton assesses him as weak and easy to manipulate. She has detected no political or material vulnerabilities in him but is certain she could make him emotionally vulnerable to her. Pendleton informs the chief that she is willing to seduce Sadegh as a means of compromising him and drawing him into spying for the U.S. She believes Sadegh will lose interest in her and will break contact if she continues to reject his advances.

Would it be morally acceptable for the CIA to allow Pendleton to engage in a voluntary sexual relationship with Sadegh as a means of drawing him into espionage?

Dr. Geoffrey Tumlin, assistant director of the Center for Ethical Leadership at the Lyndon B. Johnson School of Public Affairs at the University of Texas:

It depends. If I thought Sadegh could be very useful and the psychological "cost" to Pendleton would be marginal, I would authorize it.

Ph.D. student Margaretta Mathis:

No. It would not be morally acceptable. And it would not work, either. Sadegh would feel misled. He would know it was a ruse and would, in turn, play a double agent role and sabotage the information he provided to the CIA.

Ph.D. student Margaret Meacham:

Yes. The use of psychological techniques, including seduction, is morally acceptable. If Sadegh gets drawn in, then gets talkative, he will have to make the decision either to help out or not. Pendleton cannot be ethically asked to give her all, but if she volunteers, her part is morally acceptable.

Graduate student Jason Pogacnik of the Maxwell School at Syracuse University:

Yes. The action as described is morally acceptable. If blackmail were involved, the action would become morally questionable, but there is no indication of that here. The operation is moral because it hinges on voluntary choice. Specifically, if the operation goes forward, Sadegh will have the choice to engage in a sexual relationship with Pendleton or not. I assume he will also have the capacity for rational choice when faced with the prospect of spying on his country for the U.S., although his ability to make a clear decision will certainly be affected by the emotional vulnerability identified and capitalized on by Pendleton. From a moral standpoint, however, Sadegh is free to end the relationship and to walk away before committing espionage. Pendleton is also acting voluntarily.

Undergraduate student Laura Zandstra of Texas A&M University:
No. It would be morally unacceptable for Pendleton to engage even in a voluntary sexual relationship with Sadegh to gain intelligence. Sex should be the "cementing" of an undying love that lasts forever. Unfortunately, we live in a society where sex has been cheapened. What initially existed as a sign of true love has now become a tool for manipulation.

Lauraine Brekke-Esparza, city manager of Del Mar, California:
It depends. I think my initial reaction to this question was influenced by too many James Bond movies. I thought seduction and compromise were how it was always done! But all joking aside, my answer has to be "it depends." Pendleton reportedly volunteered to do this, but was it really "volunteerism" on her part or in fact coercion by her superiors, an understanding that this was how she could get ahead? If it is truly of her own volition, then I think it is morally acceptable for her to engage in a voluntary sexual relationship with Sadegh.

Practicing attorney Christopher Scherer:
No. All relationships are characterized by a certain degree of power and coercion, particularly sexual relationships. While it is not admirable that Pendleton has misled Sadegh about her receptivity to his advances, her voluntary action is not per se morally reprehensible. What is more troubling to me is that the CIA is willing to use the sexuality of one of its officers as a tool of the U.S. government. One must question the moral and ethical implications of such a decision, notwithstanding Pendleton's apparent volition. While in this case the CIA case officer might truly be consenting to this type of behavior, situations would likely arise where officers would feel subtly pressured to use their bodies as a state tool. I cannot think of any guiding set of standards, principles, or philosophies that would allow the Agency to evaluate whether this decision was freely made. This behavior should be prohibited in all situations.

Author's comment:
The CIA, FBI, and other U.S. government intelligence agencies have strict prohibitions on romantic relationships between officers and agents or between officers and recruitment targets. But does it happen? Of course. The CIA traitor Aldrich Ames was having an extramarital affair with his Colombian-born future wife Rosario while she worked for him as an access agent[22] in Mexico City. During my senior overseas assignments for the CIA, there were two instances in which I had to send case officers home short-of-tour for sexual misconduct, one involving an agent, the other a developmental.

I am, unfortunately, aware of other cases where CIA case officers, both male and female, have stepped across the line. Two FBI special agents, James Smith and William Cleveland, had a long-term sexual relationship with their Chinese informant Katrina Leung. Their misconduct turned into a major counterintelligence flap when it was learned that Leung was a double agent for the Chinese MSS. The rationale for the rule, I believe, is primarily moral. The U.S. government simply chooses on moral grounds not to condone such activity. It also recognizes, of course, that romantic relationships remove objectivity and cloud operational judgments.

The CIA and the FBI do not use sexual entrapment for recruitment purposes. In that regard, they may be the only major intelligence services in the world not to do so. The Soviet KGB made an art form of it during the Cold War, and the Chinese, East Germans, and others were not far behind. Sexual entrapment is still a widely used espionage technique today

Sex has sometimes been an annoying distraction and complication for female CIA case officers. A good case officer must aggressively spot potential recruitment targets and then take the lead in moving them toward developmental relationships. Even when this is done cleverly, targets often get the impression they are being pursued. Since most recruitment targets around the world are male, a female American case officer who persistently seeks to maintain social or professional contact with a male target can easily be misunderstood. Some nationalities are familiar with and accept aggressive women in the workplace, for example Europeans, but others do not, most notably Arabs, Latinos, and some Asians. A woman on the make (as case officers are trained to be) is totally alien to their cultural norms.

In Vienna, I had a young female case officer working for me under cover. She was moving around town aggressively, trying to meet as many recruitment targets as possible, just as all case officers do. I thought she was doing a good job and was off to a fine start in her operational career. One day, she met a young Palestinian official at a diplomatic reception and engaged him in small talk about his background and interests. They exchanged cards. The next day, she phoned him and invited him to lunch "to discuss the Middle East situation." He accepted without hesitation. Their lunch was pleasant and informative, and my case officer was encouraged that she seemed to have an interesting operation underway. As they were putting their coats on in the vestibule after lunch, however, the Palestinian touched my officer inappropriately and made an indecent proposal to her. When she indignantly brushed him off, he acted surprised and said to her, "Then why did you invite me out?"

Another female case officer I worked with overseas attempted to avoid the problem by targeting only other women, which, of course, was a serious limitation to her work since most of the station's high priority recruitment targets were men. This officer simply did not want the hassle of pursuing foreign men and having her intentions misconstrued. She eventually changed her career category to operations support so she would not have to recruit in her future assignments. This was an exception, however, because most CIA women case officers have learned to deal with the problem and have overcome it. Still, there is no denying that sexual undercurrents are present whenever a case officer and agent are of different sexes.

One of my good friends, a senior officer at the CIA, once commented, only half jokingly, I think, that he would like to ban sex for all case officers because it complicated operations. Fortunately, the idea of a celibate clandestine service at the CIA never caught on.

SCENARIO NO. 21:
ROMEO OPERATIONS

In its recruitment operations overseas the CIA has identified a large HUMINT target audience it is not successfully reaching: single middle-aged women. The CIA has identified hundreds of never-married and divorced women in the thirty-five to fifty age range who occupy positions with access to highly sensitive intelligence information in their countries. Some are secretaries and clerks; others are diplomats, researchers, and government officials.

CIA psychologists and operators believe some of these women would be susceptible to romantic approaches. A task force is formed to examine the possibility of recruiting a stable of handsome men of various nationalities to target these women. The participants in these "Romeo operations" would not be CIA staff officers, but would be contractors recruited and trained for this specific purpose. They would be trained in the psychological and emotional needs of middle-aged women and in techniques on how to seduce them. Once seduced, the women would be enticed into espionage.

Nadezhda Nikolayeva is a forty-four-year-old secretary for the director of the American Department of the Sluzhba Vneshney Razvedki Rossii (SVRR), Russia's foreign intelligence service. She is single and lonely. The SVRR operates aggressively inside the United States and targets U.S. military personnel, government employees, scientists, engineers, politicians, and businessmen for recruitment. Nikolayeva handles all the correspondence for the director of the SVRR's American Department and has access to his operational files.

The CIA approves a "Romeo operation" against Nikolayeva and puts one of its recruits, Bertrand Sokoloff, a French citizen of Russian origin, under cover as an employee of a French bank in Moscow. Using pattern information provided by the CIA, Sokoloff is able to engineer a "chance" encounter with Nikolayeva at a Moscow bar. They hit if off and begin to see each other socially. Before long, Nikolayeva is hopelessly in love with the dashing Frenchman. She does not report her contact with Sokoloff to the SVRR, because she knows it would not be approved.

————

Would it be morally acceptable for the CIA to use a Romeo operation against Nikolayeva in an effort to recruit her as a penetration of the SVRR?

Professor Michael Porter of the University of Missouri:
No. I would be appalled to find such a scenario rooted in fact. These are unsuspecting individuals—working-class women—who would be personally hurt by such a set up. It seems unfair to bring them into the net only to have them stung severely.

Dr. Randy Everett, M.D., from Fort Collins, Colorado:
Yes. If Nikolayeva allows herself to be recruited, she will be exchanging that which she has for that which she wants—the essence of a free trade exchange. This is manipulation, no doubt, but in the absence of coercion it is acceptable with an adult.

Undergraduate student Aaron Tatyrek of Texas A&M University:
Yes. Since the SVRR is actively targeting American diplomats, businessmen, politicians, etc., there may be several traitors inside our government like Robert Hanssen. Nikolayeva's information could provide us with information on who they are and allow us to take steps to apprehend them. A Romeo operation against Ms. Nikolayeva is morally acceptable.

Former State Department officer John Salazar:
Yes. There is no law that I know of that prohibits this. This is a classic espionage ploy used extensively by the "other side."

Michael Bohn, former director of the White House Situation Room:
Yes. This is a common recruitment tactic, and it is morally acceptable.

Colonel Cindy R. Jebb of the United States Military Academy:
[The opinions expressed by Colonel Jebb are her own and do not necessarily reflect the views of the United States Military Academy, the Department of the Army, or the Department of Defense.]
No. Romeo operations are not morally acceptable. It is tempting to approve this operation given the fact that Nikolayeva's intelligence could be

critical to U.S. national security. One could argue also that since Nikolayeva works in the Russian security apparatus she is a viable target. But I still find the operation morally objectionable. I am concerned as well that the CIA is contracting out this task to a foreign citizen. By what criteria would these contract personnel be selected? How would carrying out an operation like this affect a contract person?

Former CIA officer William Lieser:

Yes. For me, this is an easy call. An employee of an organization working against U.S. interests who clearly has access to important information affecting our security is fair game. This operational tactic was successfully used for decades by the East Germans to penetrate the West German government, and it has been used by many other intelligence services as well. I see no moral problem here.

Graduate student Sarah Forbey of the George Bush School of Government and Public Service at Texas A&M University:

No. A woman who is enticed and humiliated by a false romantic interest will likely resent the service responsible and may even lash out by inflicting damage upon it. Romeo operations traverse the boundaries that differentiate U.S. intelligence operations from those of other countries. The victim of a Romeo operation will eventually note the moral and ethical equivalency between the U.S. and the target country. Even if she was once friendly toward the U.S. and amenable to spying for ideological reasons, she will be left with nothing but emotional damage and jaded disdain for the country she associates with her seduction. Individual cases of utmost urgency might justify a Romeo tactic, but the systematic use of seduction for intelligence purposes is dehumanizing. It also produces more enemies of the U.S. than it does valuable intelligence. I see an additional danger in these operations. If CIA case officers are initiated into such callous disregard for the psychological health of their agents, they will likely engage in the cavalier devaluing of other people as well.

Author's comment:

The United States does not use Romeo operations—but they do work. The Russians and East Germans used them to great advantage throughout the Cold War. KGB documents smuggled to the West in 1992 revealed that a former British policeman named John Symonds worked for the KGB as a Romeo spy from 1972 to 1980. In interviews with the press in 1999, Symonds admitted to his role and claimed he had received training by the KGB in seduction and lovemaking techniques. His targets, he said, were lonely female employees of Western embassies.

Markus Wolf, the head of the foreign intelligence section (HVA) of the East German Ministry of State Security (MfS or Stasi), described his successes with Romeo operations in his autobiography *The Man Without a Face*. The HVA recruited a stable of usually handsome (not always) East German men and trained them as Romeo spies. They were then dispatched to West Germany with false identities to pose as West Germans. Their assignment was to seek out vulnerable women working in government jobs, to seduce them, and then to draw them into espionage. The East German operators usually had some thin pretext for why they needed the classified information, for example, support for an international peace group, research, etc., but most of the women knew early on what they were really doing. Some of the Romeo spies had more than one "romance" going on at a time. One particular cad (or very skilled operator in the eyes of the HVA) bragged that he had four or five West German women on the string at any given moment. The best estimate is that at least forty West German women were victimized by Romeo spies. Among the victims were a West German translator at the U.S. Embassy in Bonn, a secretary in Chancellor Helmut Kohl's office, a foreign ministry employee, an administrative assistant in the office of West German President Richard von Weizsacker, and a secretary for the European Economic Community in Brussels.

Wolf claimed that the intelligence from these Romeo operations was among the best the East received during the Cold War. Many of these relationships were long-term. If a woman had particularly good access and was fully cooperative, the HVA encouraged the man to keep the relationship alive. There were even some marriages, and Wolf states that at least ten of these marriages survived and have been happy. Happiness, however, was clearly the exception for the exploited women. Most of them experienced severe emotional strain and shame after being deceived in this manner. At least one, Leonore Suetterlin, committed suicide. Many of the women were tried for espionage when their spying was uncovered.

At least two American cases appear to be similar. In 1985, Sharon Scranage, an operations support assistant for the CIA in Accra, Ghana, was arrested for passing sensitive information on CIA operations to her Ghanaian lover, Michael Soussoudis. Soussoudis was cooperating with the Ghanaian intelligence service. In 1995, there was a major counterintelligence flap for the CIA when it was discovered that a female NOC in Paris had been having an unauthorized affair with a foreign national and had shared with him classified information on CIA operations in Paris. He was cooperating with French intelligence.[23]

SCENARIO NO. 22:
COERCIVE PITCH

Gennady Tokarev, a GRU[24] (Glavnoye Razvedyvatelnoye Upravleniye—Main Intelligence Directorate) officer under cover as a military attaché in the Russian Embassy in Athens, has been sloppy. His surveillance detection runs before operational acts have been too short and too predictable. As a result, CIA surveillance teams in Athens have been able to track him to meetings with four of his Greek agents. Tokarev meets with his agents in small cafés and restaurants on the outskirts of Athens. The CIA teams have been able to photograph Tokarev with these agents and to identify them by following them back to their cars, offices, and homes.

Tokarev's agents are well-placed: a high-ranking official in the New Democracy Party; the chief of counterintelligence for the EIP (Greek Intelligence Service); a journalist for *Eleftherotypia*; and a lieutenant colonel in the Greek army.

Patricia Margen, a Russian-speaking CIA officer, is sent on temporary duty to Athens to pitch Tokarev. She intercepts him on the street and informs him that four of his important agent cases have been compromised. Margen adds that unless Tokarev cooperates with the CIA, the photos and details of his clandestine meetings with his agents will be sent to the Greek government, to the Greek press, and to the Russian ambassador. Margen shows him copies of the photos. Tokarev's incompetence as a case officer will be exposed and his career will be over. The incident will cause a rift in Greek-Russian relations. The four Greek agents will be investigated and arrested. Everyone loses. The good news, however, is that Tokarev can avoid all of this unpleasantness. All he has to do is to begin working for the CIA.

The CIA would benefit greatly from a full debriefing of Tokarev on the activities, targets, equipment, and personnel of the GRU. He would be required to pass classified documents and other damaging and verifiable information to the CIA from the very beginning to establish his bona fides.[25] The CIA would also be very interested in monitoring and controlling his agent cases. Tokarev would be required to wear a concealed CIA wire at all future meetings with his agents.

Tokarev's options are extremely limited: cooperation with the CIA or professional and personal ruin. He knows that even if he turns down the CIA pitch he will be forced to report his indiscretions to his GRU superiors and to leave Athens in disgrace. The CIA not only has the compromising photos, which it can use against him at any time, but it also, of course, has a tape of Margen's pitch to him.

Tokarev is an honest and dedicated public servant, a Russian patriot, and a good family man.

————

Would it be morally acceptable for the CIA to make the coercive pitch to Tokarev as described above? Would it be morally acceptable, if Tokarev rejects the pitch, to follow through on the threat to destroy him professionally and personally? Would it be morally acceptable, if Tokarev accepts the pitch, to debrief him on everything he knows about the GRU and then to expose him and his agents to our Greek allies?

Author Ralph Peters:

Yes. It would be morally acceptable, but it would be foolish to tip what we know so clumsily, since Tokarev could pass each meeting off as a normal diplomatic conversation in a casual public environment. A photo taken in a café is not the same as one taken in a dark alley with something changing hands. You have to have evidence that something compromising—beyond just the meeting—transpired. Following through on the threat if Tokarev rejects the pitch is also morally acceptable. He's in the game. Destroying him falls within the rules of play.

Colonel Cindy R. Jebb of the United States Military Academy:

[The opinions expressed by Colonel Jebb are her own and do not necessarily reflect the views of the United States Military Academy, the Department of the Army, or the Department of Defense.]

1) Yes. It is morally acceptable to make the pitch. The CIA caught Tokarev engaging in spying against a U.S. ally, and now the CIA has an opportunity to help that ally. Tokarev is a viable target based on his capacity as an intelligence officer.

2) Yes. The CIA must follow through with the threat. If not, it would lose credibility for future operations.

3) It depends, but probably no. How would a betrayal like this affect CIA officer Margen on a personal moral level? Would she be able to conduct future operations with a clear conscience? On balance, I think betraying Tokarev would be morally unacceptable on several levels.

Former CIA and Army officer Jack Bosley:

1) Yes. He has compromised himself by his poor tradecraft and his options are very limited. Pitch the son-of-a-bitch.

2) Yes. It would be morally acceptable, if Tokarev rejects the pitch, to attempt to destroy him professionally and personally. It is likely

he will reject the pitch and take his chances back in Russia. At a minimum, though, the U.S. will be forcing him out of Athens and breaking up a major Russian spy ring.

3) No. It would not be morally acceptable or operationally beneficial to debrief him on GRU operations and then expose him. Doing that would discourage future recruitments and defections.

Former CIA polygrapher John Sullivan:

Yes. Tokarev does have a choice: he can say no and report the pitch. I do not see this as a moral dilemma. What happened to Tokarev is a risk every case officer takes. Here, Tokarev is suffering the consequences of doing his job poorly.

Professor Richard Graving of the South Texas College of Law:

1) Yes. The fact that Tokarev is an honest public servant, patriot, and good family man is largely irrelevant. He is an intelligence officer and has assumed the risks of professional failure and blackmail. A coercive pitch to him is morally acceptable.

2) Yes. Exposing him if he rejects the pitch is morally acceptable.

3) No. Exposing Tokarev to the Greeks after the CIA has debriefed him adds another dimension to the problem. What obligation do we have to our Greek allies? Can we meet our obligations as an ally without undermining our "bargain" with Tokarev? If the next Tokarev who comes along knows what happened to Tokarev, would he be likely to submit? While generally I think double-crossing is morally unacceptable, there could be payoffs that justify it, such as saving lives (or even saving the Parthenon). In this case, however, taking Tokarev's information and then exposing him and his agents to the Greeks would not be morally acceptable. That game would not be worth the candle.

U.S. Army Lieutenant Colonel Tony Pfaff:

1) Yes. As I wrote in "The Ethics of Espionage" (*Journal of Military Ethics*, 2004), intelligence officers accept the risk of this kind of coercion by virtue of being in the profession. By consenting to conduct operations that put the security of the U.S. at risk, Tokarev has consented to be the target of U.S. counterintelligence operations. He should reasonably expect such operations.

2) Yes, for the same reasons.

3) No. The success of this operation depends on Tokarev's belief that the CIA will fulfill its part of the bargain. Tokarev should not

reasonably expect to be betrayed. Thus, while coercion is permitted, lying to gain greater advantage is not.

Author's comment:
Being pitched by the CIA or the FBI can be a cataclysmic event for a foreign intelligence officer. If he does not report the pitch, he will forever be vulnerable to follow-up approaches. He assumes that the CIA or the FBI recorded the pitch and can use the tape against him at any time. Every foreign intelligence officer is required to report a hostile pitch, but the consequences of doing so can be professionally devastating. The Communist intelligence services, for example, often looked on a CIA or FBI pitch of one of their officers as an indication that the targeted officer had made a mistake or was considered vulnerable for some reason. They often resolved the doubt by quickly sending the officer home to get him out of harm's way. The officer's plum assignment in the U.S. or elsewhere in the West would be over—and future overseas assignments could also be jeopardized. His career as an intelligence officer might never be the same again.

CIA case officers who are pitched by foreign intelligence services fare much better. They are sometimes removed for their own safety, but reporting a pitch is not necessarily considered a professional black mark. The circumstances of the pitch are examined closely and if, in fact, there was exploitable behavior on the part of the case officer, corrective action will be taken. It is often the case, however, that the hostile service was simply pitching cold, without any indication of vulnerability, as an act of harassment or in the remote hope of getting lucky. It was widely known in my time at the CIA that a respected senior officer had been pitched by the Soviets early in his career. Obviously, there had been no long-term negative effects on his career. All CIA case officers know that one of the worst things they can do is to get pitched and *not* to report it. This is a cardinal counterintelligence sin and will definitely have serious consequences for the officer when it becomes known.

The situation might be different for the FBI when a target is caught in illegal activity and can be pressured into making a deal, but even those cases are rare. As a general rule, coercive pitches do not work and most Western intelligence services avoid them.

SCENARIO NO. 23:
FEEDING A DRUG HABIT

Pedram Mousavi is a thirty-four-year-old officer of VEVAK (Iranian Ministry of Intelligence and Security) under cover as a second secretary in the Iranian mission to the United Nations in New York. During his two years in New York, Mousavi has become severely addicted to cocaine. He is still able to perform his intelligence duties, but he no longer has the financial resources to support his habit. He is desperate.

Mousavi walks into the New York field office of the FBI and asks to speak to a special agent. He admits that he is a VEVAK officer and then offers the FBI a deal. He says he will work as an informant for the FBI inside VEVAK and the Iranian mission to the United Nations in return for the FBI's support of his cocaine addiction. He promises to provide the FBI with intelligence on VEVAK's operations inside the U.S., including assistance to terrorist groups. He can also give the FBI copies of classified messages between the Iranian mission and Tehran.

In his discussion with the FBI special agent, Mousavi makes it clear he is not interested in treatment. He wants a regular supply of cocaine without the expense, risk, or hassle of having to obtain it on his own. That is his offer. His proposal to the FBI is non-negotiable: take it or leave it.

———

Would it be morally acceptable for the FBI to feed Mousavi's cocaine addiction in return for his services as a penetration of VEVAK and the Iranian mission to the United Nations?

Former middle-school and high-school teacher Barbara Ziesche:
No. It is not morally acceptable to feed Mousavi's drug habit. As a taxpayer, I would be appalled to learn we were buying cocaine for a person who, in turn, was helping us in covert operations. I do not believe a drug user is a reliable person, so we should not even pursue that route.

Former FBI senior executive John Guido:
No. Providing drugs in exchange for information is not morally acceptable. Giving Mousavi money to sustain his habit, while not illegal, would be similarly wrong. In addition to the moral issue, utilizing a drug addict as a source is operationally questionable due to concerns about his reliability.

Undergraduate student Aaron Tatyrek of Texas A&M University:
No. Although the information Mousavi could provide is valuable, the fact that he is a drug addict undermines the operation entirely. He may or may not have the mental capacity to carry out the mission. He is a threat to himself and to our interests.

Former CIA officer Louise Corbin:
No. The consequences of such an operation are unpredictable, personally

destructive, and potentially life-threatening for Mousavi. Knowing what lies ahead for him, we are directly facilitating the downward spiral of a human being. In my view, it smacks a little too much of playing God with another human being's life.

Admiral Bobby R. Inman, former director of the National Security Agency and deputy director of central intelligence:

No. The moral acceptability is questionable. The operation falls apart in any case on the strong likelihood that a cocaine abuser would lie and cheat to keep the supply of drugs coming and could not be trusted.

Former FBI special agent Stanley Pimentel:

No. It has been proved that individuals with drug habits are not reliable or trustworthy. There is no guarantee that Mousavi would provide the FBI with the information he claims to be able to provide. He has no proven track record and, therefore, his offer should not be accepted. It might, however, be worth pursuing him to assess his vulnerabilities and potential. A possibility exists that Mousavi could be forced to cooperate and to provide information. Since he is a diplomat, the FBI could cause him grave embarrassment if he refuses to cooperate and could declare him *persona non grata*. In this manner, the FBI would be obtaining the information Mousavi can provide and yet not be placed in the position of fueling his cocaine habit.

Author's comment:

It is not unusual for agents to ask their case officers for illegal items or acts in return for their spying services. After all, the agents reason, the covert arrangement that brings them together is based on treason and espionage, activities that are illegal in every country. So, if the law is being broken already, what harm is there in an additional crime or two? Many agents also have an exaggerated and distorted view of what the U.S. intelligence agencies are willing and able to do for them. They often ascribe, for example, virtually unlimited extralegal authorities to the FBI and CIA. Why can't you just eliminate my hated rival in the ministry? Why can't you smuggle this package into the U.S. for me? Why can't you give me a gun with a silencer and sniper scope on it? Why can't you give me cocaine? It is not always easy for case officers to explain to these agents that such actions are illegal under U.S. law and the CIA and FBI are strictly bound by U.S. law.

The CIA has been tied to the issue of illegal drugs more often than it would like. There have been frequent allegations over the years that the CIA has been involved in drug trafficking. The charges include such things as using a CIA proprietary, Air America, to shuttle drugs around Southeast

Asia during the Vietnam War; colluding with Manuel Noriega in drug trafficking through Panama; providing trucks and mules to drug smugglers in
Afghanistan during the Soviet occupation; and distributing crack cocaine to
gangs in South Central Los Angeles. It does not seem to matter that these
charges are investigated and found baseless; the theories persist and thrive.
Not long ago, I gave a speech in a large U.S. city on the role of intelligence
in the war on terror. About ten minutes into the speech, I was interrupted
by a well-dressed and articulate member of the audience. Did I deny, he
asked, that the CIA had created al Qaida? Did I deny that the CIA had
known about 9/11 beforehand, but had let it happen so the U.S. government would have a pretext to invade Afghanistan? And why was the CIA so
eager to invade Afghanistan, he continued? So the CIA could take over the
lucrative opium trade there. He was perfectly serious.

SCENARIO NO. 24:
KIDNAPPING OR KILLING A DEFECTOR

Tommy Westlake is a forty-eight-year-old CIA officer who spent the majority of his career in the Middle East. In his last overseas assignment, he was
the CIA chief in Tel Aviv. Before that, he was an instructor at the Farm,
where for two years he trained future case officers in clandestine tradecraft.
Westlake has the reputation in the DO for being a "cowboy," a tough, ruthless, and flamboyant operator who always gets the job done, but sometimes
at the expense of cutting corners.

Westlake is sent home from Tel Aviv because of a series of drunken
escapades, including a car accident in which an Israeli citizen is severely
injured. In the security investigation that takes place after Westlake's return
to headquarters, he is polygraphed several times. During the polygraph sessions, Westlake discloses three instances of serious misconduct while he
was chief in Tel Aviv. First, he had a six-month affair with one of his female
case officers. Second, he had another affair, which was still continuing when
he left Tel Aviv, with an Israeli woman of Moroccan origin. Westlake knew
this relationship would not be approved of by the CIA and, for that reason,
did not report it to CIA headquarters, as is required by CIA regulations.[26]
On several occasions Westlake and his Israeli mistress used CIA safehouses
for their trysts. Finally, Westlake admits to having misused official funds; a
subsequent audit reveals that he in fact embezzled more than $25,000 from
official accounts, using falsified receipts to cover his tracks. Westlake is diag-
nosed by the CIA's Office of Medical Services as alcoholic and mentally ill.

The CIA informs Westlake he is being fired for misconduct and the
information on his embezzlement of funds is being referred to the Justice

Department for possible prosecution. The Agency offers to pay for alcohol treatment and psychiatric counseling for him for up to five years, but he denies he has a drinking or psychiatric problem and rejects the offer. He is furious that he is being terminated and promises to get revenge.

Westlake flees to Lebanon to avoid prosecution. He makes contact with Hezbollah and goes underground. In short order, five CIA officers are assassinated by Hezbollah terrorists in Beirut, Tel Aviv, Kuala Lumpur, Nairobi, and Lagos. The common denominator in these assassinations is that all the victims are officers Westlake knew in the Middle East or helped to train at the Farm. Hezbollah releases a videotape in which Westlake declares war on the U.S. and vows to "neutralize the CIA" wherever he can. The CIA estimates that Westlake knows the identities of over three hundred CIA case officers stationed under cover around the world. He also has extremely sensitive information on CIA and Mossad[27] operations in the region.

———

Would it be morally acceptable for the CIA to locate Westlake in Lebanon, to kidnap him, and to return him to the United States for prosecution? Would it be morally acceptable, in the event kidnapping is not operationally feasible, for the CIA to assassinate Westlake in Lebanon?

Former FBI senior official Oliver "Buck" Revell:

1) Yes. I would authorize and would find entirely appropriate the apprehension and rendition of Westlake by whatever force is necessary to secure his apprehension, including lethal force if there is no alternative.

2) No. I would not authorize and would not find morally acceptable the assassination of any American citizen, whether abroad or in the United States, by the U.S. government or any of its agencies. I also believe no person residing or located in the United States should be assassinated by the U.S. government, as alternatives are available.

Former CIA and Army officer Jack Bosley:

Yes. Tommy Westlake is a very bad guy. Morality is not the main issue here; practicality is. For that reason, kidnapping him and bringing him back to the U.S. for trial would not be a good idea. The fallout and publicity from the trial would harm U.S. intelligence collection in the Middle East. Some of the press would take up Westlake's defense. In open court, he would become a tennis ball for those who support U.S. policies and those who oppose them. I prefer termination of this problem, ▮▮▮▮▮▮▮▮▮▮▮▮▮▮▮ ▮▮▮▮▮▮▮▮▮▮▮▮ The moral issue is whether we should ask a foreign power to do our dirty work for us. My feeling is that in rare cases it is the best and safest solution to a serious problem.

Retired U.S. Army Colonel Stuart Herrington:

1) Yes. Kidnapping Westlake would be morally acceptable. He is a felon, an admitted participant in murder. We are bringing him in to face due process. Go for it.

2) No. However appealing it might be, assassinating Westlake would be an inherently evil act designed to bring about a good. The assassination of Westlake would bypass due process and would therefore be morally unacceptable.

Retired U.S. Navy Captain Richard Life:

Yes. The greater good of preserving the lives of CIA and Mossad officers and preventing the loss of critical intelligence operations warrants the kidnapping—or assassination—of Westlake.

Professor Peter Feaver of Duke University:

[The views expressed by Professor Feaver are personal and are not intended to reflect those of any particular group, institution, or organization.]

1) Yes. Kidnapping him would be morally acceptable.

2) It depends. The evidence thus far is compelling, but circumstantial. Assassinating a guilty party is morally acceptable under self-defense terms. But assassinating a suspect is more dodgy.

Undergraduate student Laura Zandstra of Texas A&M University:

1) Yes. It would be morally acceptable to kidnap Westlake and return him to the United States for trial. I assume every CIA employee signs a contract that binds him to silence. This contract should be upheld by U.S. laws. Since Westlake has broken his contract and betrayed secrets, the CIA has every right on national security grounds to kidnap him.

2) Yes. It would be morally acceptable for the CIA to assassinate Westlake in Lebanon. He has already been responsible for the deaths of five CIA case officers, and it is evident he can and will cause more deaths. To ensure the safety of others in the CIA, Westlake must be silenced.

Former CIA officer John Hedley:

1) Yes. Kidnapping is morally justifiable in an extreme case such as this, where Westlake has become, in effect, a terrorist, either

murdering or being an accessory to the murder of individuals he is uniquely able to identify and target. Depending on the relationship, liaison might be enlisted in the apprehension of Westlake (who might actually be killed in an exchange of gunfire during the attempt to apprehend him) and in arranging his extradition.

2) No. Assassination—committing murder in a noncombat situation—is neither a moral or legal option for the CIA, which by law is not allowed to assassinate.

Lieutenant Colonel Tom Ruby, USAF, Department of Joint Warfare Studies, Air Command and Staff College:

[The views expressed here are those of Lieutenant Colonel Ruby and do not necessarily reflect the official policy or position of the U.S. Air Force, the Department of Defense, or the U.S. government.]

Yes. Kidnapping would be preferable for political reasons of deterrence and to make a statement that the U.S. has the ability to track him down with clandestine forces and bring him to justice before a public court (even if that court is closed due to the nature of the material presented). U.S. law has consistently upheld the right of the U.S. to take people from third countries and to bring them back to the U.S. for justice. Assassinating Westlake is morally acceptable if the president makes the decision that doing so is necessary to protect U.S. lives and intelligence operations. The U.S. is under no obligation to bring Westlake back to the States after he has formally renounced his allegiance and has declared his intention to wage a private war against the U.S.

Anonymous active duty military officer No. 1:

Yes, without hesitation. I believe both of these options would be morally acceptable. Westlake has committed high crimes against the United States and must be held accountable for his actions.

Anonymous active duty military officer No. 2:

Yes. Westlake is a criminal who has already killed Americans and will continue to do so. Obviously, we are not going to negotiate his return, so the only option is to go get him. If assassination is the only way to neutralize him, then so be it.

Author's comment:

The most notorious of the CIA's "defectors" are Edward Lee Howard and Philip Agee. Howard was dismissed from the CIA in 1983, after a polygraph examination revealed drug use, alcohol abuse, and petty thievery. He had been in training for an assignment to Moscow and had been briefed on all the CIA's operations there. Motivated by anger and revenge, Howard made contact with the KGB and sold out, providing the Soviets with the identities of the CIA's Russian agents in Moscow and the locations of its clandestine technical operations. As the FBI began to close in on Howard, he evaded surveillance (we trained him well) and escaped to the Soviet Union, where the KGB put him up in a dacha outside Moscow and took care of his every need. He died there in 2002.

Philip Agee was a CIA case officer in Latin America. He became disillusioned with the Agency and resigned in 1969. He then became an outspoken critic of the CIA, publishing a book in 1976, *Inside the Company: CIA Diary*, that contained the names of 2,500 CIA case officers and agents. Agee continued his personal vendetta against the CIA by other publications and anti-CIA activities. He spent most of his time in Europe, but traveled frequently to the U.S. for anti–U.S. and anti-CIA lectures on college campuses. (He could not be arrested in the U.S. because revealing the identities of CIA officers under cover was not a federal crime until the passage of the Intelligence Identities Protection Act in 1982.) Agee's second book, *Dirty Work: The CIA in Western Europe*, published in 1978, revealed the names of 841 more CIA officers. It was widely assumed in the CIA that Agee was receiving assistance from the Cuban and East German intelligence services. Many believe that Agee's public disclosure of the name of the CIA chief in Athens, Richard Welch, and his call for the "neutralization" of CIA officers everywhere, led to Welch's murder in Athens in 1975. Agee now lives in Cuba.[28]

The CIA and other elements of the U.S. government monitored and tracked Howard and Agee as best they could, but did not consider kidnapping or assassination options.

Russia has taken a different approach toward its defectors and traitors. The tone was set during World War II, when the NKVD, a predecessor of the KGB, established a special unit called Smersh to hunt down and eliminate traitors, spies, defectors, and deserters. The name "Smersh" was derived from the Russian words "*smert' shpionam*" or "death to spies." Even earlier, the NKVD had been ruthless in dealing with enemies of the state. The Soviet defector Ignace Poretsky (alias Reiss) was murdered in Switzerland in 1937; Leon Trotsky was killed in Mexico City in 1940; and NKVD defector Walter Krivitsky died mysteriously in Washington in 1941. Smersh was officially disbanded in 1946, but its functions continued under the KGB. The Soviet defector Nicholas Shadrin was kidnapped and murdered by the KGB in 1975. The KGB helped the Bulgarian intelligence service, the Durzhavna Sigurnost (DS), kill Bulgarian dissident Georgi Markov in London in 1978. The assassination weapon in that case, supplied to the DS by the KGB, was an umbrella that injected the deadly poison ricin into the victim through the umbrella's tip. Although some of the facts are still in dispute, there is strong and credible evidence that the Soviets and Bulgarians were behind the attempted assassination of Pope John Paul II in 1981. An Italian parliamentary commission concluded in March 2006 that it was "beyond reasonable doubt" that the Soviets had ordered the shooting. And this pattern has continued. Two Russian intelligence officers were convicted of murdering former Chechen leader Zelimkhan Yandarbiev in Qatar in 2004.

SCENARIO NO. 25:
FABRICATING EVIDENCE

Libya is ruled by Islamic fundamentalists and has actively supported terrorist operations against Americans around the world. A bus carrying American tourists was bombed last year in the Loire Valley of France by Libyan-sponsored terrorists; twenty-two Americans were killed. Libyan terrorists were also responsible for assassinations of American officials, students, and tourists in Belgium, Switzerland, Japan, and Mexico. Two Libyan intelligence operatives were recently arrested in Omaha, Nebraska, as they attempted to contaminate a cattle-feed lot with hoof-and-mouth disease. The mastermind behind these Libyan terrorist operations is Massoud Al-Hemry, a high ranking official of the Jamahiriya Security Organization (JSO), the Libyan intelligence service. Al-Hemry served in the Libyan Embassy in Paris from 1984 to 1988. He is now based in Tripoli.

The FBI and CIA devise a plan that they hope will eliminate Al-Hemry. A JSO officer under cover in the Libyan Permanent Mission to the United Nations in New York has been aggressively developing an Arab-American who works as a translator for the FBI in New York. The translator reports his contact with the JSO officer to his FBI superiors and seeks their guidance. The FBI decides to try to run the translator as a double agent against the Libyans. The translator agrees and is given the code name THUNDER WALKING (TW).

TW is instructed to maintain contact with the JSO officer and, under FBI control, to allow himself to be recruited. TW, a practicing Muslim, pretends to be sympathetic to the Arab cause and to be deeply troubled by U.S. military operations in Islamic countries. He also pretends to be venal. The JSO officer recruits TW as a penetration of the FBI and agrees to pay him a salary of $2,000 a month.

At the urging of his JSO case officer, TW accepts an offer to transfer to the FBI's headquarters in Washington, where he will work as a translator in the joint FBI-CIA counterterrorism center. The JSO is delighted with this transfer and believes its agent will have greatly improved access in his new position.

The plan to eliminate Al-Hemry is ready to be implemented. Al-Hemry travels to Paris on official business and is monitored by the CIA while he is there. Two weeks later, TW reports to his JSO case officer (falsely) that he has just finished transcribing audio tapes of a meeting Al-Hemry had in a hotel room in Paris. The meeting was with an Arabic-speaking case officer for DGSE (Direction Générale de la Sécurité Extérieure, or General Directorate for External Security), the French foreign intelligence service. Al-Hemry and the DGSE thought their meeting was secure, but the CIA was able to install an audio device in the room before the meeting took place. TW provides a copy of the fabricated transcript to his JSO case officer.

It appears from the transcript that Al-Hemry has been an agent of the DGSE for several years, probably since his assignment in Paris in the 1980s. He receives large payments from the DGSE that are deposited in a secret Swiss bank account. Al-Hemry also makes several disparaging remarks on the transcript about the Libyan regime.

Would it be morally acceptable for the CIA to use THUNDER WALKING to plant false evidence against Al-Hemry in an effort to have him arrested and executed?

Former CIA officer David Edger:
Yes. This scenario would be morally justifiable in my opinion. The target is known for his past actions and his elimination greatly enhances our security. While a false document is involved, there is no harm from this document other than to the terrorist himself.

Professor Mark Moyar of the U.S. Marine Corps University:
Yes. Stirring up dissension within the enemy's ranks by surreptitious means has been a common practice throughout history. If America's terrorist adversaries kill one another by mistake, it is no less morally acceptable than if American forces had done the same. For someone guilty of crimes against humanity, there should be few constraints against his elimination. Whether the fabricated information will lead to Al-Hemry's execution or only to incarceration is uncertain.

U.S. Army Lieutenant Colonel Tony Pfaff:
It depends. Normally, fabricating false evidence to frame an enemy

intelligence officer is morally permissible. It is up to the officers and their agencies to protect themselves against such operations. There are limits, of course. For example, one should not fabricate evidence in such a way that nonoperators, such as family members or friends, are implicated. The possibly troubling part here is that we have implicated the French (DGSE). Given that this evidence could lead to retaliation against the French, they should be consulted first.

Professor Bruce Gronbeck of the University of Iowa:

Yes. I have a great deal of difficulty in making this judgment, given my objections to capital punishment and the rule of force vs. the rule of law. And yet, I believe that terrorism works outside civilized social-political institutions in that it permits random slaughter. The scenario apparently is based on solid evidence of Al-Hemry's guilt and suggests that other ways of capturing him have been tried and failed over a relatively long period of time. The case, therefore, is set up as a kind of trial in absentia of a person guilty of capital crimes. It also suggests he is not assassinated but, rather, returned to his own culture for judgment. In other words, I find myself forced to assess a series of circumstances that permit me some flexibility in how I interpret the actions taken. I take my judgment, therefore, to be a product of life in the New World Order, where situational ethics are being rewritten.

Former CIA officer Richard Corbin:

No. This approach could be acceptable if there were no other options, but there are better options that are clearly morally acceptable. Al-Hemry was behind the bombing of the bus in the Loire Valley. Thus, the French have justification for arresting him. He could be remanded to the U.S. for trial, if the French, Belgians, or Swiss do not try him. The trial could be a propaganda coup focusing international attention on Libya's terrorist activities. Also, interrogation of Al-Hemry could yield valuable information on his operations.

Retired U.S. Army Colonel Stuart Herrington:

It depends. It is not clear if Libya and Al-Hemry have taken credit for the terrorist acts in Europe and Asia or how strong the evidence against them is, which to me is key. I will take it as a given that this is not loose speculation or outdated demonization of Libya, JSO, and Al-Hemry (a significant leap these days given the Iraq/WMD fiasco). But assuming Al-Hemry is a dyed-in-the-wool, certified bad guy whose organization was behind the terrorist attacks, I find the scenario morally acceptable.

Former USIA officer Philip Brown:

Yes. I just wonder why it is necessary to go through all this effort and use all this time to have Al-Hemry arrested and executed. If he is as bad as we think, can we wait for the wheels of Libyan justice to turn? If laws are not a concern, why not simply murder him? But will eliminating one man, albeit the mastermind, really end Libya's terrorism? Ronald Reagan had a simpler solution to this problem back in the 1980s. He just bombed Libya and, if I'm not mistaken, it had a chastening effect on the regime.

Author's comment:
Assiduous readers of spy fiction will recall that a devious fabrication of evidence to eliminate an adversary was a key element in John Le Carré's novel *The Spy Who Came in from the Cold.* In that book, MI6 planted false clues and went to great lengths to convince East German intelligence that one of its counterintelligence officers, who was threatening an important MI6 operation, was a British spy. Le Carré's portrayal of the world of spying as dark and heartless has been criticized by some intelligence professionals as extreme, but there is no doubt that Le Carré has captured well the moral ambiguities of intelligence operations.[29]

The operational use of fabricated evidence has not been limited to fiction. In their excellent book *The Main Enemy*, James Risen and Milt Bearden describe an ingenious CIA operation that was designed to determine whether the KGB had penetrated CIA communications and was reading top-secret CIA cable traffic. The CIA had suffered devastating losses of Russian agents in 1985, and there were competing theories inside the CIA about the cause of the debacle. We know now that the compromises were due to the treachery of CIA officers Edward Lee Howard and Aldrich Ames and FBI Special Agent Robert Hanssen, but, at the time, some CIA counterintelligence officers thought the problem could be technical. The KGB had already shown itself capable of highly sophisticated bugging operations against the U.S. embassy in Moscow.

CIA officers Burton Gerber, Milt Bearden, and Paul Redmond came up with the idea of testing the security of CIA communications by fabricating an operation in a CIA station in Africa involving the recruitment of a local officer of the GRU, Russia's Main Intelligence Directorate. The restricted handling cable traffic on the bogus operation was sent from the station back to headquarters, and headquarters responded just as if the operation had been real. If the GRU officer in question suddenly disappeared, the CIA would know that in all probability its communications had been compromised. For moral reasons, however, the CIA built an escape hatch into the operation. The CIA did not want the incriminated GRU officer actually to be tried and executed for spying for the CIA. If the officer disappeared, the

CIA would quietly inform the KGB that the cable traffic had been a ruse and the officer was innocent. When nothing happened, the CIA felt better about its communications and redoubled its efforts to find a human spy.

SCENARIO NO. 26:
L-Devices

Three years ago, the CIA successfully tapped a secret communications cable inside Iran. This cable serves the Iranian military and other government organizations, including the highly classified agency that is responsible for developing Iranian nuclear weapons. The intelligence from this tap has been invaluable. Six months ago, however, the tap developed serious technical problems. The CIA concluded that it had not been tampered with but had simply malfunctioned. Tensions with Iran are at an all-time high, and the U.S. is seriously considering aggressive military action, including a possible preemptive strike against Iran's nuclear facilities. The NSC informs the CIA that it desperately needs the intelligence that was previously supplied by the cable tap. It authorizes the CIA to carry out a special covert operation in Iran to repair the tap.

The CIA trains a team of three volunteers from the Special Operations Group (SOG) to conduct the operation. Their mission is to parachute into Iran "black," that is, without being detected, to proceed to the tap site, to repair it, and to escape by land to Pakistan. The team is told that it is absolutely vital that the cable tap be reactivated and that the Iranians not learn of its existence. For that reason, each team member is issued an L-device (L stands for "lethal") to use in the event he is about to be captured. The L-device in this case is a needle containing deadly shellfish toxin. The CIA and NSC are certain that if the team is captured alive its members will be tortured and will reveal everything they know about the tap. The three SOG officers agree to use the L-devices if their capture is imminent and if they are ordered by the CIA to do so.

———

Would it be morally acceptable for the CIA to give the officers the L-devices and to order them to use them in the event they are about to be captured inside Iran?

Undergraduate student Aaron Tatyrek of Texas A&M University:
Yes. This is an important mission, and with the stakes so high I would authorize the CIA to order its officers to use the L-devices if capture were imminent.

Kyu Mani Lee, Ph.D., former superintendent of Larned State Hospital in Kansas:

Yes. The three SOG officers understand the true nature of the mission and voluntarily agree to use the L-devices if the need arises. I see no moral problem.

Former CIA officer Richard Corbin:

Yes. The CIA's order notwithstanding, it would be the team members' choice to use the L-device. They could opt not to use it (like Francis Gary Powers) or to use it (like Aleksandr Ogorodnik). In effect, all the CIA is doing is giving the operatives an option they might not otherwise have.

Graduate student Sarah Forbey of the George Bush School of Government and Public Service at Texas A&M University:

It depends. It would be morally acceptable to issue the L-devices to the officers, so they have the option of ending their lives if capture and torture are inevitable, but not to order them to use them.

Former CIA officer John ▮▮▮▮▮:

No. In my view, the operation should not be mounted at all. We have an obligation, which transcends strict adherence to the oath of office, not to needlessly put our officers in harm's way. While the stream of intelligence from the Iranian cable tap has clearly been critical, this operation should not be assessed in a vacuum. In the later years of my career, I began to get the feeling that intelligence operations, like military operations, were not integrated into a broader strategic palette. It was easy for policy makers to look for the critical piece of intelligence or the critical tactical victory to make their decisions easier, and to look at intelligence operations through a very small diameter pipe. There was not enough thought being given to crafting an approach to any given problem which would include diplomatic, economic, social, cultural, and financial factors, as well as military and intelligence. Specifically, and restricting the argument to the intelligence arena:

a)   Do not lose the high ground. The Iranians do not know of the operation, so the intelligence collected thus far is reasonably certain not to have been compromised. In case of capture, apart from the unacceptable risk to the officers, there is a good chance the Iranians will learn of the operation.

b)   Aggressively look for other technical options. Can the operation be reconstituted remotely? Can another tap point be secured by other technical means? Is there another channel that can be attacked?

c) How does the intelligence collected so far stack up with other collection? Has it been corroborated? In particular, has the intelligence identified HUMINT targets who could provide the same stream of reporting? Are there opportunities to mount recruitment operations against them?

We have a moral obligation not only to the officers and their families, but also to our superiors, to know when to say "no." This is one of those times.

Author's comment:

Francis Gary Powers was the pilot of the U-2 spy plane that was shot down over the Soviet Union on May 1, 1960. The U-2 overflights of the USSR, which took place from 1956 to 1960, were a flagrant violation of Soviet sovereignty and international law. The Eisenhower administration, therefore, wanted to do everything possible to keep the flights secret and to retain plausible deniability in the event something went wrong. A surviving, captured, and talking pilot would be inconvenient, to say the least. For that reason, the U-2 pilots were issued poison-tipped needles to use, at their discretion, if they were about to be captured. The rationale was that a pilot might wish to commit suicide rather than to face torture at the hands of the Soviets. Also, by dying and not talking, the pilot could render one last patriotic service to his country. The CIA, which ran the U-2 program, did not order the U-2 pilots to use the needle to avoid being captured alive. Each pilot was to make his own decision. Powers chose not to die. He parachuted to the ground after his plane was hit and was captured by locals. When he was released from Soviet prison and returned to the U.S. in 1963, Powers was severely criticized in some circles for having talked too much and for having confessed to his crime. The tacit message to Powers was that a braver man would have killed himself.

L-devices, usually potassium cyanide capsules, were sometimes issued to OSS operatives on high risk missions during World War II. They were also carried by some infiltration teams into Communist countries in the late 1940s and early 1950s.

SCENARIO NO. 27:
INSERTION OPERATIONS

The United States and North Korea appear to be headed for war. Negotiations on easing tensions have broken down and North Korea's rhetoric has become increasingly bellicose. The need for intelligence on North Korean intentions and capabilities has never been greater.

The CIA is trying to establish a covert presence inside North Korea for intelligence collection and sabotage, not only for current requirements but also as a stay behind capability in the event of hostilities. For that reason, the CIA has been conducting insertion operations into North Korea for the last two years. These operations are conducted jointly with the South Korean intelligence service, the Agency for National Security Planning (ANSP).

The CIA and ANSP recruit South Koreans, many of whom have family ties to North Korea, to be secretly inserted or infiltrated into North Korea. They are all volunteers, motivated by patriotism, anti-Communist convictions, and financial gain. They know these operations are extremely high risk. The volunteers are well paid and receive substantial life insurance. After thorough security vetting, they are trained in clandestine tradecraft, communications, recruitment operations, and sabotage. When their training is completed, they are inserted into North Korea from the air or by submarine. They can request exfiltration[32] once their assignments are completed, but they are responsible for casing the appropriate pickup sites and for arranging all the other details.

Thirty-four of these agents have been inserted into North Korea in the last two years. None have survived. As best the CIA can determine, they were all captured by North Korean security forces. No useful intelligence was obtained.

For security reasons, future volunteers for these insertion missions cannot be told anything about the previous operations.

———

Would it be morally acceptable for the CIA to continue sending these volunteers into North Korea without telling them the previous insertion operations had all failed?

Dr. Geoffrey Tumlin, assistant director of the Center for Ethical Leadership at the Lyndon B. Johnson School of Public Affairs at the University of Texas:

No. There is enough data (n=34) to suggest either something is terribly flawed with the operational procedures or the North Koreans have the operation penetrated. It is not ethical to continue sending agents into North Korea unless they know the odds.

Former CIA officer Robert Mills:

Yes. While it might not be operationally acceptable to continue sending in agents without a thorough review of what is going wrong, I would have no moral problem with not telling the agents about the failure of the previous insertions. Telling them, in fact, would be a violation of operational security. Historically, there have been numerous examples of compromises that resulted in the loss of all agents being inserted into denied areas. Kim Philby's activities come to mind immediately.

Ph.D. student Margaret Meacham:

No. While we may think telling the truth would limit volunteers, telling the truth will simply bring in a new type of volunteer. Rather than those who do it for patriotism, family, or glory, we will get mercenaries and survivalist types who are much better equipped mentally and physically to succeed. This will be more expensive financially for the U.S., but less costly in lives.

Ph.D. student Margaretta Mathis:

No. The CIA must be clear on the risks to the volunteers. Clarity and truth are important so the volunteers know they can trust and rely on the CIA as they go off on the mission.

Professor Howard Prince, director of the Center for Ethical Leadership at the Lyndon B. Johnson School of Public Affairs at the University of Texas:

No. While the potential benefits of a successful agent insertion could be great, the likelihood of that appears so small that only informed agents should be sent. In other words, let the potential agents decide whether they are prepared to participate in what appear to be suicide missions with a low chance of success.

Lieutenant Colonel Tom Ruby, USAF, Department of Joint Warfare Studies, Air Command and Staff College:

[The views expressed are those of Lieutenant Colonel Ruby and do not necessarily reflect the official policy or position of the United States Air Force, the Department of Defense, or the U.S. government.]

Yes. It would be morally acceptable to send volunteers into the North. First of all, these are inherently high-risk operations that the volunteers understand are not guaranteed to succeed. Second, the volunteers are motivated toward the ends desired by both the United States and the Republic of Korea. They are well compensated and trained. Finally, there is no concrete evidence that all thirty-four were killed or captured. It may be that their training was sufficient and some survived. The fact that none have requested exfiltration does not mean they have been captured. They may simply be lying low until the conflict commences.

Anonymous active duty military officer No. 1:

Yes. All the personnel are volunteers and are aware of the risks to their life before taking on the mission. Notifying them of the prior failed missions would substantially impact their motivation and ability to carry out the operation. That said, it is imperative that the CIA personnel who are aware of the failures do their best to derive the lessons learned from the failed missions and to ensure that their tactics, techniques, and procedures are revised, if possible, to reduce the risks to future missions.

Anonymous active duty military officer No. 2:

It depends. I do not see why the security of the future missions would be compromised if the volunteers were told the truth about the past failures. Only if there is, in fact, an absolutely compelling security reason to keep the truth from them would I find it morally acceptable to send them in without that knowledge.

Author's comment:

The CIA has a long history of inserting covert action teams into denied areas. The tradition began with the famous OSS and Special Operations Executive (SOE) Jedburgh teams[33] that were parachuted into Nazi-occupied Europe during World War II. Until recently, all CIA case officer trainees went through jump training at the Farm. This training is no longer required, but most candidates today still try to do it on a voluntary basis. Officers being prepared for insertion operations, of course, receive specialized training in all the necessary skills.

In the early years of the Cold War, intelligence on Communist countries was so hard to come by that the CIA resorted to extraordinary means to try to fill the gap. It trained teams, ███████████████████████████████ ██████ for insertion by parachute, sea, or land. Their mission was to collect intelligence and, in some cases, to assist anti-Communist guerilla forces in those countries. The fatality rate for these operations was very, very high.

SCENARIO NO. 28:
FAKE DIAGNOSIS

Abdul Rashad al-Dobhani is a thirty-five-year-old mid-level official in the Ministry of Interior of Yemen. He is not well paid. Al-Dobhani is involved in counterterrorism operations in Yemen and has access to a great deal of sensitive information. He has occasional liaison contact with the U.S. Embassy in Yemen.

Over time, al-Dobhani develops a good professional and personal relationship with Fred Ballesteros, an FBI special agent working in the embassy as an assistant legal attaché. Al-Dobhani confides to Ballesteros that he is very concerned about the health of his nine-year-old daughter Amal. He says that Amal suffers from weakness, loss of appetite, rapid heartbeat, and chest pains. She has recently shown a slight difficulty in walking. Al-Dobhani is beside himself with worry. The Yemeni doctors he has consulted have not been able to determine the cause of Amal's illness.

Ballesteros shares this information with a CIA colleague. Al-Dobhani has long been a high-priority CIA recruitment target, but the available assessment data on him shows him to be a loyal Yemeni, unlikely to cooperate with the CIA. The FBI and CIA agree on a carefully crafted recruitment approach to al-Dobhani.

At their next meeting, Ballesteros tells al-Dobhani that he has been thinking about Amal's illness and might be able to help. He says that an American doctor will be visiting the U.S. Embassy in two weeks and could examine Amal if al-Dobhani wishes. Al-Dobhani accepts the offer.

The CIA arranges for one of its doctors to make the trip to Yemen. He does a thorough examination of Amal, including a series of laboratory tests. When the tests are analyzed, it is determined that Amal is suffering from juvenile pernicious anemia, a serious but very treatable disease. If al-Dobhani is told the truth, he would certainly be relieved and grateful, but probably not to the point of agreeing to cooperate with the CIA.

Would it be morally acceptable for the FBI and CIA to tell al-Dobhani that his daughter is suffering from acute lymphoblastic leukemia, a deadly disease, and that in return for his cooperation she can receive the expensive Western medication and treatment she needs to recover?

Graduate student Jason Pogacnik of the Maxwell School at the University of Syracuse:

No. Treatment for leukemia is very invasive and causes significant trauma to the patient. Presumably, the "fake" treatment would have to be made as realistic as possible to keep the sham believable. Therefore, there is no question that the daughter, Amal, would suffer. Al-Dobhani's cooperation would be involuntary on account of his love for his daughter. Moreover, Amal is a total "innocent," and it would be immoral to cause her suffering in the service of some "greater good," in this case, learning more about Yemeni counterterrorism efforts.

Former CIA polygrapher John Sullivan:

No. Not only is this morally unacceptable, it is also stupid. To use a sick child to get a father to cooperate might, and I stress the word "might," get some cooperation from the father, but it could also engender some real hatred on his part later on. My way of handling this would be to make the pitch directly, without strings, and to hope for the best. We are supposed to be the good guys. Good guys don't do things like this.

One of our most productive assets in Vietnam was supposedly working for us because we got her mother a cataract operation. She turned out to be in collusion with her husband to run a scam on us.

Lauraine Brekke-Esparza, city manager of Del Mar, California:

No. I do not think it is morally acceptable to trick the father into believing his daughter is suffering from a serious disease when a simple and straightforward treatment is easily available to him. His gratitude for the correct diagnosis and treatment might be enough to cultivate over time the kind of relationship the CIA would like to have with him. I do not believe that using children as "pawns" in the game of espionage is morally acceptable.

Writer, poet, and teacher Burke Gerstenschlager:

No. Although al-Dobhani is a high-priority CIA recruitment target, it would be highly unethical to use his daughter as leverage to gain his cooperation. It would likewise be immoral to deceive al-Dobhani about the nature of his daughter's disease. The CIA and FBI, having arranged for the daughter to be examined by a CIA doctor, are under a positive obligation to tell the truth to the father and to ensure his daughter receives the proper treatment. Doing otherwise would be cruel and unusual. It might also back-fire. If al-Dobhani discovers that the CIA has lied to him, his relationship with the CIA will be forever ruined.

Practicing attorney Christopher Scherer:

No. Using the life of a child as a chip is blackmail. Giving the girl's father a fake diagnosis would be morally equivalent to poisoning her and holding the antidote in front of him. Forcing a man to choose between his daughter and his state is morally indefensible. He is being coerced; he is not being allowed to make his decision on the basis of principle or reasoned reflection. An intentional misdiagnosis would be morally unacceptable as malfeasance (misleading and coercing the father) and nonfeasance (denying the daughter the treatment she needs).

Former CIA officer Louise Corbin:

No. At the risk of sounding trite, children are the hope and future of our world. Withholding a diagnosis that clearly has an easy cure in the inter-ests of operational intelligence is reprehensible. As a parent, I could not be a party to it. To cause this kind of anguish and conflict in a father, even for the reasons cited, is morally wrong.

Randy Everett, M.D., of Fort Collins, Colorado:

No. Exploiting the anxious concerns of a parent with the deception of a possibly fatal disease strikes me as blackmail of a rather sinister kind. Though the threat to the daughter is not real and I might condone the exploitation of an adult's emotional needs or weaknesses under other cir-cumstances, this plan represents a type of torture that the U.S. should not use. It is torture because it applies mental anguish to the father in such a way that he would likely prefer physical torture to having harm come to his child. Hence, this represents coercion that is real and violent. If al-Dobhani is told the truth and is relieved and grateful, he may yet cooperate and do so with a higher level of trust and reliability.

Author's comment:

The CIA has several doctors who provide assistance to agent opera-tions overseas. It might be, for example, that an agent needs special medical care or medications that are not available in that country.

Agents agree to work for the CIA for many different reasons. The incentive for an agent's cooperation can be money, some other material consideration, or a special favor. Expensive medical care for an agent or a family member, such as major surgery in the United States, could conceivably be used as a quid pro quo in a recruitment pitch, but I have never known it to be used on a misleading or coercive basis as in the scenario above.

SCENARIO NO. 29:
DRUGGING A FOREIGN DIPLOMAT

The United States and Iran have agreed to conduct a series of meetings in Paris to negotiate the future of Iran's nuclear weapons program. This is seen as an important diplomatic breakthrough by the U.S., which is prepared to offer Iran significant concessions and aid in exchange for a verifiable cessation of its program. The Iranians are pushing hard for the best possible terms and, as a result, the discussions have been very difficult.

The chief Iranian negotiator, Mostafa Ghorbani, is a careless man. He has been observed putting large stacks of Iranian official documents in his briefcase and taking them with him to his private suite in the Hotel Crillon.

The CIA has been able to conceal video devices behind the ceiling molding in Ghorbani's suite. Night after night, he is monitored as he works on his papers in his room. He then orders his dinner from room service before retiring. The CIA would very much like to have access to the documents in Ghorbani's briefcase.

Without much difficulty, the CIA is able to recruit one of the cooks in the kitchen of the Hotel Crillon. In return for a lump sum payment of $10,000, he is willing to do whatever the CIA wishes.

The CIA has a drug that can put a person into a deep slumber for up to four hours. The person wakes up after that time not realizing he has been drugged. There are no harmful after effects to the drug.

A CIA surreptitious entry[35] specialist can easily defeat the locks on the doors of the hotel and enter the room without leaving a trace.

———

Would it be morally acceptable for the CIA to drug Ghorbani's food, to enter his room while he is sleeping, to take the briefcase to another room where the documents can be photographed, and then to return the briefcase just as it was to his room?

Former CIA Information Management Officer Ray Brewer:

Yes. The information in these documents will be invaluable to U.S. representatives in their negotiations with the Iranians. Halting the Iranian nuclear program will reduce the chance of nuclear war and also close off a source of nuclear material for terrorists.

Professor Richard Graving of the South Texas College of Law:

No. The goal here seems to be to gain an advantage in negotiation rather than to acquire military or scientific intelligence. The possible product is an insufficient end to justify the serious assault on physical integrity and human dignity involved in the administration of psychotrophic drugs to a diplomat. If for no more than practical reasons in the conduct of international relations, the diplomat is entitled to rely on a reasonable expectation of privacy and immunity with respect to drugging. I would have no moral objection to a surreptitious entry if drugs are not used. Ghorbani has no reasonable expectation of privacy with regard to his suite at the Crillon or his unaccompanied work papers. He should know they are fair game.

Former USIA officer Philip Brown:

Yes. If we can halt Iran's nuclear weapons program by letting Ghorbani get some much needed rest, let's do it (but I bet the cook in the Crillon kitchen will ask for payment in euros rather than dollars).

Colonel Cindy R. Jebb of the United States Military Academy:

[The opinions expressed by Colonel Jebb are her own and do not necessarily reflect the views of the United States Military Academy, the Department of the Army, or the Department of Defense.]

No. This operation would not be morally acceptable. It would also be an imprudent course of action. There are several considerations. Since it appears that these negotiations are indicative of a significant diplomatic breakthrough, then anything that would endanger the negotiations would be too risky. Ghorbani is a diplomat. Both he and his U.S. counterparts are working toward some level of trust to establish a foundation for future U.S.–Iranian relations that would be beneficial to U.S. security. For Ghorbani, it appears there would be no physical harm. However, he and other Iranian diplomats would lose all trust in the United States if they ever discovered what happened. It also seems unwise to use a local cook for such a delicate, high-stakes operation. In fact, on that basis alone I would be opposed to the operation. There is simply too great a danger that the CIA's operation would derail a promising diplomatic process.

Former CIA officer Eugene Culbertson:

Yes. It would not only be morally acceptable but absolutely imperative to use clandestine resources to support U.S. negotiating tactics, long-term national interests, and global stability. The United States has already made and implemented the decision to install video devices in Ghorbani's hotel suite. Surreptitious entry is the logical next step operationally.

Practicing attorney Christopher Scherer:

It depends. This scenario is morally complex for me. On the one hand, the CIA is drugging Ghorbani and, therefore, engaging in coercion. However, it seems that the drug's sole purpose is to confirm that Ghorbani will sleep through the night. One could argue, then, that the use of the drug is actually justifiable to ensure the safety of the CIA officer who will enter the room and take the papers.

One must ask, though, whether it is morally defensible for the CIA to break into the negotiator's room in the first place. Ghorbani has a legitimate presumption of a certain degree of security in his hotel room. There is nothing in this scenario to suggest Iran is such an immediate threat to the U.S. that a violation of Ghorbani's security and privacy would be justified.

What is the objective of this exercise? It is to view the papers in Ghorbani's briefcase. Doing that would force the Iranian state to do nothing; it would simply enhance the bargaining position of the United States. Would that be worth drugging a person? I have my doubts. That being said, however, limiting a nation's ability to kill millions is morally admirable and therefore may justify a certain degree of unsavory behavior. In the end, this operation is probably morally defensible. But it is a very close call.

Author's comment:

Drugs and spying share a long and troubled history. KGB defector Oleg Gordievsky reported that the Soviets first started using drugs in intelligence operations as early as the 1920s. In his book *KGB: The Inside Story*, cowritten with Christopher Andrew, Gordievsky related how a Finnish diplomatic courier was given drugged tea on a Soviet train so Soviet intelligence could photograph the contents of the diplomatic bag he was carrying. There have been numerous accounts of how the KGB experimented with drugs that would induce apathy, create confusion, cause deep sleep, undermine will power, and produce illogical thinking. There was widespread concern that China, North Korea, and other Communist countries were doing the same. The West watched in shock as Hungarian Cardinal Joszef Mindszenty at a staged trial in Budapest in 1949 admitted to treason and other illegal acts against the Communist government. He appeared listless and compliant throughout the proceedings, giving rise to speculation that he had been subjected to mood-changing drugs by the Hungarians. The fear of Communist mind-control drugs came to a head in the early 1950s with reports of their use against American and British POWs in Korea. Also, by the early 1950s the CIA was aware that the Soviets were conducting tests of a new hallucinogenic drug called LSD. Political prisoners and other criminals in Soviet gulags were the unfortunate guinea pigs for the Soviet drug tests. Later, the KGB made systematic use of drugs against dissidents in an effort to influence their behavior and attitudes, or simply to punish them for their "antisocial behavior." During my CIA training at the Farm, we were warned that drugs could be used against us by hostile intelligence services and we needed to be constantly alert to this threat.

In a 1953 press interview, CIA Director Allen Dulles warned the American public that the Communists were using "brain warfare" and "brain-perversion" techniques against their enemies. In that same year, Dulles approved a secret program at the CIA, code-named MKULTRA, to conduct research on mind-altering drugs and techniques. The original intent of MKULTRA was defensive, addressing the question of how to protect the United States against these dangers, but the project eventually evolved into studies of offensive applications as well. The horrors of MKULTRA have been amply disclosed by the Church Committee in 1975 and in DCI Stansfield Turner's testimony before the Senate Select Committee on Intelligence in 1977. It is hard to believe now that the U.S. government actually conducted drug tests on unwitting subjects and set up brothels for sex and drug experiments. But it did. And the most tragic consequence of MKULTRA was the death of Army scientist Frank Olson (no relation) in 1953. Olson was administered a seventy-microgram dose of LSD in a glass of Cointreau, without his knowledge, so that CIA scientists could observe his reactions. He went into a highly agitated psychotic state and eight days later jumped to his death from the tenth floor of a New York hotel.

Also shocking to many was the 1977 revelation that MKULTRA had received research support from forty-four American colleges and universities, fifteen research institutes, and numerous hospitals, clinics, and prisons. In all, according to the MKULTRA documents, 189 nongovernmental researchers and assistants had collaborated in the project.

MKULTRA was terminated in 1963. The CIA considered using LSD against Fidel Castro at about that time, but, according to Stansfield Turner in his 1977 testimony to Congress, no actual operational use was ever made of any of the drugs tested in the MKULTRA project.

SCENARIO NO. 30:
PRESS PLACEMENTS

The United States is taking a beating in the European press. Anti-American sentiment is at an all-time high. U.S. political leaders are routinely ridiculed in the European media and their policies are consistently opposed.

The National Security Council asks the CIA to determine if there are covert ways to influence European reporting and editorial commentary to make them more favorable to the United States. The CIA tasks its stations around Europe to begin spotting, assessing, and developing European journalists, editorial writers, and TV commentators for possible recruitment as press placement sources.

After several months of work, the CIA stations report to their headquarters that they have identified possible agents at *Le Monde Diplomatique* (France), Agence France-Presse (France), national television station TF1 (France), *Frankfurter Allgemeine Zeitung* (Germany), *El Pais* (Spain), and *L'Espresso* (Italy). Key personnel at each of these press outlets appear ready to accept money from the CIA in return for subtle pro–U.S. slanting of their reporting and editorials. Once these journalists are fully recruited, their CIA case officers will meet secretly with them to provide them with themes, facts, and, on occasion, disinformation serving U.S. interests. The CIA expects that some of the favorable reporting and editorial comment will be replayed in other publications in Europe, thereby adding to the operation's overall impact.

Would it be morally acceptable for the CIA to recruit European journalists to serve as paid press placement assets?

Professor David S. Allen of the University of Wisconsin-Milwaukee:
No. The problem in this scenario is not only with the ethically questionable actions of the European journalists, but also the lack of recognition by the CIA of the importance of a free press. It is obviously true that governments around the world—including the United States—engage in this type of action, but that does not make it ethical. Some of these European journalists may decide on their own accord to write stories favorable to the United States. But paying a journalist to write something hinders that journalist's legitimacy. The real danger, of course, is the chance that these opinions will gain credibility and influence public opinion far beyond the borders of Europe. The ultimate question is whether people would find it acceptable for the CIA to pay U.S. journalists to report favorably on the

Agency. I imagine most people would find that practice unethical. The same standard should hold for journalists everywhere in the world.

Graduate student Jason Pogacnik of the Maxwell School at Syracuse University:

No. Freedom of the press and, to a lesser extent, journalistic objectivity, are closely held values in American society. By paying off journalists to say certain things, the U.S. government would effectively counter some of the same values upon which it was founded and continues to operate. Moreover, the foreign journalists would have little to lose and much to gain by exposing the CIA's advances, revealing this essential hypocrisy. As a result, press coverage of the U.S. in Europe would likely become more negative, making the situation worse than before. Finally, the press is often a good gauge by which policymakers can read the morality of their decisions. By telling journalists what to write, the U.S. government loses an important source of feedback, potentially leading to immoral decisions in the future.

Ph.D. student Margaret Meacham:

No. Since the toll on lives is negligible, this issue could go either way. I would find it tipping toward morally unacceptable, though, because we are using disinformation and fabrications to distort the perceptions of others for our own financial (capitalistic) gain. We want these journalists to write facts, not fabrications, to change perceptions. If the facts are not in our favor, changing our behavior is better than changing the facts.

Ph.D. student Margaretta Mathis:

No. There are good ways to forge letter-writing and article-writing campaigns that are legitimate without paying under the table. Establishing an education and communications strategy seems more direct and fruitful.

Los Angeles Times journalist Bob Drogin:

It depends. I do not have a problem with the CIA's hiring non-Americans—even foreign journalists—to act on the CIA's behalf to carry out assigned U.S. foreign policy objectives. The CIA has long done so. I can see how stories that are sympathetic to U.S. policies or that attempt to sway public opinion in favor of U.S. policies are useful. I'm less convinced that U.S. taxpayers should use the CIA to boost support for "U.S. political leaders," but that's another issue.

The problem is the growing likelihood that disinformation the CIA secretly pays to place in major overseas media will spread back to the United States via the Internet or other channels and quickly appear in the U.S. media.

One of the press outlets mentioned, for example, Agence France-Presse, is an international wire service that distributes reports to major U.S. newspapers, magazines, and TV networks. The CIA thus would be presenting disinformation—even indirectly—to Americans, and that would be morally unacceptable.

Dr. Geoffrey Tumlin, assistant director of the Center for Ethical Leadership at the Lyndon B. Johnson School of Public Affairs at the University of Texas:

No. I would not approve of this operation because it violates the principle of a free press. Also, the ramifications if this plan, if leaked, would be much worse than the "good pub" gained by the operation.

Ambassador Henry Grunwald, former editor-in-chief of Time, Inc.:

No. It would involve corruption that would be very hard to justify. Obviously, changing public opinion about the U.S. is very desirable, and I can imagine certain roles the CIA could play in this—I especially remember *Encounter* [see author's comment]—but this is a very different situation.

Former USIA officer John Williams:

No. Over the years, the U.S. has expended considerable effort and resources to foster institutions and practices that promote an unfettered press as critical to the maintenance of a free society. To undercut these principles so that items more gratifying to America, its policies, and leaders might appear is not justifiable. The fact that these same journalists might be guilty of anti–U.S. bias at the behest of their European editors is not relevant; that's their issue.

In any case, there is a better way. Foreign journalists, including Europeans, do not hew to the ban that U.S. news organizations impose on accepting "educational travel" or similar programs. USIA had considerable success for several decades exposing foreign journalists firsthand to American life and values. While the insights thus gained may not immediately be translated into more favorable coverage of the U.S., they provide a permanent frame of reference through which perceptions of American behavior and policies are filtered, often leading to more accurate reporting.

Author Thomas Powers:

No. It sounds as if the White House seeks the rosy glow of apparent success for domestic political purposes. I can identify no clear short-term benefit, and over the long term what good would it do for the U.S. to generate shallow and dishonest approval from venal journalists? The CIA appears to lack the courage to tell the NSC that this idea is foolish and shortsighted.

Former USIA officer Philip Brown:
No. This is just not the way the United States should operate (that's my moral judgment). And in practical terms, it isn't going to work. Many of our policies are so at odds with European thinking that it will take much more than "subtle pro–U.S. slanting" to have any impact. When the bribery becomes public knowledge, the consequences will be much more serious than having our president kicked around in the European press. For that matter, who cares anymore what the French, Spanish, and Italians say about us?

Author's comment:
CIA interference with a free press seems anachronistic and generally unacceptable to a majority of Americans today, but the U.S. government has not always taken this view. It is easy to forget how dangerous the world looked to the United States in the immediate post–World War II years. All of Eastern Europe was under Communist rule, China was about to fall, and Soviet expansionism was on the move everywhere. Presidents Truman and Eisenhower believed that the Cold War was a battle for minds and the main battleground would be in Europe.

In 1950, the CIA clandestinely organized a group in Paris called the Congress for Cultural Freedom. The purpose of this new organization was to bring together non-Communist leftist intellectuals in Europe to promote democracy, to undermine Communist influence, and to defeat the neutralist tendencies of many left-of-center European intellectuals. The Congress for Cultural Freedom was funded through a series of CIA front organizations; the participants were not aware of CIA sponsorship.

In 1953, the Congress for Cultural Freedom launched its flagship journal *Encounter*, with its offices in London. *Encounter* emphasized politics and culture and quickly became a respected forum for non-Communist intellectual discussion. Many of the articles criticized Communist infringements on cultural expression and political thought. The CIA, through its well-placed agents on the editorial staff, gingerly guided *Encounter* away from any strong criticism of the U.S., but in general the publication had editorial freedom. Writers like Bertrand Russell, James Baldwin, Vladimir Nabokov, Isaiah Berlin, Jorge Luis Borges, Stephen Spender, Mary McCarthy, and W. H. Auden were contributors. Most of them would have been horror-struck if they had known they were supporting a CIA covert action operation.

The Congress of Cultural Freedom eventually published about twenty similar journals in Germany, France, Italy, Africa, Asia, and Australia. While all of this activity was going on, the CIA secretly subsidized the publication of several hundred anti-Communist books aimed at the same audience. The overall impact of this covert action is hard to measure, but it was certainly considerable. CIA sponsorship of the Congress of Cultural Freedom was exposed in the U.S. magazine *Ramparts* in 1967. The CIA discontinued all support in 1970.

The Congress of Cultural Freedom was not the CIA's only press-related covert action operation during the Cold War. There were other front groups, press placements, and propaganda mechanisms. All major intelligence services, in fact, have conducted press operations of one kind or another, and many are still doing it. Journalists, as it turns out, have not been hard to buy.

The CIA used two front organizations, the National Committee for a Free Europe and the Crusade for Freedom, to operate two Munich-based radio stations transmitting anti-Communist programming to Eastern Europe and the Soviet Union. Radio Free Europe, broadcasting primarily to Czechoslovakia, Romania, Hungary, Poland, and Bulgaria, was launched in 1950. Radio Liberty, aimed at the Soviet Union, started operations in 1953. Radio Free Europe and Radio Liberty became the voice of freedom and hope for millions of listeners behind the Iron Curtain. CIA sponsorship of the stations was revealed by the *New York Times* in 1967, and clandestine funding was cut off in 1972.

The purpose of the Crusade for Freedom was to collect "freedom dollars" from Americans around the country to help bring the "voice of truth" to the "enslaved peoples of Eastern Europe." In reality, the Crusade for Freedom generated only a small portion of the operating expenses of Radio Free Europe and Radio Liberty (most came directly from the CIA budget), but it was a convincing and patriotic front. I remember going to the movies and seeing Crusade for Freedom appeals when I was a boy in Iowa. After a short film showing the evils of Communism, the lights came up and a can in the shape of the Liberty Bell was passed around for donations. I felt very proud of myself for putting the dime my mother had given me for popcorn into the can. I was doing my part to fight Communism!

Another example of an "information operation" surfaced in December 2005, when the U.S. Army was revealed to have paid Iraqi journalists to print articles favorable to the Iraqi government, coalition forces, the democratic process, and U.S.–led reconstruction efforts. The Army used a private "strategic communications" firm as an intermediary to conceal the direct U.S. government sponsorship. Iraqi journalists were reportedly paid $25 for a favorable story, $45 if photos were included. The going rate for a positive television report was $50. Some Iraqi journalists received total payments of up to $900 a month. The U.S. government's role in making the payments, "suggesting" story topics, and providing "guidelines" to the Iraqi journalists was kept secret—until the story broke in the U.S. press. A U.S. military spokesman in Baghdad pointed out that al Qaida leader Abu Musab al-Zarqawi was aggressively using the Iraqi media to promote his anti-American terrorist agenda. He said the U.S. Army operation was simply an effort to counter the propaganda being disseminated by "an enemy intent on discrediting the Iraqi government and the Coalition, and who are taking every opportunity to instill fear and intimidate the Iraqi people."

SCENARIO NO. 31:
FABRICATING ACADEMIC CREDENTIALS

Syed Arif Sadiq is a senior advisor to Pakistani President Ashfaq Yusuf. Sadiq has access to large quantities of classified documents in the office of the president, including secret reports of President Yusuf's meetings with foreign leaders. Sadiq has regular professional contact with Walter McHenry, the deputy chief of mission at the U.S. Embassy in Islamabad. Through McHenry, Sadiq meets CIA officer James Thurman. Sadiq and Thurman have sons who attend the same international high school in Islamabad. The two boys become friends and spend time together in each other's home. The parents become better acquainted at school functions for their sons and soon begin socializing together.

The Sadiqs' dream is to have their son Jamaat study at a top university in the United States. The problem is that Jamaat did not apply himself in high school and made poor grades. He also has a reputation for having a bad attitude and for getting into trouble. His SAT and TOEFL (Test of English as a Foreign Language) scores are excellent, but without grades and good recommendations his prospects for getting into a selective U.S. university are dim. Sadiq shares all of this with Thurman and asks for his advice.

Thurman believes he can recruit Sadiq as a CIA source in return for getting his son into the right U.S. university. The CIA has the capability of fabricating an impressive high school transcript for Jamaat and of forging glowing recommendations for him from teachers and administrators. In addition, the CIA can agree to secretly pay for Jamaat's schooling, since the cost of an education at an elite private university in the U.S. would be beyond the family's means.

Sadiq wants his son to apply to Georgetown, Rice, Duke, Stanford, and Dartmouth.

———

Would it be morally acceptable for the CIA to fabricate academic credentials for Jamaat and to pay for his education in return for Sadiq's agreement to work for the CIA as a source inside the president's office?

Former CIA officer John Hedley:

It depends. It is morally unacceptable to falsify academic records and recommendations for use in the U.S.—in effect conducting a domestic operation by deceiving an American university. Doing something known to be prohibited by U.S. law would be immoral. Questions of legality and illegality are easily determined; an action either is or isn't. But are there degrees of moral and ethical behavior? Are there extenuating circumstances that might cause the CIA to cross the line? That, in my view, is what is at issue in this case. It might be different if a non–U.S. university were involved or if the source could provide critically needed information pertaining to U.S. national security. That is why "it depends." If Sadiq's recruitment would provide access to valuable counterterrorist information, that would merit a fabrication outside the United States. Does this amount to the end justifying the means? Possibly. This is a case where, at a non–U.S. university, the stakes could be high enough to justify the fabrication.

Professor Bruce Gronbeck of the University of Iowa:

No. This is a comparatively easy case for a university professor, whose job depends on accurate intellectual and academic information. Institutional integrity—even for private institutions—is in trouble. Furthermore, there is no sense here of extenuating circumstances, for example, that Sadiq could provide vital information to protect societies or individuals. This operation reeks of mere opportunism, not necessity in special circumstances. This is a no-brainer case.

Professor Mark Moyar of the U.S. Marine Corps University:

Yes. In light of the potential benefits for the United States, it would be morally acceptable to fabricate credentials for Jamaat and to fund his education. Universities often lower the standards for certain types of students, and almost always for reasons less important than the protection of U.S. national security. Because the CIA would be paying the full costs, the university would not suffer financially. The main victim would be the student who was denied a place so that Jamaat could go. This student has also likely been passed over in favor of other less qualified applicants for reasons much less compelling than national security, so this injustice is a relatively minor one. One would hope that this procedure could be avoided completely by having the CIA appeal directly and overtly to the university, though in today's climate it is far from clear that the university would agree to such an arrangement.

Former CIA officer Gena Mills:

It depends. While I have no objection in principle to the idea of fabricating credentials (which is probably done anyway by citizens from several countries), there are other aspects to consider in this scenario. There is the issue of CIA involvement in visa fraud. Jamaat would presumably apply for and receive a U.S. student visa as a result of his admittance to a U.S. university, and that admittance would be based on false credentials. Even more important is the issue of the financial circumstances of Sadiq and his family. The question of how Sadiq is able to afford this foreign education is a security risk and might well spark an investigation by the Pakistani security services. Only if these issues are addressed should this operation go forward, though withdrawing from it would not necessarily be based on moral issues.

Graduate student Jason Pogacnik of the Maxwell School at Syracuse University:

No. All practical issues aside, this operation would be morally unacceptable. Jamaat clearly has no right to be accepted at one of the elite universities his father would like to see him attend. By forging documents that would facilitate Jamaat's acceptance, the CIA would effectively deny the acceptance of another student who is more deserving. That person, if admitted, could go on to accomplish great things for his or her country. Those accomplishments could far outweigh the benefits to be gained from Sadiq's agreement to work for the CIA. It is also morally problematic that Jamaat himself cannot voluntarily decide whether to participate in this operation.

Former middle-school and high-school teacher Barbara Ziesche:

No. It would be grossly unfair to all the other students wanting to study in the U.S. to let this young man come into the country just because his father is making a deal with the CIA.

Professor Harry Mason of the Patterson School at the University of Kentucky:

No (class vote). The graduate students in my course on intelligence found it morally unacceptable to fabricate academic credentials for Jamaat by a vote of 1-16. The prospect of having an excellent source for the CIA in Pakistan convinced only one student to vote yes. Most of the other students attended undergraduate programs with rigid honor standards. They have also signed on to the Patterson School code of conduct and are not willing to see academic integrity betrayed.

Author's comment:

I once handled an agent ████████████████ who wanted no compensation from the CIA other than a U.S. college education for his daughter. The agent was extremely productive, cooperative, and loyal. The CIA valued his services highly and wanted to do everything possible to accommodate his request. Unfortunately, the daughter was a mediocre student with below average SAT and TOEFL scores. Using guidance from CIA headquarters, I worked closely with the agent to prepare application packages to suitable U.S. schools for his daughter. The daughter, of course, was not aware that the CIA was in any way involved with her father or with the application process. The agent and I spent long hours in a safehouse analyzing his daughter's records, filling out forms, and "editing" her reference letters and essays. There was no outright fabrication, but the end product certainly presented her in the best possible light. She was accepted at a fine, but less competitive, private liberal arts college with a beautiful campus. She loved it there and did well. No one ever knew that she was, in effect, going to school on a "CIA scholarship." Her father was forever grateful and continued to be one of the best agents the CIA had in that region.

SCENARIO NO. 32:
PLAGIARIZING A PH.D. DISSERTATION

Qiang Song is a twenty-eight-year-old Chinese Ph.D. student in Computer and Information Sciences at the University of Minnesota. He hopes to have his dissertation completed by the end of the year but is having a great deal of difficulty in writing it.

Song walks into the FBI's Minneapolis field office and asks to speak with a special agent. He says he desperately needs help with his Ph.D. dissertation and is willing to make a deal with the FBI to get it. Song reveals that he is actually a People's Liberation Army (PLA)[36] intelligence officer in the U.S. under cover as a graduate student. His PLA mission, he says, is to do everything possible to stay in the U.S. once he has his Ph.D. and to get a job in the computer industry. If he can acquire permanent resident alien status, he is to proceed along the path toward U.S. citizenship. Eventually, with citizenship, he would plan on applying for a position in a U.S. national laboratory or with a high-tech government contractor. In the meantime, Song is expected to help the PLA in identifying computer technology to steal, to advise the PLA on setting up front companies, and to spot Chinese-American engineers and computer scientists for possible recruitment.

Song states that he will be professionally and personally disgraced if he fails to complete his Ph.D. The PLA will recall him to China, and his once-bright career prospects will be destroyed. Song offers to work for the FBI as a penetration of the PLA in exchange for assistance in writing his dissertation. He says he can identify Chinese intelligence officers in the United States and can also help the FBI uncover illegal PLA front companies and other illegal acquisition mechanisms. He says he is prepared to commit himself to a long-term clandestine relationship with the FBI.

————

Would it be morally acceptable for the FBI to help Song write a plagiarized dissertation and obtain a fraudulent Ph.D. from the University of Minnesota in exchange for his services as a long-term penetration of the Chinese PLA?

Former CIA officer William Lieser:

Yes. This seems to be a relatively easy and, to me, noncontroversial means of gaining the cooperation of a potentially very valuable long-term penetration of the PLA. And it provides important leverage in keeping the loyalty of the agent, as the prospect of revealing the plagiarized dissertation would compromise the agent's professional credentials and career. While someone in the academic world might strongly disagree, I feel that the operational advantages outweigh any moral reservations.

Professor Michael Porter of the University of Missouri:

No. While it may sound good on the surface, what happens to this individual—with Ph.D. in hand—once the sting is over? We cannot have individuals with false academic credentials in society, teaching, etc. It looks like a bad situation from the start, and the false granting of an advanced academic degree should not be used as bait in such a situation. The FBI now knows that Song is a spy for his government, so any espionage career he would have had in the U.S. is over.

Professor Peter Feaver of Duke University:

[The views expressed by Professor Feaver are personal and are not intended to reflect those of any particular group, institution, or organization.]

Undecided. This is a tough call. I know the standards for a Ph.D. are elastic and there are many "unworthy" Ph.D.s out there. Moreover, is a fraudulent Ph.D. any worse than a fraudulent back story to justify employment? Yes, it is worse, but how much worse? On the other hand, this cuts pretty close to the core essence of my profession, so I am uneasy! One could argue that this is morally acceptable on the grounds that the university has already compromised itself by admitting a spy, albeit unwittingly. On the other hand, this is compromising an entire system that has the presumption of innocence otherwise.

Former FBI senior executive John Guido:

Yes. The no-risk solution would be for the FBI to reject Song and to let him go home in disgrace. With that approach, however, the U.S. would gain no intelligence advantage and would learn nothing about Chinese intelligence operations and possible front companies. The FBI should provide Song with the requested assistance. Morally, there would be no real difference between doing this and providing false identification or a false legend to an agent, which we do all the time. Song's falsely obtained credentials will not put anyone at risk or in danger except Song himself. While this may not be fair to the university, it is much more operationally secure than involving a number of people at the university in creating a false record of Ph.D. completion. This operation is within acceptable operating procedures.

Graduate student Jason Pogacnik of the Maxwell School at Syracuse University:

Yes. Normally, academic dishonesty is highly immoral. Here, it is a question of relativity. China is notorious for large-scale industrial espionage and copyright infringement, two morally questionable activities. Because Song could help identify Chinese intelligence officers and illegal acquisition mechanisms, employing his services as a spy for the United States will help to prevent China from engaging in such immoral pursuits. Specifically, plagiarizing Song's dissertation can be directly linked to decreasing an immoral and harmful activity of a similar type and larger scale elsewhere. Therefore, academic dishonesty would be acceptable in this scenario. A caution: the relative "weighing" of morality like this should be done only in cases where we can compare apples to apples (here, for example, individual plagiarism versus large-scale industrial espionage and copyright infringement).

Kyu Mani Lee, Ph.D., former superintendent of Larned State Hospital in Kansas:

Yes. Song can be tremendously beneficial to U.S. counterintelligence efforts, and the opportunity to recruit such a valuable penetration of Chinese intelligence does not come around very often.

Author's comment:

It is not uncommon for foreign intelligence officers, like Song, to approach the FBI or the CIA to try to make a deal. Some are venal and simply want money to finance a more lavish lifestyle. Others are politically or professionally disaffected from their own systems and hope to defect and resettle in the U.S. There are, in fact, multiple reasons why foreign intelligence officers and others "walk in" to the FBI or the CIA to volunteer their services.

Many of the best operations the FBI and the CIA have had over the years started as walk-ins. A favorite venue for walk-ins during the Cold War was Vienna, a city crawling with spies. In nearly seven years, I saw a steady stream of them—and, inside the CIA, Vienna deservedly earned the reputation of being the "walk-in capital of the world."

Many of the walk-ins are kooks, peddlers, or con men. I remember one very well-dressed and distinguished-looking gentleman who walked in to the Embassy in Vienna. I met with him in the lobby and asked how I could help him. In impeccable, educated German he told me he would like me to deliver a message for him to the CIA. He said the CIA was using a long-distance ray gun to fire electronic beams into his rear end, and he was in great pain. He had come to the U.S. Embassy, he said politely, to see if the CIA would turn off the gun. I told him I would pass the message to the CIA immediately and was certain the beams would soon stop. A week later, he sent a thank-you note to the U.S. ambassador, saying he greatly appreciated the CIA's kindness in turning off the ray gun.

SCENARIO NO. 33:
EXPOSING UNWITTING PERSON TO RISK

Madeleine Martineau is a seventy-four-year-old Belgian widow living in a luxury apartment on Rue de la Loi in Brussels. Her husband was a French diplomat. When he died, Martineau returned to her native Brussels to live in this apartment, which has been in her family for many years.

Ambassador Dieter Bothner, the deputy permanent representative of Germany to the European Union, lives in an apartment immediately adjacent to the apartment of Martineau. He meets often with high-level government officials there, not only from Germany but also from other European Union countries. It is also known that Ambassador Bothner holds weekly meetings in his apartment with his senior staff, usually on Saturday mornings.

U.S. relations with the European Union have reached a low point. Ambassador Bothner has been particularly strident in his criticism of the U.S. and has been the leader of a large anti–U.S. bloc inside the EU. The CIA would very much like to put a listening device inside Ambassador Bothner's apartment to record his conversations with his European colleagues and with his staff. An audio operation of this type, however, obviously has considerable political risk, and it is imperative that the American hand not be shown.

Martineau spends the month of August on the Côte d'Azur in France. The CIA proposes to make a surreptitious entry into her Brussels apartment while she is gone. The plan is for CIA technical officers to drill through the adjoining wall and to place audio devices behind the plaster and wood-work of Ambassador Bothner's apartment. The CIA already has an apart-ment nearby that can be used as a listening post where it can receive the low-powered transmissions from the audio devices. The drilling damage to Martineau's wall will be completely restored so there will be no trace of the operation. All the equipment used in the devices will be of French manufacture.

In the unfortunate event the audio devices are discovered by the Ger-mans and the incident is reported to the Belgian police, suspicion will im-mediately fall on Martineau. Her ties to France are extensive and the devices themselves appear to be of French origin. There will be absolutely no proof the U.S. was in any way involved.

Would it be morally acceptable for the CIA to expose Martineau to potential criminal and civil liability by making use of her apartment without her knowledge for a technical operation against Ambassador Bothner?

Former CIA officer John ████████:

Yes. Accepting the premise that the EU is a high-priority collection target and that the entry and installation can be made without detection, I think we should proceed. With regard to the risk to Martineau, I would argue that her ignorance may well be her best protection. If the operation is compromised, Mme Martineau can legitimately protest that she knows noth-ing about the affair. I expect that this would be believed. In any event, there would be no proof against her.

If the Germans detect the installation, presumably from their side of the wall, they might choose to turn the operation into a disinformation channel. This would be difficult to do, however, since they would not know for sure who the target is. If the Germans remove the devices and determine their French origin, they would have to decide if the evidence is sufficient to make a démarche to the French. If they do, the French will truthfully deny everything, including any intelligence relationship with Martineau. The Ger-mans (and the French if they are informed) may suspect a CIA operation, but they will not be able to prove it. Martineau will have a great story to tell her grandchildren.

Lauraine Brekke-Esparza, city manager of Del Mar, California:

It depends. Is there a way Martineau can be protected in the event the hidden listening device is discovered? Obviously, from her background, she has some knowledge and sophistication in these matters, but I do not think it would be morally acceptable to set up an innocent third party and then just stand aside when a discovery is made. If we can put some protections in place, then I think it would be morally acceptable to bug Ambassador Bothner through Martineau's apartment.

Mike Hannesschlager, former executive director of the Texas Christian Coalition:

No. As valuable and important as the information from Ambassador Bothner's residence would doubtless be, it would be wrong to pin suspicion and blame on an innocent person. This operation could conceivably end in Martineau's prosecution for a crime she did not commit, and that would be a terrible moral failure on our part.

Former CIA officer Richard Corbin:

Yes. Martineau is unwitting of the activity and can plausibly deny involvement. Actual attribution for the bugging would be difficult to prove, so the risk to her would be minimal.

Professor Abraham Clearfield:

No. I am totally against involving innocent people without their knowledge in clandestine operations. In this case, if the listening devices are discovered, the CIA will certainly not come to Martineau's defense. Her life could be ruined. It would be immoral to involve an innocent person. But does the CIA care?

Author's comment:

I was once involved in a similar operation. The CIA was very interested in knowing what was going on inside the offices of an Asian group that was hostile to the United States. Using a recruited local citizen as a front, the CIA was able to rent an apartment with an adjoining wall to the target office. The recruited asset actually lived in the apartment to give it a normal pattern of activity and to serve as the "listening post" operator once the bug was installed. The setup looked perfect.

Late one night, when the Asian target office was empty, a CIA technician started to drill from the asset's apartment into the adjoining wall of the office. The idea, of course, was to stop just short of the plaster in the target office so the installed microphone would have the best possible position for high-quality audio. Despite all his training and all the technical devices he had available to prevent such a mishap, the technician broke through the other side, leaving a big hole. That was a disaster. The sophisticated Asians in the target office would see the hole the next morning and immediately recognize what it was. The CIA's asset would be exposed and arrested. We had no choice but to get the asset out of the country that night and resettle her safely in the United States. This flap cost the CIA a lot of money—and the poor technician had a lot of explaining to do. Rule No. 1 for audio technicians: don't poke through.

SCENARIO NO. 34:
KAMIKAZE DOLPHINS

The CIA received an unconfirmed intelligence report two years ago that Iran was training frogmen to carry out terrorist attacks against Western targets. A little over a year ago, an underwater explosion blasted a large hole in the hull of the USS *Kentucky* (SSBN 737), a nuclear powered ballistic missile submarine, while it was docked at its homeport in Bangor, Washington. Twenty-two crewmen were killed and damage to the submarine was extensive. Navy and FBI investigators concluded that an explosive device had been placed on the hull of the submarine by an underwater swimmer. Three months later, the luxury cruise ship *Carnival Conquest* was rocked by an underwater explosion in the port of Cozumel, Mexico. Forty-seven passengers and crew, including thirty-eight Americans, were killed. Again, it was ruled that the cause of the explosion was terrorism, mostly likely by an underwater swimmer.

In response to the attack on the USS *Kentucky*, the U.S. Navy and the CIA's Counterterrorism Center joined forces to create a new counterterrorism program similar to the Navy's earlier Marine Mammal Program. In this new top-secret project, bottlenose dolphins are trained to use their sensitive natural sonar to locate underwater swimmers. When a swimmer is detected, the dolphins attack the swimmer with a harpoon-like device attached to their backs. In extensive trials, the dolphins proved to be more effective than any other available countermeasure in detecting long distance underwater swimmers and striking them with the harpoon. When the dolphins are operational, the harpoon will trigger an explosion, killing both the swimmer and the dolphin. Alternate methods of having the dolphins simply sound an alarm or perform other non-lethal actions have proved to be less effective.

———

Would it be morally acceptable for the Navy and the CIA to use trained dolphins in suicide attacks against underwater swimmers to protect U.S. ships from terrorism?

Undergraduate student Laura Zandstra of Texas A&M University:
Yes. It would be morally acceptable to use trained dolphins for national security purposes. The value of human life is much greater than the value of

an animal. Animal protection rights should exist and there should be extra measures to ensure the proper treatment and care of animals. But if the loss of the life of a single animal would save the lives of many humans, the death of the animal is justifiable.

Former CIA officer Eugene Culbertson:

Yes. This is morally acceptable, but only as a stopgap measure to prevent terrorist attacks against American military and civilian maritime targets. As soon as an alternate method is developed to intercept terrorist frogmen, the sacrifice and use of dolphins should be stopped.

Undergraduate student Aaron Tatyrek of Texas A&M University:

Yes. This counter-measure is morally acceptable to protect our fleet and to save American lives.

Lauraine Brekke-Esparza, city manager of Del Mar, California:

Yes. While I love animals dearly, I do not see this as morally unacceptable.

Author Ralph Peters:

Yes. Absolutely. Flipper's great, but if we can use him to stop terrorists and save human lives, there's no moral issue for me.

Stephanie Boyles, wildlife biologist for People for the Ethical Treatment of Animals:

No. Wars are human endeavors. Animals do not wage war, so why should they suffer just because humans do? Like civilians, animals often become innocent victims of war. The armed forces conscript various animals into intelligence and combat service, sending them on "missions" that endanger their lives and well being. With no guarantee or even likelihood that these animals will save human lives, this forced service is reprehensible.

Bottlenose dolphins are highly intelligent animals, but they have no idea that lives will be lost if they fail to perform their tasks properly. They cannot have any reasonable sense of accountability, and reliance on them to protect our citizens is unfair to the animals. Our citizens deserve the best protection available, which comes from leadership, technology, and training—not from using animals. These animals do not enlist, and the attitude that any creature is an expendable tool to be used and tossed away by the CIA and the military is immensely disturbing. All citizens of the world should come together for the peaceful purpose of condemning and demanding an end to this abuse of innocent animals.

Author's comment:

In 2002, the FBI issued a nationwide warning that attacks by scuba divers could threaten U.S. ships and port facilities. The information came from CIA interrogations of al Qaida detainees in Afghanistan. All U.S. divers, dive instructors, and dive centers were asked by the FBI to report any suspicious events or individuals. The threat is certainly out there.

The U.S. Navy has trained bottlenose dolphins for various military duties since the early 1960s. The dolphins proved to be very skilled at detecting mines, recovering underwater objects, and intercepting underwater swimmers. The Navy later added sea lions and white beluga whales to the program. Dolphins were used successfully to protect U.S. ships and harbors in Vietnam in the 1960s and 1970s. They also played a similar role in the Persian Gulf in 1987 and 1988. The Navy used dolphins to protect nuclear submarines at the Trident Missile Base in Bangor, Washington, in the late 1980s, but protests from environmentalists and animal rights activists forced a discontinuation of the operation. Today, U.S. Navy dolphins and sea lions are actively engaged in mine-clearing and anti-swimmer operations in the waters off Iraq.

The Navy has been sensitive to complaints from animal rights groups that it has misused and abused the marine mammals, particularly the dolphins. The Navy insists the animals are well cared for and are not used to disarm explosives, to emplace limpet mines, or to carry out any other dangerous missions. There were widespread rumors during the Vietnam War that the Navy had a secret "swimmer nullification program" that used dolphins to attack underwater swimmers with a harpoon-like device. The Navy denies such a program ever existed.

The bottlenose dolphins and sea lions have not, in fact, used lethal force. Instead of attacking underwater swimmers, they have been trained to mark them with a buoy or other signal so Navy personnel can spot them and intervene. The current procedure is for the dolphin or sea lion to approach a swimmer from behind and to clamp a cuff on his leg. The cuff is attached to a rope and buoy, so the swimmer is stopped and marked at the same time.

The Navy has developed torpedo-like robots in an effort to duplicate the functions of the marine mammals, but the machines have been less effective than the animals. Bottlenose dolphins will be tough to beat. They are intelligent, reliable, and particularly good in shallow water, where Navy sonars are not dependable. If the terrorist threat from underwater swimmers increases and the cuffs turn out to be unreliable, I think it is possible deadlier options will be considered.

SCENARIO NO. 35:
SPYING ON AMERICANS OVERSEAS

The Russian foreign intelligence service, the SVRR, remains very active in recruiting Americans. Whenever possible, the SVRR prefers to meet with its American sources in ███████, Costa Rica, Austria, or Switzerland. The SVRR considers it dangerous to conduct clandestine meetings in the United States because of tight surveillance by the FBI. Therefore, it instructs its American agents to make quick trips to one of the above "safe countries" for meetings there with their SVRR case officers. The CIA has just learned from a sensitive penetration of the Chinese MSS that the Chinese are doing something similar, that is, meeting American agents outside the United States.

The U.S. National Counterintelligence Executive, the senior coordinating body for U.S. counterintelligence activities, proposes to create and maintain a database of all American citizens with top secret clearances. Counterintelligence officials will use travel information from U.S. Customs, the FBI (through cooperative contacts in the airline industry), and NSA (from travel industry computer files) to cross-check the data to identify Americans with top-secret clearances who are traveling to ███████, Costa Rica, Austria, or Switzerland. Nonbusiness trips of short duration will be particularly scrutinized. Suspicious patterns of previous travel—such as a quick trip to Switzerland every three months—will also be flagged.

If the FBI is unable to verify a valid reason for the foreign travel by these Americans citizens, the information will be passed to the CIA for possible physical and electronic surveillance overseas.

———

Would it be morally acceptable for the FBI, NSA, and CIA to monitor the overseas travel of American citizens with top-secret clearances as part of an expanded U.S. counterintelligence program, including physical and electronic surveillance of them while they are overseas?

Former CIA officer William Lieser:

Yes. Individuals who have accepted the responsibilities of having a top-secret clearance must be prepared to accept potentially significant intrusions into their personal lives, for example, the regular polygraph exams[37] administered to CIA and other intelligence personnel. Top-secret clearances are a privilege, not a right, and counterintelligence officials must have authorization to conduct reasonable investigative procedures.

Michael Bohn, former director of the White House Situation Room:

It depends. I cautiously support such a measure if safeguards are adequate to ensure proper legal procedures are followed in the aftermath of identifying a suspect. Also, there must be a review and oversight process that is watertight.

Mike Hannesschlager, former executive director of the Texas Christian Coalition:

Yes. This just makes good security sense. It is not too invasive to monitor the travel of those Americans entrusted with our most sensitive secrets, particularly if that travel happens to fit the profile of SVRR or Chinese tradecraft. It is true that "ordinary" Americans are not given this kind of treatment, but then "ordinary" Americans don't possess top-secret information, either.

Graduate student Russell Rodriguez of the George Bush School of Government and Public Service at Texas A&M University:

Yes. Anyone who is entrusted with the nation's secrets should be willing to give up some of his or her freedoms to ensure that the government's trust is not misplaced. One idea would be to have people with top-secret clearances sign a release that specifically authorizes such procedures. Signing the release would be a condition of maintaining one's clearance.

Author's comment:

Sometimes the line between effective counterintelligence and protecting civil liberties is a fine one. The rights of U.S. citizens vary considerably depending on whether they are physically present in the United States or overseas.

There has never been a problem with monitoring suspicious activity by Americans overseas. The CIA has primary counterintelligence jurisdiction for the U.S. government outside the country and routinely exercises it. This means that U.S. citizens overseas can be surveilled, tapped, photographed, and otherwise monitored if there are reasonable grounds to believe they are involved in intelligence activity. No warrants or court orders are required.

The real difficulty arises with regard to U.S. citizens at home. U.S. law is appropriately solicitous of their privacy and individual rights. The U.S. government clearly has the right to conduct background investigations of prospective employees, and many agencies conduct periodic reinvestigations of their cleared employees. At the CIA, for example, employees are reinvestigated at about five-year intervals. Use of the polygraph varies from agency to agency, but it has always been standard practice at the CIA and NSA. The FBI has used polygraphs for its employees less routinely, but there is a trend now for more frequent use, especially for applicants. The State Department, like many other U.S. government agencies, has staunchly resisted polygraphs of its employees.

Except for these authorized and routine security clearance procedures, U.S. counterintelligence and law enforcement officials are severely limited in their ability to monitor and investigate government officials. They cannot currently, for example, monitor the travel, tax forms, bank accounts, credit card charges, or other nonpublic personal records of U.S. citizen employees without probable cause. The big "mole hunt" at the CIA from 1985 to 1994, which eventually uncovered CIA officer Aldrich Ames as a Soviet spy, was significantly handicapped by the investigators' difficulty in getting approval for intrusive investigative techniques against the suspects. It was only after there were substantial indicators pointing to Ames that the FBI could get approval for physical surveillance, wiretaps, surreptitious entry into his home, and a trash cover.[38]

When I was in counterintelligence at the Agency, I proposed that CIA security officers discreetly drive through the CIA's parking lots once or twice a week to look for expensive luxury vehicles. They were to take down the plate numbers of any vehicles that fit that description and identify the owners through the Department of Motor Vehicles. The CIA's Counterintelligence Center and Office of Security would then quietly verify that the employees in question had sufficient explainable income to justify that kind of car. I thought this would be good, low-cost counterintelligence. The CIA's lawyers, on the other hand, said the program would be an invasion of CIA employees' right to privacy without probable cause. They killed the idea.

SCENARIO NO. 36:
SPYING ON FRIENDS

Relations between the United States and its NATO ally Turkey have improved greatly since the 2003 tension over the Turkish refusal to allow U.S. troops to use Turkey as a staging area for the invasion of Iraq. Turkey has been especially helpful in allowing the U.S. to establish new SIGINT facilities in southeastern Turkey along the border with Syria, Iraq, and Iran. From these new facilities, the U.S. is able to intercept Syrian, Iraqi, and Iranian phone calls, faxes, emails, telexes, and radio communications. Coverage of both civilian and military targets in these countries has been excellent. The intelligence produced from these sites has been of high value to the United States.

The agreement signed by the United States and Turkey strictly prohibits the U.S. from using the SIGINT facilities in Turkey for collection against

Turkish targets. The U.S. government, however, is concerned about Turkish military activities in the area, particularly along the border with Iraq, and would like to begin intercepting Turkish military communications in addition to the authorized collection against Syria, Iraq, and Iran.

Would it be morally acceptable for the United States to violate its agreement with Turkey by secretly intercepting Turkish military communications in southeastern Turkey?

Admiral Bobby R. Inman, former director of the National Security Agency and deputy director of central intelligence:
Yes.

Professor David S. Allen of the University of Wisconsin–Milwaukee:
No. It would be wrong for the U.S. to purposefully target messages that it had agreed not to intercept. While those messages might provide beneficial information, agreements should be honored and promises kept. While I am not willing to say there are no situations in which breaking a promise is justifiable, I see no evidence in this scenario that breaking the promise is necessary.

Former CIA officer David Edger:
Yes. Spying on friends is a reality of the world. In this case, we are talking only about SIGINT coverage. Modern organizations are well aware of the possibility of SIGINT, and methods exist to encrypt message traffic to such a degree that interception of messages is unlikely to prove worthwhile. I see no moral objection to using our equipment to listen in on the Turkish military. If the Turks are sending traffic we can read, or if traffic analysis alone proves interesting, there is no moral reason for us not to take advantage of the situation. The fact that signals intelligence is passive to some extent makes this case easier to justify. Recruiting a human source inside an allied military power might be a tougher moral question. Picking up message traffic that is "out there" for anyone to receive is less of a moral problem.

Former CIA Information Management Officer Ray Brewer:
Yes. All nations should know that when they go into intelligence agreements of this kind, national interests on either side can override the accord.

Kyu Mani Lee, Ph.D., former superintendent of Larned State Hospital in Kansas:

Yes. Spying on friends is a standard part of intelligence work.

Professor Terry H. Anderson of Texas A&M University:
No. If the Turks discovered this U.S. illegal behavior against them, then the trust and confidence both sides had been developing for years would be destroyed.

Author's comment:
It is axiomatic in the spy world to say there are friendly countries, but no friendly intelligence services. With very few exceptions, everyone today with the capability to do so spies on everyone else.

Israel, despite all the security assistance and other support it has received from the United States over the years, was caught red-handed in 1985 handling U.S. Navy intelligence analyst Jonathan Pollard as a spy against the United States. Pollard was convicted of espionage and is serving a life sentence. The United States, even though it expressed outrage that Israel would do such a thing, cannot really claim the moral high ground in these matters. In 1987, an Israeli court convicted Israeli Army intelligence officer Yossi Amit of spying for the Americans. Israel has insisted repeatedly that it has stopped spying against its American ally, but in 2006 William Franklin, a Pentagon analyst, was sentenced to twelve years in prison for passing classified information to an Israeli diplomat and two members of the pro-Israel lobbying group American Israel Public Affairs Committee.

France has been notorious for conducting intelligence operations against the United States. French operations have included technology theft, economic espionage, listening devices, surreptitious entries, and phone taps. American business and government officials traveling to France for negotiations with their French counterparts have often been spied upon. Here again, however, the spying was not one-sided. In 1995, the French wrapped up a major CIA spying operation in Paris and expelled four American "diplomats" assigned to the U.S. Embassy and one American "business person."

It is generally asserted that the U.S. has "special relationships" with certain countries that prohibit spying on each other. There have been no documented cases of espionage by the United States against ███████ ███████████████████████████—or vice versa. There is speculation that a small number of other countries enjoy this special status as well.

It has not always been so. Even our great friends the British, when their national survival was at stake at the beginning of World War II, did not hesitate to conduct massive covert action operations inside the United States in an all-out effort to bring America into the war. British intelligence officer William Stephenson brilliantly headed up the effort, which involved influence agents, propaganda, and forgeries. Even today, I am struck by how brazen the British were and cannot understand why President Roosevelt, J. Edgar Hoover, and William Donovan let them get away with it.

SCENARIO NO. 37:
SPYING ON THE UNITED NATIONS

The United States has adopted a foreign policy that is more multilateral, consultative, and cooperative than it was previously. As one manifestation of this policy, it has upgraded its representation at the United Nations and has made a strong effort to work within the framework of that organization. The results, however, have been mixed. It has become increasingly clear that there is a great deal of anti-American sentiment at the U.N. Many U.N. decisions, in fact, have been directly inimical to U.S. interests, and voting blocs have formed in the Security Council and the General Assembly to oppose U.S. initiatives. The Counter Terrorism Committee of the Security Council, for example, has obstructed U.S. demands for full enforcement of resolution 1373, which requires all member states to take specific actions to combat international terrorism. The U.S. also believes the International Atomic Energy Agency has been lax in enforcing safeguard regimes at the nuclear facilities of proliferation threat countries, including Iran and North Korea. Finally, in what has become a very contentious issue, seven members of the Security Council have urged that U.S. military commanders be tried before the International Court of Justice for alleged war crimes in Iraq.

The National Security Council and the president decide that the U.S. must have better intelligence on what is going on at the U.N. so it can better protect its interests.

Would it be morally acceptable for the FBI and CIA to recruit agents inside the U.N., for example, diplomats, top officials, Secretariat employees, and safeguards inspectors? Would it be morally acceptable for NSA to intercept phone calls, emails, and other communications to and from U.N. officials? Would it be morally acceptable for the FBI and CIA to plant listening devices inside the offices and residences of the secretary general and other top U.N. officials?

Former State Department officer John Salazar:
1) and 2) Yes. No laws that I know of would prohibit the recruitment of agents within the U.S. or the intercepting of their phone calls.
3) No. Detection of the listening devices would be a major embarrassment, with very serious diplomatic consequences.

Professor Abraham Clearfield:

I do not think the U.S. should ever recruit agents inside the U.N. In fact, if such efforts were ever revealed, the U.S. would lose credibility and stature among the world's nations. I believe we should work through our State Department to determine what is behind the charges against the U.S. military. We should pose the questions directly to the governments involved. If they do not comply, then I think we might have to resort to intercepting their communications. However, we should not plant listening devices inside the U.N. Secretary General's office. Our U.N. ambassador should take up the matter directly with the secretary general and request a closed-door review of the charges against our military commanders.

Randy Everett, M.D., of Fort Collins, Colorado:

1) No. I suspect I am unqualified to answer this question because of ignorance of the U.N. charter and additional treaties we may be a signatory to as host of the U.N. But I think it would be morally unacceptable to recruit agents inside the U.N. because of our agreements with that organization. It would also be very dangerous to our international standing to do so.

2) and 3) Yes. As I believe intelligence gathering is morally acceptable in general, I have no problem with monitoring communications, even at the U.N.—perhaps even more so there than in individual countries. The high level of corruption at the U.N. and abuses by the General Assembly and Security Council, primarily but not exclusively by nondemocratic states, increase the need and justification for such intelligence.

Los Angeles Times journalist Bob Drogin:

Yes. This is neither new nor wrong. U.S. intelligence agencies bugged the international conference in San Francisco in 1945 that created the United Nations, and President Roosevelt lobbied to set up the new U.N. headquarters in New York specifically to facilitate spying on the international delegations. Every U.N. delegation since then has known that its communications are routinely intercepted. Every government knows that intelligence agencies from around the world, including the United States, actively spy at the U.N. Many take counter-measures and factor the danger of spying into their work. The CIA was created to spy on foreign governments, and their presence at the U.N. makes it imperative for the CIA to do so.

Former CIA officer Burton Gerber:

The first duty in an operation such as this is to determine the requirements that U.S. policymakers have and to assure that other intelligence programs are tasked appropriately. Then, the question becomes, what cannot be obtained by those other intelligence means? Recruitment of human sources is the last resort, but that does not mean it is inappropriate or unnecessary in defense of a just political community. I see no ethical impediment to recruiting the kinds of persons described above if other means of intelligence acquisition—diplomatic reporting and technical collection systems—have proven inadequate. There will certainly be some operational and political issues that may become impediments, but that is not the issue here.

In defense of a just political community, I have no moral objection to intercepting communications to and from U.N. officials as long as this is done based on clear and important requirements from our political leaders. And this technical collection should be important in reducing or better targeting any human intelligence programs the FBI and CIA may undertake.

I believe the issue of planting listening devices in the homes or offices of the Secretary General and other top U.N. officials is not so much a moral or ethical question as it is a political and operational question. Again, if there is a strong need to obtain information to defend the just political community and it is not otherwise available, I see no ethical objection. I do expect that the political consequences of such a flap would be so huge that the political and intelligence leaders of the United States ought to stay away from this one.

Former FBI special agent Stanley A. Pimentel:

Yes. Spying has been going on since the time of Adam and Eve. It is common knowledge that every country spies on its neighbors, its friends, and its enemies. It is morally acceptable for the FBI and CIA to recruit agents inside the United Nations, for NSA to intercept U.N. communications, and for the FBI and CIA to plant listening devices inside the offices and residences of top U.N. officials.

For many years, the Foreign Intelligence Surveillance Act[39] court has authorized certain actions against diplomatic establishments for the purposes of collecting intelligence, combating espionage, countering terrorism, and fulfilling other intelligence requirements. The U.S. government has the duty to protect U.S. citizens and property from harm. Using intelligence devices and methods against countries, organizations, and individuals inimical to the best interests of the United States is morally acceptable. Laws or presidential executive orders may be needed to exercise these options, but once legally approved, they should proceed.

Author's comment:

There is nothing new about spying at the United Nations. Several nations have been caught in the act of using U.N. cover for espionage purposes. During the Cold War, the U.N. was packed with spies from the Soviet Union, Eastern Europe, and other countries. More recently, diplomats from the Cuban, Iraqi, and Iranian official missions to the U.N. have been expelled for intelligence activity. Perhaps most disturbingly, two Iranian officials from the Iranian Mission to the U.N. were expelled in 2004 for secretly videotaping tourist attractions and other landmarks in New York City, including St. Patrick's Cathedral, Rockefeller Center, subways, and buses. Iran is a known sponsor of international terrorism.

Great Britain was accused in 2004 of having conducted electronic surveillance on U.N. Secretary General Kofi Annan before the U.S.–British invasion of Iraq in 2003. There were also allegations that the United States had engaged in widespread intelligence operations at the U.N. in 2003 in an effort to determine the voting intentions of Security Council members concerning Iraqi resolutions. More specifically, the charge was that U.S. intelligence had monitored the home and office phones and emails of key U.N. diplomats and had then used this intelligence to try to influence their votes. According to one alleged NSA document that was leaked to the press, the United States was specifically targeting the U.N. delegations of Security Council members Angola, Cameroon, Chile, Guinea, Mexico, and Pakistan. Not surprisingly, there were strong protests against U.S. spying in those countries, especially in Mexico and Chile.

Senior U.N. officials, like Boutros Boutros-Ghali, Hans Blix, and Rolf Ekeus, have all stated publicly that they assumed they were targeted by foreign intelligence services, including the United States. Former U.N. chief weapons inspector Richard Butler reported that he knew his U.N. communications were intercepted, at a minimum, by the United States, Britain, France, and Russia.

The United States has frequently been accused of using various U.N. organizations, missions, and teams overseas as cover for intelligence operations. Ekeus, the chairman of the U.N. Special Commission (UNSCOM), established to investigate the existence of weapons of mass destruction in Iraq, stated in 2002 that U.S. spies in UNSCOM attempted to plant listening devices in offices and installations around Iraq.

Spying at the U.N. is a violation of the U.N. Charter and the Vienna Convention on Diplomatic Relations . . . but everyone is doing it. Does that make it morally acceptable for the United States?

SCENARIO NO. 38:
INDUSTRIAL ESPIONAGE

Datalog Technology, a Canadian company based in Calgary, is a world leader in mud logging and other oil field data acquisition services. It is active in all the major oil and gas exploration regions in the world, including the Middle East, South America, Kazakhstan, the North Sea, and West Africa. Logging data is critical in determining the geological characteristics and potential yields of new oil and gas wells. The information derived from logging operations is considered sensitive and is strictly protected by the companies involved. Multimillion dollar investment decisions are based on logging data.

Paul Markowitz is a forty-eight-year-old Canadian engineer employed by Datalog at its headquarters in Calgary. In his position as a senior supervisor in the Mud Logging Division, Markowitz has access to confidential logging data for Datalog clients around the world. By reviewing the computerized mud logging and stand-alone gas detection data, he is in a position to know which oil and gas sites appear particularly promising and, on the contrary, which sites have shown disappointing results.

The CIA assesses Markowitz as pro–U.S. and totally venal. He lives beyond his means and is deeply in debt. His information from inside Datalog would be of great assistance to the CIA in monitoring and analyzing worldwide oil and gas developments.

———

Would it be morally acceptable for the CIA to recruit Markowitz at a salary of $250,000 a year as a clandestine source on international oil and gas exploration? Would it be morally acceptable for the CIA to pass selected sensitive information from Datalog to major American oil and gas companies to give them inside information on what their foreign competitors are doing in key exploration areas?

Admiral Bobby R. Inman, former director of the National Security Agency and deputy director of central intelligence:
1) Yes.
2) No.

Former CIA and Army officer Jack Bosley:
1) Yes. It would be morally acceptable to recruit Markowitz at $250,000 a year. However, this recruitment should be carefully planned. Does this recruitment contravene an agreement with the Canadian government not to deal unilaterally with Canadian citizens? If yes, then recruitment should be done by a semiofficial

organization which could provide cover, such as Battelle, ARPA, or even a fictitious oil and gas company from Houston.

2) Yes. It would be morally acceptable to pass information from Markowitz to major U.S. oil companies. Oil exploration and production are defense issues.

Retired U.S. Army Colonel Stuart Herrington:

1) No. This one is tricky, a minefield. It is hard to keep out of my mind how the French, South Koreans, and Israelis are doing it. We need to have a level playing field in the economic sphere, particularly since the health of the U.S. economy was declared (appropriately) by President Bush No. 1 to be a national security matter. All of this said, purchasing the disloyalty of an employee of a Canadian company is an inherently evil act, however tempting. If he were North Korean, the act would not be evil. It is also the kind of thing that, if done and compromised, would cause far more bad things to happen than any good that might come from it. I realize this latter point is not purely a moral one, but I could argue that this kind of boomerang does have a moral dimension. When we suffer a huge setback like this in the public domain, we have hurt our ability to constitutionally defend our country, and stupidity like that would be immoral.

2) Yes. If we do not recruit Markowitz, we have no information. But let's assume that somehow, without recruiting him, perhaps through open source collection or an anonymous mailing, we have the information. Even though we have for political and legal reasons always forbidden the Agency from feeding the U.S. private sector when it acquires such information, this is not a moral issue.

Ambassador Joseph E. Lake:

1) It depends. Is the data truly needed for national security reasons? Is it truly unavailable from other sources? Much "confidential" petroleum information can in fact be obtained through overt means. If, however, the information meets national security requirements and is truly not available from other sources, then it would be morally acceptable.

2) No. It would not be morally acceptable for the CIA to pass selected sensitive information to major American companies for commercial purposes.

Graduate student Roxana Botea of the Maxwell School at Syracuse University:

No. This operation would be morally unacceptable for several reasons. First, Canada is a U.S. ally and such behavior seems unethical between friendly countries. The situation would be different if the target were China, since China routinely engages in such activity. Second, I am uncomfortable with the idea of having the CIA pass this information to U.S. firms. The reason is that the link to national security here is tenuous. While oil and gas are important resources, they are not exactly issues of national security. If a country were developing chemical weapons, it would be acceptable to pass this information to a U.S. chemical company to encourage R&D on an antidote. But that would be an exceptional case. Industrial espionage contradicts the American ideals of free markets and honest competition. The CIA and other national security agencies have a duty to the American people. U.S. companies are primarily responsible to their stockholders, who may or may not be American. The duty of the U.S. government is to ensure a secure environment in which commerce can take place and not to intervene in industrial competition when there is no direct security interest at stake.

Author's comment:
The United States' "special relationship" with Canada would preclude recruiting Markowitz under current intelligence guidelines. Those guidelines could change, however, at the stroke of a pen if it were decided that vital U.S. national interests were sufficiently at stake.

Industrial espionage against the United States is a huge and rapidly increasing phenomenon. Hundreds of cases a year are detected by the U.S. government and by the American companies concerned. In some cases, the industrial espionage is official government policy and the operations are conceived and orchestrated by that country's intelligence service. In other cases, a foreign competitor mounts its own industrial espionage operation against a U.S. leader in the field. Some of these "private" operations are just as professional and sophisticated as anything an intelligence service could do.

The major fields being targeted by these foreign governments and firms are U.S. defense technology, telecommunications, aerospace, biotechnology, pharmaceuticals, energy, semiconductors, and computer software and hardware. Any American firm that has a technological or manufacturing advantage over its international competitors is likely to be the target of industrial espionage.

The U.S. government has determined that more than twenty countries actively engage in industrial espionage against the United States. The major offenders are China, France, Russia, Japan, Israel, Cuba, South Korea, and Taiwan. The Chinese program is probably the most pervasive, with hundreds, if not thousands, of Chinese businessmen, graduate students, diplomats, journalists, and others aggressively stealing U.S. technology. In terms of sheer audacity, the French program is probably the most egregious. The French foreign intelligence service, the Direction Générale de la Sécurité Extérieure (DGSE), does everything in its power to promote the interests of French businesses, including bribery and technology theft on a large scale. In 1994, U.S. intelligence uncovered French attempts to bribe senior government officials in Saudi Arabia and Brazil so French companies could win lucrative contracts there. Thanks to this intelligence, the U.S. was able to approach the Saudi and Brazilian governments, to nullify the bribes, and to salvage the big contracts for Boeing, McDonnell Douglas, and Raytheon. The French were furious.

One of the DGSE's favorite techniques is to place cooperating French citizens inside U.S. high-technology companies. Once they are there, they steal software, marketing strategies, technology, and trade secrets to give to their DGSE handlers. The inside information is then passed by the DGSE to the appropriate French competing firm. French technology moles were discovered inside IBM, Corning, and Texas Instruments in the 1980s. In this age of globalization and multinational corporations, large U.S. companies are vulnerable to this threat whenever they hire non–U.S. citizens and make them privy to company secrets.

In 2005, several Israeli companies and private investigators were charged with a relatively new and pernicious form of industrial espionage: Trojan horse software. The Israeli operators were able to introduce their "malware" (malicious ware) into the computer systems of competitors via innocent-looking emails or attachments. The software not only disabled the competitor's computer security systems, but also allowed unlimited future access to the target's computerized databases. The Israeli operation was a totally private affair, with no known involvement of Israeli intelligence. Some of the targeted firms were American.

Many cases of industrial espionage are never uncovered or are not reported by the victimized company, but it is clear that losses to American companies are in the billions of dollars annually. The FBI, State Department, Department of Defense, and CIA provide awareness training and defensive briefings to American companies to help them protect themselves against industrial espionage.[40] If U.S. intelligence learns that an American company is losing an overseas contract because of a foreign competitor's bribe, it will generally inform the U.S. company of what is happening. Likewise, if U.S. intelligence learns that a U.S. company is being targeted by a foreign intelligence service or firm, it usually finds a way to let the company know about the danger. This notification is often done through the FBI.

The United States government, however, does not do offensive industrial espionage against foreign companies on behalf of U.S. businesses. The rationale is as follows:

1) U.S. intelligence has better things to do with its resources;
2) helping U.S. companies with their bottom line is not a national security matter; and
3) it would be impossible to decide which U.S. company or companies would be the beneficiaries of such intelligence, without being unfair to others.

Most senior U.S. intelligence officers agree with this policy, but there are some who argue that commerce is in fact a national security issue and the U.S. is being foolish and naive not to do what every other major trading nation in the world is doing.

SCENARIO NO. 39:
BRIBING A FOREIGN GOVERNMENT

Brazil's recent purchase of twelve Dassault Mirage advanced jet fighters has created a military imbalance in Latin America. In response, Argentina has announced that it is in the market for a $850 million purchase of jet fighters to modernize its aging fleet of combat aircraft. The leading contenders for the Argentine contract are Russia's Sukhoi SU-35 and Lockheed Martin's F-16.

The CIA learns from sensitive sources that the Russians are offering bribes to Argentine government officials in an all-out effort to win the contract. Lockheed Martin is legally prohibited from doing the same by the U.S. Foreign Corrupt Practices Act, 15 U.S.C. The U.S. government, however, is very concerned about having a U.S. company lose out unfairly in such a profitable deal, particularly since it would create a significant number of new jobs in the United States. There is considerable concern also about giving the Russians such an impressive breakthrough victory in the lucrative Latin American arms market, which the United States would like to see dominated by U.S. companies like Lockheed Martin, Boeing, United Technologies, Litton Industries, Raytheon, General Dynamics, and McDonnell Douglas.

By carefully tapping into its discreet contacts in the Argentine government, the CIA determines that well-placed bribes totaling $25 million would be enough to swing the contract away from the Russians and to Lockheed Martin.

———

Would it be morally acceptable for the CIA to pay $25 million in bribes to government officials in Argentina to win the $850 million jet fighter contract for Lockheed Martin?

Author Thomas Powers:

No. The plan here appears to involve using federal dollars to break the law for the benefit of a particular U.S. firm. Why should the U.S. care if Lockheed benefits? What has Argentina done for us lately? The whole plan reminds me of the origins of the Iran-Contra affair. If this plan blows up, the CIA is going to take the fall. Why doesn't the CIA face the facts and tell the National Security Adviser that he or she is way off base?

U.S. Army Lieutenant Colonel Tony Pfaff:

No. Bribing the foreign government would not be morally acceptable, any more than it would be acceptable to cheat in a sports event because the other team is cheating. To use Kantian language, it would be treating the target of the bribery as a means and not as an end, thus failing the "universalizability" test. One might argue that a bribe would be permissible as a reprisal, but that would be the case only if the bribe were aimed at getting the other side to cease bribing, not to gain advantage. It would, however, be acceptable to expose the bribe in order to invalidate the contract. A similar incident happened in the 1990s, except it was the French who were trying to bribe the Saudis to get an Airbus contract. The U.S. government informed King Fahd of the bribe and the French lost the contract.

Professor Michael Porter of the University of Missouri:

Yes. Go for it. Corrupt away. Something tells me no one is following the U.S. Foreign Corrupt Practices Act anyway. While the rationale for bribing the government of Argentina seems a bit shallow, to be honest, if it will help the American aeronautical industry and will only cost $25 million to do so, O.K. I feel a bit "dirty" agreeing to this, but I can't help believing that such practices are common. I'm not sure the CIA needs to be in on this; in fact, why isn't Lockheed Martin doing the corrupting? Or can we assume it will be providing the $25 million?

Former CIA officer Mary Lee Lieser:

Yes. I would not break the law, but if the law were changed, I would find the bribes morally acceptable.

Retired U.S. Navy Captain Richard Life:

No. This is not a national security issue. Using the CIA to advance the competitive edge of U.S. industry for the benefit of stockholders would be totally inappropriate.

Author's comment:

Bribery of foreign governments by U.S. companies was common practice before the passage of the Foreign Corrupt Practices Act of 1977. More than three hundred U.S. firms were known to have made undisclosed questionable payments to foreign officials, amounting to hundreds of millions of dollars. The United States strengthened the law with the passage of the International Anti-Bribery and Fair Competition Act of 1998, which was the implementing legislation for U.S. commitments under the international "Convention in Combating Bribery of Foreign Public Officials in International Business Transactions." Thirty-six nations have signed this convention, which is administered under the auspices of the Organization for Economic Cooperation and Development (OECD). Almost all of the thirty-six countries have passed implementing legislation similar to the 1998 U.S. act. When President Bill Clinton signed the legislation, he stated, "We have long believed bribery is inconsistent with democratic values, such as good governance and the rule of law."

That's fine, but is the international agreement working? The State Department reported in 2004 that it had identified forty-seven contracts worth $15 billion that had been affected by bribery in the previous year alone. U.S. companies lost eight contracts worth $3 billion because of these bribes. The offending countries included Canada, Korea, Norway, Sweden, France (*quelle surprise*), Italy, and Switzerland.

One problem is that many important international trading nations have not signed the OECD convention. China, Russia, Israel, and Taiwan, for example, are nonsignatories. Moreover, some of the signatory countries have been slow to enact legislation or to enforce it. As of 2006, for example, Japan had not initiated a single bribery prosecution under its law.

U.S. firms face fierce competition from foreign companies for international contracts. In some parts of the world, bribes are still expected and are considered part of the cost of doing business. Many foreign competitors tend to be less punctilious than their American counterparts on the issue of bribery. Their governments, in fact, are often willing to look the other way if the contracts are big enough. Before the OECD convention, some countries even allowed their companies to deduct bribes on their tax returns as a business expense.

It is not surprising, therefore, that some American companies still succumb to the temptation to bribe. Their dilemma is simple: pay the bribe or lose the contract. In 2005, the U.S. agrochemical firm Monsanto paid $1.5 million in fines to the Justice Department and the Securities and Exchange Commission for bribing an Indonesian official. In the same year, the U.S. telecommunications company Titan was fined $28.5 million for bribing officials in the West African nation of Benin.

The United States has taken the position that bribery tarnishes the image of American democracy, damages the reputation of American business, and undermines public confidence in capital markets. That is all true. But it is also true that strict enforcement of U.S. anti-bribery laws puts American firms at a competitive disadvantage in bidding for lucrative international contracts.

SCENARIO NO. 40:
TAMPERING WITH U.S. MAIL

The United States officially designates Iran, Syria, Libya, Cuba, North Korea, and Sudan as states sponsoring international terrorism. Not all of these countries are directly involved in terrorist acts themselves, but all provide some form of funding, training, arms, sanctuary, or other support to terrorist groups.

Through painstaking research and analysis, the CIA, FBI, and NSA have compiled a list of over 1,200 addresses of individuals, companies, and other entities in the above countries that are known or suspected to be associated with terrorist groups, including Hezbollah, Hamas, Palestine Islamic Jihad, al Qaida, Egyptian al-Gama'a al-Islamiyya, Popular Front for the Liberation of Palestine-General Command, and others. An additional 400 addresses of groups and individuals sympathetic to terrorists have been identified in Pakistan, Saudi Arabia, Lebanon, Yemen, and elsewhere.

U.S. counterterrorism officials would like to monitor the mail to and from the approximately 1,600 addresses on the above watch list. This effort would include intercepting all letters and packages sent from inside the United States to any of the addresses on the list, as well as any letters or packages mailed from overseas with any of these return addresses. It is not legally or practically possible to obtain warrants for such a high volume of mail. Moreover, many of the individuals who receive and send such mail through the U.S. postal system would not previously have come to the attention of U.S. authorities. Monitoring the mail in this fashion could provide U.S. law enforcement officials with valuable leads to individuals in the U.S. with ties to terrorist groups.

————

Would it be morally acceptable for the U.S. government to set up a secret unit in the U.S. Postal Service to monitor (that is, to record the names, frequency, dates, locations, etc., but not to open) mail to and from addresses on the terrorism watch list? Would it be morally acceptable to open the particularly suspicious letters, to copy their contents, and to reseal them without leaving a trace before sending them on their way?

Michael Bohn, former director of the White House Situation Room:

Yes. This is not much different from monitoring voice communications. Opening mail is the analog of breaking a cipher system, but it should require a warrant from a designated court. Also, the process needs oversight from a designated outside secret unit.

Former middle-school and high-school teacher Barbara Ziesche:

No. It is not morally acceptable to open private mail. At what point can "Big Brother" do anything and everything in the name of homeland security? People are going to be labeled as suspects based on their ethnicity. We already have "ghost prisoners" who are being denied due process.

Graduate student Russell Rodriguez of the George Bush School of Government and Public Service at Texas A&M University:

1) Yes. The information on the outside of the letter is already being processed, so the technology is there. It just needs to be modified to do the job. I do not see any constitutional problem.

2) It depends. Actually opening the letters is acceptable only if authorized by a judge. Otherwise, it would violate a right protected by the Fourth Amendment.

Former CIA officer John ███████:

Yes. The enemy is using many aspects of our society and our legal system against us. We conduct intrusive pat-downs of airline passengers who would not normally attract any attention, yet we refrain from profiling likely suspects to avoid any appearance of discrimination. Accordingly, our actions protect the enemy and inconvenience our citizens. We need targeted initiatives that have a high probability of success but preserve the rights of law-abiding citizens.

In this context, I would support a mail monitoring and opening program for correspondence to and from suspected terrorist organizations. Some constraints need to be put in place, as follows:

a) The individuals who participate in the program should be from a number of organizations; the CIA, FBI, Department of Homeland Security, Department of Justice, U.S. Postal Service, and NSA come immediately to mind.

b) The program needs to be small and bigot-listed (restricted to a small group of authorized individuals).

c) Personnel should be carefully screened to ensure they understand the significance of the operation and the need for absolute secrecy.

d) Enabling legislation and judicial approval procedures need to be put in place.

e) Restricting the scope of review to terrorist-related activity would have to be enforced; unrelated criminal activity that would be uncovered would have to be discarded.

When I was on active duty with the CIA, I used an Iowa benchmark to calibrate the morality of my operations. If my wife's mother, Phyllis, an Iowa farm wife, who is intelligent, shrewd, and skeptical, were to read about one of my operations in the local Red Oak press, would she be satisfied that the taxes on her Iowa farm were being well and appropriately spent? In this case, I think she would say yes.

Author's comment:
Americans have always had a special sensitivity about the inviolability of the U.S. mail. There is a high expectation of privacy when it comes to personal or business correspondence. For most U.S. citizens, it would be almost as unthinkable for the government to be inside their envelopes as inside their bedrooms. Tampering with the U.S. mail is a federal offense that carries heavy penalties, and most Americans would say rightly so.

The country was shocked, therefore, to learn in 1975 that the CIA had been engaged in a massive mail monitoring and opening program from 1952 to 1973. The main focus of the top secret operation, code-named HTLINGUAL, was mail to and from the Soviet Union, but some mail to and from Communist countries in Asia was also included. HTLINGUAL was approved by three postmasters general and at least one attorney general (John Mitchell, attorney general in the Nixon administration). The FBI was briefed on the program in 1958, agreed the CIA should continue running it, and from that point on became a primary recipient of the product. The FBI also provided the names of individuals, including U.S. citizens, to be included on the mail watch lists.

The CIA misled the Post Office Department about the extent of the program. The Post Office officials were told the operation would be only a mail "cover," that is, the surreptitious photographing of the outside of the envelopes, with no actual opening of the envelopes. It is clear from the CIA documents of the period, however, that the CIA intended from the beginning to extend the operation to mail "openings." Some openings, in fact, without the knowledge or consent of the Post Office Department, were taking place as early as 1953. The CIA officers handling the mail secretly removed certain items from the Post Office to another location, where CIA experts opened the mail and photographed the contents. The letters were then professionally resealed and returned to the Post Office for onward delivery. By 1959, some 13,000 letters a year were being opened in this manner. In HTLINGUAL's last full year of operation (1972), the New York branch alone examined over four million pieces of mail and photographed the exteriors of 33,000 envelopes. Approximately 8,700 letters were opened. There were smaller branches of HTLINGUAL in San Francisco, Hawaii, and New Orleans. Information of counterintelligence interest was disseminated to the Counterintelligence Staff of the CIA and to the FBI. The database for the project contained over two million entries.

Despite the "approvals" from the postmasters general and the attorney general, CIA officials knew from the beginning that HTLINGUAL was illegal. They simply reasoned that the national security needs of the United States justified a violation of the law. DCI James Schlesinger called HTLINGUAL a "basic counterintelligence asset designed to give United States intelligence agencies insight into Soviet intelligence activities and interests." He concluded, however, that the counterintelligence value of HTLINGUAL was insufficient to justify the risk of discovery. He terminated the project in 1973.

During World War II, Americans accepted the legalized opening and review of international mail for national security purposes. When, if ever, will a majority of Americans decide the war on terror justifies a similarly extreme measure?

CIA officers can legally intercept and open mail outside the U.S. for counterintelligence and counterterrorism purposes. For that reason, most CIA case officers receive training in how to secretly open and reseal envelopes in the event a specialized technical officer is not immediately available. "Flaps and seals," as we call it, was one of my favorite subjects at the Farm.

SCENARIO NO. 41:
PROTECTION OF CODE BREAKING

Four months ago, the CIA pulled off a major intelligence coup. It recruited a Syrian code clerk, encrypted NVBISON, working in the communications center of the Syrian Ministry of Foreign Affairs in Damascus. NVBISON is providing the CIA with not only the texts of hundreds of encrypted cables but also the key lists, one-time pads,[41] wiring diagrams, manuals, and computer disks used in Syria's cryptographic systems. Thanks to NVBISON, the National Security Agency is able to read virtually all the classified cable traffic to and from the Syrian Ministry of Foreign Affairs.

One of the major revelations of the traffic is the extent to which Syria is actively supporting Middle Eastern terrorist groups, particularly Ahmad Jibril's Popular Front for the Liberation of Palestine–General Command (PFLP-GC). It was previously known that Syria was providing funding, training, and refuge to Jibril and his group, but the new intelligence shows that Syria is also deeply involved with the PFLP-GC in the planning and execution of actual terrorist attacks.

The information from the Syrian code-breaking operation is an intelligence gold mine. The U.S. president and other senior policy makers are getting close to real-time information on Syria's support for terrorism, its activities in Lebanon, its relations with other Arab countries, its reactions to U.S. foreign policy decisions, and its aggressive secret assistance to anti–U.S. elements in Iraq and elsewhere.

Several deciphered communications indicate that Syria and the PFLP-GC are planning a suicide truck bomb attack against the Paris offices of El Al, the Israeli national airline. The traffic indicates a target date for the attack in three weeks.

The U.S. intelligence community is reluctant to share the intelligence with the French or the Israelis for fear of revealing or even hinting to them its ability to break the Syrian codes. The U.S. is also concerned that if Syria observes heightened security measures around the El Al offices in Paris, it might logically conclude its communications are no longer secure. The investigations and tighter security that would result could jeopardize NVBISON and limit his ability to continue his cooperation with the CIA. There is a high risk the U.S. could lose its ability to break the Syrian codes.

——————

Would it be morally acceptable for the U.S. to allow the terrorist attack against the El Al offices in Paris to proceed without telling the French and the Israelis?

Professor David S. Allen of the University of Wisconsin–Milwaukee:
No. If warning someone about an imminent attack could save lives, I believe the CIA is morally obligated to warn the intended victims.

Former CIA Information Management Officer Ray Brewer:
No. To allow a bomb to explode in a large European city when this could be avoided would be unconscionable.

Professor Harry Mason of the Patterson School at the University of Kentucky:
No (class vote). Only four of the seventeen graduate students in my intelligence course thought allowing the attack to take place would be morally acceptable. The fact that the target was the Israeli national airline was a big factor for those voting no.

Dr. Geoffrey Tumlin, assistant director of the Center for Ethical Leadership at the Lyndon B. Johnson School of Public Affairs at the University of Texas:
It depends, but probably not. What is the code-breaking operation for

if not to save lives? I would be likely to warn the French and the Israelis of the El Al attack unless I thought there might be a much bigger payoff from NVBISON in the fairly immediate future.

Former CIA officer Haviland Smith:

No. There is no reason to start with the assumption that warning friendly services has to be an admission that we have broken the Syrian codes. What we are talking about here is what the clandestine service has always done well. This is an operational problem, no more, no less. There have to be literally dozens of ways to put the information in the hands of the Israelis or the French in a way that does not threaten the source. Since we have NVBISON on the string, we must know volumes about what the Syrians are up to. Are they running taps, audio, double agents? Is there some way we can get the information to the people who need it without raising the suspicion, either by the recipients or by the Syrians, of codes being broken? Is there some way we can cast suspicion on some other source for the material? There has to be, and we simply have to find it.

Professor Howard Prince, director of the Center for Ethical Leadership at the Lyndon B. Johnson School of Public Affairs at the University of Texas:

No, but this is a tough one. If the intelligence is not shared, we will continue to collect highly valuable intelligence until the agent quits or is compromised. There is a chance that NVBISON will be exposed if the United States acts now, but this is not certain. We should inform the French and Israelis without revealing our source . . . and hope for the best.

Ph.D. student Margaret Meacham:

No. The French and Israelis are our allies in the war on terrorism. It would be morally unacceptable not to tell them about the planned attack. If this jeopardizes the agent, he must be extracted and hidden away. His disappearance might cause the Syrians to redesign their codes, but perhaps NVBISON can tip us off to another code clerk still there who might be willing to help us.

Ph.D. student Margaretta Mathis:

No. Imagine if we found out the French or Israelis had advance information about the World Trade Center attacks and had decided to withhold it.

Former CIA officer Mary Lee Lieser:

No. I would trust the ingenuity of CIA officers to come up with some other plausible sourcing for the information. It would be morally unacceptable to have prior knowledge and to allow the bomb attack to proceed.

Admiral Bobby R. Inman, former director of the National Security Agency and deputy director of central intelligence:

No. An acceptable story of a human source can be constructed to provide suitable warning to the French and Israelis without jeopardizing our cryptographic success.

Former CIA officer Robert Mills:

It depends. This was a very difficult scenario for me. There appears to be no other plausible method of warning that could be attributed to another source. While it might appear morally unacceptable to allow the attack to continue with the inevitable loss of innocent lives, there is precedent under the greater good theory. Historically, there have been examples where the source of intelligence was so significant, such as the Enigma machine and the breaking of the Japanese codes, that it was deemed acceptable to allow incidents to occur which resulted in the loss of life rather than to risk exposing the sensitive source. In these cases, the greater good made the actions morally acceptable.

Author's comment:

The ability to break another country's codes has always been one of the most closely guarded intelligence secrets. The constant problem with SIGINT is that if you use it you can lose it. Intelligence services, therefore, take elaborate measures to conceal the fact they are reading the other country's codes. Their hope is that, even if they take an observable action as a result of the SIGINT, they can sufficiently obfuscate the source so the other country does not change its codes.

Sometimes, however, as pointed out by Robert Mills, the decision is made not to act in the interests of protecting the code-breaking secret. The long-term value of the operation is deemed so critically important that it simply cannot be jeopardized. The most famous example of this was in November 1940, when British Prime Minister Winston Churchill made the difficult decision not to warn the city of Coventry that a large-scale German air attack was coming. Churchill knew of the planned attack because of ULTRA,[42] but he feared that if the Germans observed an evacuation of the city before the attack or unusual defensive measures, they might conclude their codes had been compromised. He chose not to take that risk. He believed that ULTRA, if the secret held, could save thousands if not hundreds of thousands of allied lives during the course of the war. About three hundred residents of Coventry perished in the Luftwaffe bombing of the city on the night of November 14, 1940. Some contemporary historians challenge this version of events, but all agree that extreme measures are occasionally taken to protect vitally important cryptographic successes.

In 1943, the United States intercepted and decoded a Japanese message indicating that Admiral Isoroku Yamamoto, commander in chief of the Japanese Navy, would be visiting Japanese bases in the Solomon Islands on April 18, 1943. The message included precise times and locations, as well as the fact that Yamamoto's aircraft would be escorted by six fighters. Admiral Chester W. Nimitz, the U.S. commander in chief in the Pacific, had a tough decision to make. It was highly tempting to try to shoot down Yamamoto's aircraft, but doing so might tip off the Japanese that their codes were being read. Nimitz consulted with Vice Admiral William F. Halsey, his number two in the area, and they decided to take the risk. There are unconfirmed reports that Nimitz obtained approval for the operation from Secretary of the Navy Frank Knox and President Franklin Roosevelt because of the high stakes involved in risking the U.S. code-breaking capability. In any event, Yamamoto's plane was shot down by U.S. fighters on April 18, 1943, and he was killed. The Japanese concluded that Yamamoto had been the victim of a routine patrol and did not change their codes. The United States took a huge chance and got away with it. If this high-risk decision had not, in fact, been made by President Roosevelt, it should have been.

A fascinating example of a clever scheme to protect code-breaking was the Zimmerman Telegram incident in 1917. The British intercepted and decrypted a message sent by German Foreign Minister Arthur Zimmerman to the German ambassador in Mexico on January 16, 1917. In the message, Zimmerman directed the ambassador to offer Mexico an alliance against the United States in return for a promise that after the war Mexico would recover its "lost territory" in the southwestern United States. The British, eager to get America into World War I, recognized how helpful this explosive message would be to their cause if they could safely get it into President Wilson's hands. Their problem was that they had obtained the message from a secret tap of the transatlantic cable, and they were reading U.S. diplomatic traffic on those cables as well as German. Only after the British obtained a second version of the Zimmerman telegram from an agent in Mexico City did they share the message with the United States. The Americans and Germans were led to believe the compromise had occurred in Mexico City and was of human origin, not cryptographic. A month later, the United States declared war against Germany.

On April 14, 1986, the United States bombed several targets in Libya in retaliation for the Libyan bombing of La Belle Disco in Berlin, a favorite hangout of U.S. servicemen. An American sergeant was killed, as well as a Turkish woman, and more than 200 people were injured, including fifty U.S. servicemen. To justify the attack on Tripoli, President Reagan acknowledged that the U.S. had "irrefutable proof" of Libyan responsibility for the Berlin bombing in the form of intercepted Libyan diplomatic communications. A short time later, Libya changed its codes. Losing the Libyan codes was a major setback to U.S. intelligence, but President Reagan made the decision that the cost was justified.

SCENARIO NO. 42:
BREAKING A PROMISE TO AN AGENT

Rolando Gutierrez, a twenty-eight-year-old Mexican citizen, walks into the U.S. embassy in Mexico City and asks to speak with a representative of the FBI. He states he is a member of the Tijuana Cartel, which has become the largest of the Mexican narcotics trafficking organizations. Gutierrez says he wishes to volunteer his services to the U.S. government as a penetration of that organization. In return, he wants ample compensation, which he says he will discuss in detail at a future meeting. A follow-up meeting is sched- uled for the next weekend at a safe location in the suburbs of Mexico City.

FBI, CIA, and DEA traces confirm that Gutierrez is a known member of the Tijuana Cartel. He started his career as a hit man, then progressed through the ranks to major responsibilities in the transportation area. He is considered ruthless and dangerous.

Washington decides that the Gutierrez case will be run as a combined FBI-CIA-DEA operation, with the CIA having the lead for handling him inside Mexico. Under heavy protective countersurveillance,[43] Art Shoeman, a thirty-two-year-old CIA case officer, meets that weekend with Gutierrez.

Gutierrez, now encrypted QAREINDEER, drives a hard bargain. He says the Tijuana Cartel has developed a very close relationship with the Revo- lutionary Armed Forces of Colombia (FARC) and the two are planning a massive shipment of pure uncut cocaine to the United States. QAREINDEER offers to provide specific details on the shipment in return for a cash pay- ment of $100,000, resettlement in the United States, citizenship, and a new identity. He demands that $25,000 of this total be paid up front, with the remaining commitments to be honored only if the seizure is successfully completed. QAREINDEER states that he wants to get out of the narcotics business and start a new life for himself in the United States. He says his demands are non-negotiable. In addition to providing actionable intelligence on the major shipment, he agrees to a full debriefing on the Tijuana Cartel, including everything he knows about its personnel, activities, and transport mechanisms. Finally, he claims he has been the primary middleman with FARC and can provide useful intelligence on that organization.

All of QAREINDEER's information appears to check out, and he passes a series of CIA-administered polygraph exams. On the polygraph, he admits to several murders earlier in his career. The deal is made. QAREINDEER discloses that a three-ton shipment of cocaine with a street value of over $500 million will enter the United States through Portland, Oregon, aboard a Panamanian registered freighter. He gives the name of the ship and the estimated date of arrival. The ship is inspected when it arrives in Portland and the seizure is made. In fact, the amount of pure uncut cocaine seized is nearly four tons.

———

Would it be morally acceptable for the United States to pay QAREINDEER the remaining $75,000—but to renege on its agreement to resettle him in the United States with citizenship and a new identity because he is so clearly undesirable?

Former CIA officer Eugene Culbertson:

No. It would be morally unacceptable to renege on the resettlement part of the agreement. The murders to which QAREINDEER confessed and the unknown number of deaths he caused by his complicity in drug dealing are certainly troubling. But if that had been a decisive factor, then the United States should not have entered into the deal with him in the first place. Couldn't it be argued, rather, that the operation, if successful, would save many lives and warrant QAREINDEER's resettlement in the United States? A secret agreement of this kind would not be enforceable under U.S. law, but reneging on it would be operationally unsound and immoral. QAREINDEER has not only burned his bridges and put his life on the line by betraying the cartel and FARC, he has also delivered on every facet of the agreement. Moreover, his actions tend to validate his declared intent to turn his back on his past and start a new life. Abandoning him now would result in his demise and also impact negatively on the U.S. intelligence community's efficacy in future counternarcotics operations.

Rabbi Peter Tarlow:

No. If the United States is willing to give taxpayer money to someone it considers undesirable, then the question becomes why would we not keep our word? How do we know he will continue to be undesirable? There is always the chance that he will perform repentance and restart his life. I would admit him to the United States, and if he ever becomes involved in illegal activity, then deport him.

Former CIA officer John ███████:

Yes. The bottom line is that we cannot expose innocent Americans to grave risk in the interests of a one-time operation. QAREINDEER represents a clear downstream threat to U.S. citizens, a risk no U.S. intelligence organization should be associated with. Here are a few alternatives, which may actually be more acceptable to QAREINDEER:

a) Give him more money—a lot more money.
b) Resettle him in a third country.
c) Offer him the option of standing trial for his crimes, accepting possible incarceration, and then receiving U.S. citizenship after his release. (His cooperation with U.S. authorities might mitigate his sentence.)

Writer, poet, and teacher Burke Gerstenschlager:

No. Thanks to QAREINDEER's actions, the United States was able not only to make a substantial drug bust but also to infiltrate a major drug cartel and an international insurgency movement. The United States has never sought to extradite QAREINDEER, so his slate, domestically, is clean. He has upheld his part of the agreement. It would be morally unacceptable for the United States to renege on its part. Traditionally, the United States is a country that prides itself on giving individuals an opportunity to start their lives anew. Although QAREINDEER has circumvented the customary paths for immigration, he has crossed the treacherous battle lines of the Drug War on our behalf and should be met halfway.

Professor Harry Mason of the Patterson School at the University of Kentucky:

No (class vote). My students voted 3-14 against breaking the promise to QAREINDEER. The class understood that it would be legal under U.S. law to break such promises, but deemed that it would be unprofessional. The no votes were based on a belief that the United States should never renege on a spy promise and on the fact that this one case was insignificant given the large number of illegal immigrants.

Former CIA polygrapher John Sullivan:

No. Once the deal is made, it would be morally unacceptable to renege on it. QAREINDEER more than lived up to his end of the bargain. We knew what he was going into the deal. To break our promise after pumping him dry would make us no better than he is, and, in all probability, would be a death sentence for him. How moral would that make us?

If QAREINDEER had committed human rights violations, I would not have offered him a new life in the United States as part of any deal. If Saddam Hussein or his sons, for example, had offered us Osama bin Laden in exchange for asylum, I would have turned that deal down.

On a practical note, breaking promises can come back to haunt the breaker. The word gets out that the promise-maker is untrustworthy.

Author's comment:

It is paradoxical that the spying profession, as rooted in deception as it is, is so scrupulous about honoring commitments to agents. I am not aware of a single case in my career in which a promise to an agent was broken. Undoubtedly, there is a moral component to keeping one's word, but spy services also recognize in pragmatic terms that developing a reputation for breaking promises is bad for business.

CIA case officers are drilled in how important it is to be careful in making commitments to agents. In my overseas assignments, we made it a practice to post on the inside front cover of every agent's soft file two things: our emergency contact plan with the agent and our commitments to him or her. These two issues in agent handling demand special clarity and precision. Any changes to either area had to be reported and posted immediately.

The problem with commitments is that they sometimes get fuzzy over time. What exactly was said to the agent at the pitch meeting twelve years ago? Was the agent ever promised a guaranteed interest rate on his escrow account?[44] What specifically was said about resettlement in the United States? CIA case officers are usually reassigned ███████████████, so a typical long-term agent will deal with a succession of them. It is not unusual for an agent to claim that a previous case officer made an oral commitment that is not in the record. Sometimes this is a genuine misunderstanding; a case officer and an agent sitting around drinking vodka together in a safehouse can hear different things. Other times, a manipulative and greedy agent can try to exploit a turnover or ambiguity to extract additional benefits. "But Ed [the previous case officer's alias] told me I would get a 25 percent raise every five years." "But Laura told me the CIA would cover my expenses to the Paris conference." Unless a case officer is absolutely clear and keeps accurate records, the issue of promises can become a big sticking point in any agent operation.

I was once handling a sensitive agent from a denied area who was providing incredibly high-level intelligence on his country. We had given him a generous compensation package, including eventual resettlement in the

United States. After several years of faithful and productive service to us as an in-place source, the agent, with our help, defected to the United States to start a new life. The CIA's defector resettlement staff[45] took good care of him, and everything seemed to be going well. Suddenly, however, the defector claimed I had promised him a lump-sum bonus of one million dollars when he arrived in the States. That was totally untrue. It would have been preposterous for me to have made such an offer without headquarters approval and to have done so without making it a matter of official record. Nevertheless, the agent persisted and caused a lot of administrative hassle before the CIA finally agreed to settle with him by paying a lesser amount. I thought we had been robbed.

SCENARIO NO. 43:
UNAUTHORIZED COVER

Becky Polk, a twenty-eight-year-old American originally from Cleveland, Ohio, earned an honors degree in marketing from the University of Pittsburgh. She worked as a petroleum marketing account executive for ExxonMobil in Houston for four years. After that, she attended the Wharton School of the University of Pennsylvania, where she completed her MBA degree. In her last year at Wharton, Polk began sending her resume out to potential employers, both in the private and public sectors. She received several offers. One of them was to return to her previous employer, ExxonMobil, where she would work in Saudi Arabia as a marketing liaison officer with the International Operations Division of Saudi Aramco. Another was to enter the Clandestine Service Training Program of the CIA.

After lengthy discussions with the CIA, Polk expresses an interest in serving in the CIA as a nonofficial cover officer, or NOC. The CIA is eager to improve its coverage of international oil markets and is keenly interested in Polk's offer from ExxonMobil to work in this area in Saudi Arabia. ExxonMobil is willing to postpone the start of Polk's employment for one year after her graduation from Wharton to allow her time for "travel and personal business."

———

Would it be morally acceptable for the CIA to give Becky Polk intensive training in clandestine tradecraft and Arabic language for one year and then to assign her as a CIA NOC inside ExxonMobil without informing anyone in ExxonMobil's management?

Mike Hannesschlager, former executive director of the Texas Christian Coalition:

Yes. Without a doubt, ExxonMobil has extensive, long-standing, and very intimate ties with the Saudi royal family, some of whom are strong supporters of radical Islam, and all of whom are wealthy. Polk could obtain important information for our government with this excellent cover as a backstop. It is true that it might not be fair to ExxonMobil to place a CIA officer in its ranks without its knowledge. But ExxonMobil deals in the world's most coveted natural resource in the world's most dangerous and unpredictable region. The question ExxonMobil's senior managers ought to ask themselves is not "Do we have any CIA officers on the payroll," but rather, "How many CIA officers do we have on the payroll?"

Professor Terry H. Anderson of Texas A&M University:
Yes. This seems like normal procedure for the CIA or any spy agency.

Former CIA officer Haviland Smith:
Yes, but stupid. I have no moral objection to this sort of cover. On the other hand, it would be the height of stupidity. I can't imagine any serious clandestine service officer wanting to see this done simply because of the incredible flap it would cause if the truth of the matter ever got out. Not only would we never see NOC cover at ExxonMobil again, we might never see it again anywhere! I would kill this one, not on moral grounds, but on a pragmatic risk vs. gain basis.

Lauraine Brekke-Esparza, city manager of Del Mar, California:
Yes. My opinion here is greatly influenced by my attitude toward "big oil," which is probably shaping our Middle East policy in ways I cannot even imagine. I see nothing morally objectionable in assigning Becky Polk inside ExxonMobil without informing its management.

Former CIA officer Burton Gerber:
No. First, the CIA must not violate its own rules or regulations (which would currently prohibit this kind of cover) without acknowledging to it-self that it is doing so. It must then decide whether to honor its rule and not approve the cover, change the rule based on the facts, or establish a waiver system (I do not mention Polk's role because she is not an employee yet, just a prospective employee. She has presented the facts and the opportunity, but she should have no role in the decision).

Following Saint Thomas Aquinas' last resort principle, I would look at whether there are other ways to accomplish the mission. I would weigh the probable benefit of what a first-tour young female officer with no interna-tional experience would likely accomplish against the importance of

ExxonMobil's role in Saudi Arabia, and even the importance of American participation in Saudi Aramco. I am not saying the decision would have to be tilted against employing Polk in this capacity, but I think there would have to be an overwhelming expectation of success to overcome the fact that CIA would be risking its relationship with a very important American company (ExxonMobil). The CIA would also be jeopardizing its relationships with other U.S. international companies, which, in the event of a flap, would for a considerable time be suspicious of the CIA.

(Full disclosure: I am a stockholder in ExxonMobil, so if I were a serving CIA officer, ethics would require me to recuse myself from this decision and, for that matter, from this operation. The same would apply to any other CIA officers who have ExxonMobil stock.)

In short, ethics, operational savvy, and political realities would require the Agency to look at this proposal with considerable skepticism. The ethical issue of "last resort" leads me to conclude there are other ways, not involving lying to an American company and risking its profits, to accomplish the same mission.

Author's comment:

The CIA could not accomplish its intelligence collection mission overseas without the patriotic support of American corporations. With few exceptions, if any, their motivation is pure patriotism. They are not usually compensated for their agreement to place CIA officers under cover in their companies. This is particularly commendable given the fact that they would suffer considerable damage if their involvement with the CIA ever became known publicly. The CIA, as far as I know, always insists on having the full-disclosure approval of an appropriate "committing authority" in each company before proceeding.

The CIA is extremely careful about how it uses NOCs overseas. NOCs would not normally participate in high-risk operations with serious "flap potential." It would be unusual, for example, for a NOC to make an actual pitch to a prospective agent, since the consequences of a turndown could be disastrous. The target, for example, might denounce the NOC to the local authorities, in which case the NOC could be arrested for espionage (without diplomatic immunity), and the U.S. employer would be seriously embarrassed. NOCs, however, more than earn their keep by spotting and assessing potential recruitment targets and by clandestinely handling assets already recruited by others. They also, by virtue of their nonofficial status, can frequently move in circles overseas where it would be awkward or impossible for a known U.S. government official to circulate.

Every NOC arrangement is different. Some NOCs, in order to sustain their cover, must work full-time in their cover jobs and then do their operational work on nights and weekends. Others, with the agreement of the committing authority, can do less than full-time work if that can be done without arousing suspicion. Sometimes the committing authority, who is usually located in the United States, is the only person who is witting of the CIA officer's true affiliation. In other cases, a senior executive in the overseas branch where the NOC is working might be informed, but not always.

Nonofficial cover is vitally important to the CIA, and I seriously doubt the CIA would ever jeopardize it by approving a Becky Polk–type operation. If the CIA wants the outstanding support it receives to continue, it is in the CIA's best interests to play fair.

SCENARIO NO. 44:
BOGUS WEBSITES AND CHATROOMS

The FBI, CIA, and NSA establish a secret brainstorming group to explore imaginative new ways to counter terrorist threats to the United States. A bright young NSA officer comes up with the idea of setting up controlled websites and chatrooms on the Internet to identify and to monitor individuals, both American and foreign, who might pose a terrorist threat to American citizens and installations.

Some of the sites would purport to be from Middle Eastern sources and would be in the Arabic language. They would adopt venomously anti-American stances and would include discussion boards and chatrooms to allow visitors to vent their hatred of the United States. FBI and CIA assets posing as anti-American militants would monitor and participate in the discussion boards and chatrooms. NSA would attempt to determine the locations and identities of those visitors to the website who appear to be particularly disposed toward violence against America. Other controlled websites and chatrooms would deal with bomb making, do-it-yourself biological and chemical weapons manufacture, and other dangerous topics. Great care would be taken to ensure that no truly new or actionable processes would be disclosed. The identities of radical participants inside the United States would be turned over to the FBI for watch listing and possible monitoring. The identities of individuals outside the United States would be turned over to the CIA.

Would it be morally acceptable for the FBI, NSA, and CIA to establish bogus anti-American and terrorist-oriented websites and chatrooms in an effort to identify American citizens and foreigners inclined to commit terrorist acts against the United States?

Author Thomas Powers:

It depends, but probably yes. This sounds like a sting operation to me. An operation like this is going to be hard to manage. Serious terrorists do not need to vent anti-American feelings; they prefer practical operational knowledge they can put to concrete use. If you're not telling them anything they don't know, why would they visit your websites? I recommend refocusing the content of the websites to attract persons of interest in other ways, perhaps by encouraging them to think a certain new technique for secure communications can be arranged, or something like that. Stop all the talk of bombs; drop all the anti-American rhetoric. Coax the villains forward the way you coax what you want to emerge from a Google search. If the operation is handled this way, I would be for it.

Mike Hannesschlager, former executive director of the Texas Christian Coalition:

Yes. Since Islamic terrorists communicate more and more on the Internet, it would be foolhardy for us not to seek to identify them. Running our own "jihad" websites would be an excellent way to do this. Of course, the nightmare scenario is that an American intelligence officer, through his undercover identity in cyberspace, would somehow incite an actual attack. Great care must be taken that the officers involved in these operations do not suggest or help plan any kind of attack. There is real risk in an operation like this, but the payoff makes it worthwhile.

Former CIA Information Management Officer Ray Brewer:

Yes. The United States must do all it legally can to disrupt, apprehend, and prosecute individuals bent on destroying the American way of life. It would be morally wrong *not* to take advantage of current technology to identify potential terrorists.

Kyu Mani Lee, Ph.D., former superintendent of Larned State Hospital in Kansas:

Yes. This method can be a very effective way of identifying individuals who need to be monitored for the sake of national security. I see no moral issue here.

Professor Terry H. Anderson of Texas A&M University:

Yes. I would think this is standard practice since the days of the Weathermen Underground and, especially, the Oklahoma City bombing. Knowledge of potential enemies does not mean arresting citizens or killing foreigners. This is morally acceptable as long as civil rights are not violated by the government; if they are violated, then it is unacceptable.

Author's comment:

It is a common practice for law enforcement officials to "lurk" or to actively participate in chatrooms and websites to flush out and identify sexual predators, child pornographers, and other criminals. Many Americans strongly object to the provision in the USA Patriot Act that allows federal law enforcement officers to monitor what books a given individual checks out from public libraries. Would they object just as strongly to having the U.S. government monitor the chatrooms and websites a person visits? Would setting up chatrooms and websites to entice virulently anti-American persons to participate be going too far?

What does it mean to turn over the names of individuals who visit the bogus chatrooms and websites to the FBI and CIA for "watch listing and possible monitoring"? Would a file be opened? Would the "posts" of these individuals be kept as a permanent record? Would they be subjected to additional scrutiny by the Transportation Security Administration when they travel by air? Would they be surveilled or otherwise tracked by the CIA when they travel overseas? Would it be acceptable to deny entry into the United States to foreigners who have voiced particularly hateful anti–U.S. sentiments in the chatrooms and websites? My gut tells me most Americans would consider the U.S. government lax if it did *not* monitor, and even manipulate to some extent, chatrooms and websites that deal with radical Islamic fundamentalism, anti-American hatred, bomb making, and chemical and biological weapons procedures. These sites attract legitimate researchers, curiosity seekers, and other nonthreatening visitors, but they have some really dangerous types on them also.

SCENARIO NO. 45:
BACK DOORS

NSA has helped to thwart dozens of terrorist attacks around the world by listening in on terrorists' satellite, microwave, email, fax, and cellular communications. Increasingly, however, the terrorists have been using commercial encryption systems that defy NSA's best efforts to decipher them. The same is true of other major targets of U.S. SIGINT, such as narcotics traffickers, organized crime groups, and money launderers. The U.S. intelligence and law enforcement communities believe they are on the verge of losing one of their best means of combating terrorism, drug trafficking, and other international crimes. If they do not get help soon, they will, in fact, lose their ability to read such communications.

NSA, CIA, FBI, DEA, and other U.S. government agencies have rec-
ommended federal legislation to require U.S. manufacturers of cryptographic
systems to build secret "back doors" into their products to allow NSA to
eavesdrop and to decipher communications to and from terrorists and other
dangerous criminals. This legislation has consistently failed because of concerns about privacy and civil liberties.

———

Would it be morally acceptable for the U.S. government to make secret
deals with U.S. cryptography manufacturers, software firms, and broadband
providers to have them provide back doors into their systems for use by
NSA against terrorists and other high-priority national security targets? Would
it be morally acceptable for the CIA to recruit or bribe key personnel in
foreign cryptography companies—Siemens, Philips, or Crypto AG—for the
same purpose?

Graduate student Roxana Botea of the Maxwell School at Syra-cuse University:

Yes. National security supersedes industrial interests and the United
States should undertake all necessary measures to protect the country.

Kyu Mani Lee, Ph.D., former superintendent of Larned State Hospital in Kansas:

Yes. If it didn't, U.S. intelligence might lose one of its best capabilities
in combating terrorism. In such cases, the issues of privacy and civil liberties become irrelevant.

Professor Harry Mason of the Patterson School at the University of Kentucky:

No (class vote). The graduate students in my intelligence course were unani-
mous (0–17) in condemning bribes to the foreign cryptographic companies.

Los Angeles Times journalist Bob Drogin:

1) It depends. It would be morally acceptable for the U.S. government to make secret deals with U.S. cryptographic manufacturers,
   software firms, and broadband providers only if sufficient congressional or other oversight were provided to prevent the use of
   such abusive techniques against U.S. citizens. Such rules were established in the 1970s to protect U.S. citizens against abuses, and
   the challenge of encryption or other new technology does not
   change that framework.
2) It depends. It would be morally acceptable for the CIA to recruit

or bribe key personnel in foreign companies as long as the same restrictions applied, namely, that communications from or to U.S. citizens would be off limits unless a FISA order or other specific oversight were imposed.

Retired U.S. Army Colonel Stuart Herrington:

1)   Yes. Assuming appropriate legislation is passed to make this legal, I would consider back doors with U.S. firms morally acceptable. The operation must be done responsibly and with "minimizing" of the intercepted communications, just as the FBI must do with today's taps.

2)   Yes, but, again, only if the U.S. law is changed.

Professor Terry H. Anderson of Texas A&M University:

It depends. There must be safeguards in place to protect the privacy and civil liberties of U.S. citizens. If the targets are proven terrorists, then 1) and 2) are acceptable, but reading the communications of people who do not have a criminal or terrorist record is immoral.

Former CIA officer John ███████:

1)   No. The likelihood that such an operation could remain secret is virtually nil, and it would be regarded with outrage by the U.S. public. Back doors in software offer essentially unlimited access to everything, and it would be *de facto* impossible to convince a skeptical public that such avenues were not being used for other purposes. The U.S. companies involved are in the business of providing security and protection to their customers. If they heard even a *soupçon* of such an initiative by the U.S. government, they would immediately cry "foul" from the rooftops and enlist the support of the ACLU and others to prosecute the people who came up with the idea. This is an extremely dynamic industry, and back doors would have to be installed on almost a daily basis to keep up with the new releases of software, firmware, and communications channels, thus increasing the risk of exposure and complicating the monitoring problem.

2)   Yes. I do not have the same objection to the exploitation of foreign companies. The encryption systems of foreign companies are probably used regularly by our anti-American targets.

Author's comment:

The U.S. government's virtual monopoly on sophisticated cryptographic systems began to unravel with the advent of so-called public key cryptography in the 1970s. Individuals and businesses began using readily available commercial systems, like RSA, PGP, and DES, that were essentially unbreakable. NSA did its best to preserve its national security equities through export controls and other limitations, but the battle was a losing one. Without some kind of help, such as back doors, clipper chips, or key escrow systems, NSA cannot defeat today's high-grade commercially available encryption systems. Foreign firms are also active in this field, so even if legally required or voluntary cooperation from U.S. manufacturers could be obtained, NSA's worldwide problem would not be solved.

NSA has made no bones about the magnitude of its predicament. Testifying before Congress in 1997, William Crowell, the deputy director of NSA, said, "If all the personal computers in the world—260 million—were put to work on a single PGP-encrypted message, it would still take an estimated 12 million times the age of the universe, on average, to break a single message."

It appears that the only way for NSA to stay in the code-breaking business is some combination of legislation and espionage. But resistance, not surprisingly, is fierce. Many Americans fear the "Big Brother" implications and do not trust the government to respect the privacy of ordinary citizens. Banks, R&D firms, hospitals, scientific institutes, and other enterprises that deal in sensitive information are also concerned about the safety of their data. U.S. companies that market encrypted products and services realize that even the slightest doubt about the security of their encryption algorithms could be fatal to their business. Microsoft, for example, vehemently denied charges in 1999 that it had built back doors into its encrypted operating systems for secret use by NSA:

> Microsoft takes security seriously. We do not deliberately leave "back doors" in our products. Microsoft has consistently opposed the various key escrow proposals that have been suggested by the government, because we don't believe they are in the best interests of consumers or the industry.

The American genius for SIGINT, a talent that has produced so many brilliant successes in the past, will not be easily beaten. Underground and undersea cables were not show-stoppers; the United States found ingenious ways to tap them. According to published reports, the formidable problems of fiber optic cables and frequency hopping transmitters have largely been overcome. Commercially available encryption systems, however, may be NSA's biggest challenge yet. Every intelligence professional knows the United States will find itself in a *grave* national security crisis if it loses the ability to listen in on the communications of terrorists and other dangerous individuals.

SCENARIO NO. 46:
BIOLOGICAL ATTACK

Deadly Israeli attacks have virtually forced the Palestinian terrorist group Hamas out of Gaza and the West Bank. As a result, the military wing of Hamas, Izzedine al Qassam, moves its forces to Iran and establishes a secret training base in the Zagros Mountains of Iran, 110 miles southwest of Esfahan. Izzedine al Qassam vows not only to avenge its losses to the Israelis but also to strike against Israel's main ally, the United States. Izzedine al Qassam is receiving full support from the Iranian government, specifically from the Iranian intelligence service, VEVAK (Ministry of Intelligence and Security).

From its remote base in the Zagros Mountains, Izzedine al Qassam trains suicide bombers for attacks against Israel and the United States. Using false documents and other logistical support provided by VEVAK, the terrorist teams are sent to their target destinations. Several Izzedine al Qassam terrorist teams have been infiltrated successfully into the United States via Mexico.

The United States is hit hard by the Izzedine al Qassam suicide bombers. An explosion in a crowded movie theater in Los Angeles kills twenty-one. A bomb on a commuter train in New Haven, Connecticut, kills seventeen. An attack at a shopping center in Baltimore on Christmas Eve kills nine. And, most recently, a suicide bomb at a church in Atlanta kills fifty-six.

The CIA has a low-level source, encrypted BTFASHION, inside Izzedine al Qassam. BTFASHION works as a mechanic and occasional cook at the training base in the Zagros Mountains. He reports to the CIA that there are about 400 people at the base at any given time. The CIA confirms this report from IMINT and other sources. The U.S. president decides that the Izzedine al Qassam base must be neutralized, but because of the international political situation, he does not believe he can order an outright military attack on Iranian territory. BTFASHION is willing and able to carry out any instructions he is given by the CIA.

————

Would it be morally acceptable for the CIA to vaccinate BTFASHION against anthrax, to train him how to deliver *bacillus anthracis* in aerosol form, to issue him the necessary agents and devices, and to order him to infect the Izzedine al Qassam base with anthrax?

Lieutenant Colonel Tom Ruby, USAF, Department of Joint Warfare Studies, Air Command and Staff College:

[The views expressed here are those of Lieutenant Colonel Ruby and do not necessarily reflect the official policy or position of the United States Air Force, the Department of Defense, or the U.S. government.]

It depends, but probably no. One could make the case that a limited biological attack would be morally acceptable if the following assurances could be made:

- That the anthrax would not be spread beyond the camp to Iranian innocents.
- That the United States would have plausible deniability.[46]
- That there is no alternative means to achieve the objective.

None of these conditions can be guaranteed here. First, from what we know about anthrax, it would probably not kill everyone in the camp. So any survivors would not only infect others with anthrax, but would also alert Iranian authorities to the attack. At that point, it would be impossible for the United States to deny involvement. Second, such a failed biological attack would not only harden terrorist will against the United States and serve as a recruiting tool for terrorists, but would also turn world opinion against the United States for a clear violation of the 1972 Biological Weapons Convention. Finally, there are other means to achieve the same end.

Anonymous active duty military officer No. 1:

No. Although attacking the terrorists in their camp is morally acceptable, doing so with a biological agent is not. First, there are ways to kill or capture the terrorists that are far more humane, causing minimal undue suffering. Second, there is no way to ensure the discriminate application of force.

Anonymous active duty military officer No. 2:

Yes. The key to this for me is to ensure it is 100 percent untraceable. If there is a reasonable possibility that the terrorist group would be able to identify this as a U.S. action, then the United States is at risk of an enormous international outcry. However, something must be done against the camp. Using a biological agent is dangerous, and I would personally prefer to use some other means, but I do not see this as morally unacceptable.

Undergraduate student Laura Zandstra of Texas A&M University:

No. It would not be morally acceptable to infect the camp with anthrax. Biological attacks, once they begin to occur, will open up a whole new frontier of warfare and terrorism. This could be deadly for the American public and cause the deaths of numerous innocent people.

Author Ralph Peters:

Yes, but only because of the exceptional nature of the situation, that is, the real and present danger. I doubt we would take this approach for a wide variety of reasons, from the practical to the ethical. It would have to be a last resort. Killing the terrorists is perfectly acceptable; the means proposed are dubious. I think we'd be too concerned about opening Pandora's box.

Former CIA officer Gena Mills:

No. Intelligence is by tradition a game of tit for tat. The last thing the United States or the CIA would want is for this type of atrocity to become known and for like revenge to be taken by the terrorist group. This would literally be a green light for the terrorists to pursue anthrax and other types of biological warfare. With such a well-placed source as BTFASHION inside the camp, we should have other options.

Rabbi Peter Tarlow:

It depends. The case of stopping a biological attack is one of pure *Pikuah Nefesh* (this principle states that under the assumption of a good inclination and only for the purpose of saving lives, religious laws may be broken). Thus, on a first reading, the answer would appear to be yes. But there are other considerations that need to be addressed. Is the United States a signatory to a nonbiological weapons treaty? Would the United States have tolerated attacks on other people's soil (the my-blood-is-redder-than-yours issue)? Would the use of a biological weapon invite other biological forms of death? Is death by anthrax worse than death by bombing? Have all other forms of attack been ethically eliminated? If we were to use more conventional forms of military action, would there be a high degree of collateral damage? With all these unanswered questions, the best I can answer is "it depends."

Author's comment:

The United States is a signatory to the 1972 Biological and Toxin Weapons Convention, along with over 140 other nations. Article 1 of the Convention states,

> Each State Party to this Convention undertakes never in any circumstance to develop, produce, stockpile or otherwise acquire or retain:
> 1) Microbial or other biological agents or toxins, whatever their origin or method of production, of types and in quantities that have no justification for prophylactic, protective, or other peaceful purposes;

2) Weapons, equipment or means of delivery designed to use such agents or toxins for hostile purposes or in armed conflict.

The United States destroyed its stockpile of biological weapons (anthrax, brucellosis, botulism, tularemia, and others) in 1975 and renounced any future use of biological weapons, under any circumstances, even in retaliation for biological attacks against U.S. forces or citizens. The United States, as permitted by the 1972 Convention, has continued to do research on biological warfare defensive measures, such as detection and testing, immunizations, decontamination, and medical treatment.

The problem, of course, is that terrorist groups do not sign or observe international conventions. Osama bin Laden has declared that Moslems have a "religious duty" to use weapons of mass destruction against Americans. There is compelling evidence that al Qaida is trying to develop the means to carry out that mandate. Al Qaida training manuals contain instructions on how to construct biological weapons. Various unconfirmed reports have stated that al Qaida terrorists have acquired biological agents, including anthrax, bubonic plague, botulinum toxin, salmonella, and the Ebola virus. In 2003, a Moslem cleric closely associated with Osama bin Laden issued a *fatwa* authorizing the faithful to use chemical and biological weapons against the United States.

The United States was prepared to use biological weapons against its enemies in the 1960s—if the United States was attacked first. Would the American people ever support using biological agents in the future? At least a dozen countries, including terrorist sponsor states like Iran and North Korea, are known to possess offensive biological weapons. If these countries ever used biological weapons against U.S. citizens, would we retaliate in kind? If they gave biological weapons to terrorists who then used them against us, how would we react?

Biological weapons have already been used against Americans and will be used again. The anthrax letters of 2001 killed four people and hospitalized at least a dozen more. The perpetrator of that attack remains unknown. In 1984, the Bhagwan Shree Rajneesh cult sprinkled salmonella on salad bars in eleven restaurants in The Dalles, Oregon, killing no one, but hospitalizing several hundred people.

Biological agents can be easily obtained from nature, universities, laboratories, or clinics. The expertise and facilities needed to produce and deploy them are well within the reach of many international terrorist groups. I am surprised we have not been hit by a large-scale attack of this kind already. I know it's coming.

SCENARIO NO. 47:
FORGING DOCUMENTS FROM FRIENDLY COUNTRIES

The United States has broken all relations with North Korea. American citizens have been expelled, and it is strictly forbidden for any American to travel to North Korea. Tensions between the two countries have not been higher since the Korean War. The CIA is under intense pressure to continue producing high-quality intelligence from inside North Korea. It has three valuable intelligence sources in Pyongyang: DBFEATHER (a general in the North Korean Army); DBMONSOON (a senior official of the Choson Central Bank); and DBSLED (the deputy chief of the American Department of the North Korean Foreign Ministry). Contact with all three of these valuable agents has been interrupted.

The CIA urgently needs an on-the-ground operational presence in Pyongyang to recontact DBFEATHER, DBMONSOON, and DBSLED and to handle them securely inside the country. Given the political situation, U.S. documentation and cover for a CIA case officer to travel to North Korea are out of the question.

Would it be morally acceptable for the CIA to forge documents from a friendly Anglophone country—for example, Canada, Britain, Ireland, Australia, or New Zealand—and to send a CIA case officer under appropriate cover into North Korea using those documents, without informing the friendly country?

Former USIA officer John Williams:

No. We can be just as effective without endangering our relationships with these friendly countries. I see two possibilities:

1) ask a friendly nation to use its existing in-country intelligence resources to reestablish contact with our agents and to share with us the intelligence obtained; or

2) ask a friendly nation to send in a specially trained case officer for this purpose.

Since the countries named share our need to learn as much as possible about internal North Korean developments, I see no fundamental impediment to either arrangement. On the other hand, if we use a friendly country's documentation without its knowledge, we run the risk of considerable bilateral damage if the operation is ever compromised. In a purely moral context, an operation like this would violate accepted norms of international conduct as well as international law.

I concede, however, that moral constraints in this case might dissipate if certain factors came into play. For example, if none of the Anglophone nations is willing to cooperate and the need for actionable intelligence from inside North Korea becomes extremely urgent, I might see it the other way.

Former CIA and Army officer Jack Bosley:

No. A more practical way, with less danger to the case officer, would be to run a joint operation with a friendly power. Several nations want to know what North Korea is up to. For me, morality is not a major factor here. I am basing my decision on practicality and the chance of success.

Professor Harry Mason of the Patterson School at the University of Kentucky:

Yes and no (class vote). My students were split 8-8 with one abstention on the issue of forging friendly country documents. Most agreed that forging the documents would be morally acceptable, but those who voted no thought we should inform the friendly government of what we were doing, without providing operational details.

Ph.D. student Margaret Meacham:

No. Our relationship with the other Anglophone country would be compromised if the officer were caught and the document deception exposed. Both countries need to know all the facts before entering into an operation like this.

Dr. Geoffrey Tumlin, assistant director of the Center for Ethical Leadership at the Lyndon B. Johnson School of Public Affairs at the University of Texas:

Yes, provided there is a valid operational reason for not informing the friendly country. I am not sure what that would be, but if there is such a reason, I have no moral problem with forging the documents.

Author's comment:

Every good intelligence service employs professional forgers. Spies operating under cover and in alias in foreign countries, particularly in hostile countries, need forged passports, driver's licenses, and other documents to protect their identities. I used many forged identity documents in my career—and depended on them heavily for operational security and personal safety. It was comforting, when I was crossing international borders, checking into a hotel, or renting a car overseas, to know I had the best false documents the forger's art could produce.

It is getting more and more difficult for intelligence officers to use forged identity documents today. Antiforgery technology is now widespread, with many countries using special papers, watermarks, sensitive inks, holograms, etc., to make their passports and other documents difficult, if not impossible, to forge. Airport and other security controls have also gotten much tighter. Gone are the days of a quick glance and a stamp from a bored passport control officer. Passports are now electronically scanned in several countries, and in the age of terrorism, security officials everywhere are far more attuned to fake passports, visas, and entry/exit stamps. Computerized databases also make it easier today for security officials to probe the backstopping of suspect documents. Does the address on the document exist? Is the holder of the document listed in phone or other directories at that address? Is there a professional listing anywhere for the alleged occupation? Serious intelligence services do an excellent job of backstopping their forged documents, but the level of scrutiny to which the documents are subjected today is far greater than in the past.

Forgeries have a rich and illustrious history in intelligence operations. In addition to making false identity documents, the great intelligence services of the world have used forgeries for disinformation, propaganda, psyops,[47] and other covert action purposes. The OSS in World War II forged German stamps and currency. The Germans forged millions of British pounds in an effort to disrupt the British economy during the war. The brilliant but ruthless Reinhard Heydrich, the head of the Nazi security service, used masterful forgeries in 1936 to convince Josef Stalin that Soviet Chief of Staff Mikhail Tukhachevsky and thousands of other Soviet Army officers were disloyal, which led to their execution, imprisonment, demotion, or banishment. The Russian KGB made *dezinformatsiya* a major prong of its anti–U.S. covert action machine during the Cold War. Skillful KGB forgeries, for example, convinced many Africans and others that the United States was behind the AIDS epidemic. The CIA and the U.S. military made extensive use of forgeries for psyops in Vietnam in the 1960s and 1970s.

It is unlikely the CIA would want to share sensitive denied-area operations like DBFEATHER, DBMONSOON, or DBSLED with other intelligence services, even friendly ones. Some of the Anglophone countries listed do not even engage in overseas espionage operations of this type. The CIA would definitely want one of its own specially trained case officers handling these cases, but the close U.S. ties with these Anglophone allies would probably preclude any undeclared use of their documentation. The CIA would have to find another way to recontact its agents inside North Korea.

SCENARIO NO. 48:
COLLATERAL DAMAGE

After a short period of appearing to renounce the development of nuclear weapons and other weapons of mass destruction, Libyan leader Moammar Gadhafi has secretly eased back into the business. U.S. intelligence is particularly concerned about Gadhafi's efforts to achieve a biological weapons capability.

Unfortunately, Gadhafi has been aided in his efforts by a renegade American microbiologist named Edgar Blake. Dr. Blake, formerly a research scientist at Rockefeller University in New York, left the United States two years ago in an angry response to some perceived academic or professional slight, the details of which are not entirely clear to his U.S. associates. In any event, Dr. Blake made contact with Libyan officials in Italy and offered his services to Gadhafi in building a sophisticated biological weapons program in Libya. Dr. Blake is widely recognized as a brilliant scientist and an expert in the production of biological agents suitable for weapons use.

According to sensitive intelligence sources, Gadhafi accepted Dr. Blake's offer, agreed to pay him royally, and set him up in an apartment building in downtown Tobruk. In what was once a series of adjoining apartments, Dr. Blake and his Libyan staff have built a modern laboratory, using equipment purchased by cutouts in Europe.

U.S. intelligence believes Dr. Blake has produced large quantities of anthrax, botulinum toxins, and plague for weapons use by Libya. According to CIA sources, Dr. Blake and his staff members live and work inside the apartment building, along with several Libyan families who are not connected with the secret laboratory.

The U.S. president decides to conduct a preemptive strike against the villa but is deeply concerned about civilian casualties and collateral damage.

———

Would it be morally acceptable for the CIA to destroy the laboratory with two Hellfire missiles fired from a Predator RQ-1B unmanned aerial vehicle, even though civilian casualties and collateral damage could not be avoided? Would it be morally acceptable for the CIA to specifically target Dr. Blake in the attack?

Pastor Tom Nelson of Denton Bible Church in Denton, Texas:
No. The U.S. should find a way to take Dr. Blake out in a less damaging way. Only if the civilians in his building are aiding and abetting the enemy in some way would this be morally acceptable. Here, they are innocent

bystanders; so another way must be found. As a Christian, I do not feel that a righteous decision will ever put us at a disadvantage. God, I believe, will provide an alternative. God is the wild card. Morality does not put a nation in a cul-de-sac.

Former CIA officer William Lieser:

It depends. This is a really tough call. The American scientist has given up his rights to protection as a U.S. citizen with his collaboration on the development of biological weapons. But the potential loss of innocent civilian lives in a preemptive strike does trouble me deeply. The age of terrorist acts designed for massive loss of life has changed my perception about the morality of preemptive actions, but the moral conflict involved in killing innocent persons still remains huge for me.

Dr. Geoffrey Tumlin, assistant director of the Center for Ethical Leadership at the Lyndon B. Johnson School of Public Affairs at the University of Texas:

Yes. There is enough evidence of possible catastrophic losses via biological warfare that the collateral damage in this case is morally acceptable.

Ph.D. student Margaret Meacham:

Yes. Once Dr. Blake and his staff moved from the talking stage to the implementation stage, they invited all U.S. efforts to stop them. The civilians in the building are acceptable collateral damage when compared to the potential for lost lives if the biological weapons program is not obliterated.

Professor Howard Prince, director of the Center for Ethical Leadership at the Lyndon B. Johnson School of Public Affairs at the University of Texas:

1) It depends. Here the key seems to be whether there are alternatives and the president's willingness to consider them. Absent an imminent threat or strong indicators that Libya is about to use WMD, the president should proceed cautiously or risk an immoral action. This situation is similar to Israeli strikes on Hamas in Gaza after suicide bombing attacks in Israel. But in this case, there has been no use by Libya of the biological weapons. What other means are there short of a missile attack? This question must be answered before conducting a preemptive strike and risking the lives of innocent civilians.

2) Yes. Blake is a hired gun, not a neutral scientist. It would be morally acceptable to target him specifically, subject to my concerns above.

Ph.D. student Margaretta Mathis:

1) Yes. Destroy the laboratory if it is being used for producing biological agents.
2) It depends. Assassinating Dr. Blake in this manner is morally acceptable only if the U.S. government knows for a fact he is guilty
   and if nonlethal alternatives, such as kidnapping or arrest, are not
   possible.

Anonymous active duty military officer No. 1:

1) It depends. As a nation, regardless of whether the CIA or DOD
   is taking the action, we have a moral imperative to limit collateral
   damage. However, we are not bound to eliminate it. If the Predator with the Hellfires is believed to be an option that reasonably
   limits collateral damage, then this operation would be morally acceptable. My driving factor here in answering "it depends" is what
   type and how much collateral damage are we talking about. With
   the presence of WMD, it is possible the collateral damage through
   contamination could be catastrophic and thus make the attack
   unacceptable. If we cannot reasonably assess the extent of collateral damage, then we must refrain from attacking.
2) Yes. It is morally acceptable to target Dr. Blake.

Anonymous active duty military officer No. 2:

1) Yes. It would be morally acceptable to destroy the building with
   Hellfire missiles. Collateral damage should be avoided when possible, but the value of this legitimate target makes it necessary to
   strike it.
2) Yes. Dr. Blake is in every way, shape, and form an enemy of the
   United States. Negotiating his return is not going to happen. He
   must be stopped. I guess this in some ways smells of vigilantism,
   but so be it. The end justifies the means.

Lieutenant Colonel Tom Ruby, USAF, Department of Joint War-
fare Studies, Air Command and Staff College:

[The views expressed are those of Lieutenant Colonel Ruby and do not
necessarily reflect the official policy or position of the United States Air
Force, the Department of Defense, or the U.S. government.]

No. Neither question is morally acceptable. First, Dr. Blake has not
done anything overtly threatening to the United States. As an agent of the
government of Libya, he should be immune to prehostility action. The United
States cannot wage war against an individual working for a sovereign state.

If the United States has a beef with the individual, it needs to go through Libya and the instruments of power one state uses against another. There is no clear necessity to kill this scientist. The only acceptable killing of non-combatants is when the proportionality of the attack is outweighed by the necessity of the action. In this case, the noncombatants in the Tobruk apartment complex do not have any inherent expectation that they can be killed by another state. We are not at war with Libya.

Author's comment:
The United States considers itself legally and morally obliged to limit civilian casualties to the extent possible in any armed conflict. Innocent civilians may not be the target of the attack; the civilian casualties must be unavoidable; and the number of civilian casualties must be minor compared to the importance of the legitimate military objective.

The U.S. Department of Defense has codified these principles into its Law of Armed Conflict (DoDD 5100.77), which contains three criteria for determining whether a military action is lawful: military necessity, distinction, and proportionality. Key provisions are as follows:

Military necessity requires combat forces to engage in only those acts necessary to accomplish a legitimate military objective. Attacks shall be limited strictly to military objectives. In applying military necessity to targeting, the rule generally means that the United States Military may target those facilities, equipment, and forces which, if destroyed, would lead as quickly as possible to the enemy's partial or complete submission . . .

Distinction means discriminating between lawful combatant targets and noncombatant civilians . . .

Proportionality prohibits the use of any kind or degree of force that exceeds that needed to accomplish the military objective. Proportionality compares the military advantage gained to the harm inflicted while gaining this advantage. Proportionality requires a balancing test between the concrete and direct military advantage anticipated by attacking a legitimate military target and the expected incidental civilian injury or damage. Under this balancing test, excessive incidental losses are prohibited. Proportionality seeks to prevent an attack in situations where civilian casualties would clearly outweigh military gains. This principle encourages combat forces to minimize collateral damage—the incidental destruction that occurs as a result of a lawful attack against a legitimate military target.

Who makes these determinations? According to the USAF Intelligence Targeting Guide, Air Force Pamphlet 14-210, of February 1, 1998,

> Determining collateral damage constraints is a command responsibility. If national command or theater authorities do not predetermine constraint levels for collateral damage, a corps or higher commander will normally be responsible for doing so.

The United States has often been accused of violating its own guidelines with respect to collateral damage, most recently in the Balkans, Afghanistan, and Iraq. Human rights and other watchdog groups keep close tabs on how many civilian deaths are caused by U.S. forces and use these figures to accuse the United States of indiscriminate use of force and, in extreme cases, of war crimes. Critics of the United States frequently refer to the U.S. attacks on essentially civilian targets during World War II: the fire bombs against Dresden and Tokyo and the atom bombs against Hiroshima and Nagasaki. The numbers of civilian deaths caused by those attacks are difficult to determine, but most historians agree they were roughly as follows: Dresden 30,000; Tokyo 100,000; Hiroshima 140,000; and Nagasaki 70,000.

Nothing on that scale is likely to occur today, but civilian casualties are inevitable in the war on terror. The CIA adheres to the same principles as the Department of Defense in attempting to limit civilian deaths when it carries out covert action operations against terrorists. The nature of the current war, however, raises special problems. First, to what extent are nonstate actors like terrorists entitled to the protections of the Geneva and Hague Conventions? Second, do the actions of the terrorists themselves somehow justify higher levels of civilian casualties than might otherwise be tolerated? Terrorists hide in cities and wear civilian clothing. They store their weapons, train, and place their headquarters in civilian neighborhoods, often in homes or mosques. In some cases, they employ human shields to protect their personnel and facilities. In essence, terrorists, by design, present U.S. counterterrorism forces with a dilemma: you have to kill innocent civilians to kill us.

In January 2006, the United States fired a missile into the Pakistani border village of Damadola, about four miles from Afghanistan, in an effort to kill Ayman al-Zawahiri, the number two leader of al Qaida. Al-Zawahiri was not killed in the attack, but at least seventeen people were, some, if not all, of whom were innocent Pakistani civilians. The Pakistani government condemned the U.S. action and issued a formal diplomatic protest. Anti–U.S.

demonstrations broke out all around Pakistan. In a statement to the press, Senator John McCain offered his view: "This war on terror has no boundaries. We have to go where these people are, and we have to take them out."

SCENARIO NO. 49:
FOREIGN OFFICER VISITORS

The U.S. Army's Command and General Staff College (CGSC) in Fort Leavenworth, Kansas, admits more than 1,000 company and field grade officers a year for graduate-level training in military doctrine and tactics. The standard course is ten months in duration.

Although the overwhelming majority of the students who attend the CGSC are U.S. military officers, approximately eighty to a hundred foreign military officers are invited to attend each year. These foreign military officers tend to be the "cream of the crop" from their respective countries and many go on to become heads of state, defense ministers, chiefs of staff, ambassadors, or other high ranking officials. They come from more than seventy-five different countries, including Algeria, Egypt, Chile, Iraq, Bulgaria, Poland, Turkey, Bosnia, France, Israel, Latvia, Lithuania, Kenya, Afghanistan, Colombia, Jordan, Saudi Arabia, and many others.

U.S. intelligence considers several of these foreign military officers to be attractive recruitment targets, not only because they are likely to attain senior ranks in their countries' military services, but also because some of them will rise to high civilian positions in their governments. During their ten-month stay at Fort Leavenworth, the foreign students will have daily contact with their American military colleagues and with civilian sponsors in the community. Close friendships generally develop. The presence of these foreign officers in the United States in the controlled environment of the CGSC offers an excellent opportunity for assessing their political views, personalities, strengths, and vulnerabilities.

———

Would it be morally acceptable for the CIA, FBI, and DIA to collect biographic and assessment information on the foreign students at Fort Leavenworth, using cooperative American officers and civilians as the sources, to determine which, if any, of the foreign officers are susceptible to recruitment? If so, would it be morally acceptable to develop the foreign students aggressively and to pitch them on behalf of U.S. intelligence while they are in the United States?

Mike Hannesschlager, former executive director of the Texas Christian Coalition:

Yes. But before judging whether this operation is morally acceptable, a more fundamental question needs to be asked: Why does the United States allow the future leaders of foreign countries to train at an elite U.S. military college if it is so concerned about their countries of origin that it tries to recruit them as spies? It seems paradoxical. As incongruous as this arrangement may be, it does represent a legitimate opportunity. Not only is it morally acceptable to assess these foreign military officers while they are here; if the chance presents itself, they should be recruited on the spot. These foreign officers have access to information we need for our security. It's as simple as that.

Professor Terry H. Anderson of Texas A&M University:

Yes, it is acceptable, and probably expected on both sides. Pitching the foreign officers, however, could be counterproductive, diminishing the friendships and good will developed during the ten-month program.

Retired U.S. Army Colonel Stuart Herrington:

Yes, in general. There are certainly valid questions, however, on the wisdom of attempting to recruit an officer from a country that is a good ally of the United States (cost of possible compromise vs. gain).

Former CIA officer Gena Mills:

Yes. This is the price of doing business. When foreign governments send their officers to the United States for training, they are certainly aware the students are potentially susceptible to becoming cooperative sources or actual agents recruited by U.S. intelligence services. It would be foolish for the United States not to pursue this avenue. Some of the students are from "unfriendly" countries and, as aspiring leaders, they could be expected to use the knowledge obtained in their U.S. training to further their careers in their home countries and quite possibly to use such training against U.S. interests.

Retired U.S. Navy Captain Richard Life:

1) Yes. I consider this to be SOP, and I am confident the counterintelligence organizations in most countries alert their officers to this probability when sending them to U.S. military schools.
2) No. Pitching the foreign officers while they are still in the United States is not morally acceptable—or prudent. With very few exceptions, they are too junior in rank to be worth the risk of recruitment. I am comfortable with pitching only officers from potential

enemy countries, or from countries closely aligned with our current and possible future enemies. However, this should be accomplished later in the officers' careers, after they have risen to higher, more responsible positions with greater access and/or influence.

Author's comment:

Every year the United States host tens of thousands of foreign military officers and other potential leaders in a variety of programs all around the country. The U.S. Army's Command and General Staff College is perhaps the best known for admitting international students, but there are significant international contingents as well at the National War College, the Naval War College, the Army War College, the Air War College, and other military schools. The International Military Education and Training Program, overseen by the U.S. State Department and operated by the Department of Defense, provides training to thousands of foreign military officers each year in counterterrorism, counternarcotics, counterintelligence, and other fields. On the civilian side, the United States admits approximately 1,300 Foreign Fulbright Fellows annually. The International Research & Exchange Board, since its founding in 1968, has given scholarships and research grants to thousands of foreign students, teachers, government officials, journalists, and others. The Edmund S. Muskie Graduate Fellowship Program has sponsored more than 3,000 graduate students and professionals from the former Soviet Union since 1992 for study trips to the United States. The Hubert S. Humphrey Fellowship Program brings in approximately 175 midcareer professionals a year, from over 140 countries, for study and professional development in the United States.

From an intelligence standpoint, there is no better venue for recruiting penetrations of foreign governments than in the United States. The visitors get a good look at American values and way of life; some will develop attachments to the United States that might be exploitable in a recruitment pitch. Others will simply be assessed as venal, and perhaps a deal can be made with them on that basis. Finally, the visitors are on U.S. soil and to some extent are dependent on the U.S. government for benefits and privileges. They can be assessed and developed far more easily in the United States, where we control the turf, than they could ever be in their home countries.

Many Americans would be appalled that the international good will and understanding generated by these programs could ever be tainted by "crass" U.S. intelligence activity. Obviously, any such activity would have to be done discreetly because of the political sensitivities involved, but should the United States totally forgo such a golden intelligence opportunity?

SCENARIO NO. 50:
INTERROGATION

America's war against terror is in full force. The United States has troops throughout the Middle East and South Asia. In joint raids with friendly countries and in unilateral preemptive strikes, U.S. forces have destroyed training camps used by terrorists, seized their weapons stockpiles, tracked them to their hiding places, and captured or killed thousands. Eight hundred terrorist suspects are in U.S. military and CIA custody on the island of Diego Garcia in the Indian Ocean.

U.S. Army and CIA interrogators at Diego Garcia hope to obtain actionable intelligence from the suspects through interrogation. They have devised a sliding scale of techniques ranging from mild discomfort to serious stress. Their intention is to move progressively through these techniques until the suspect breaks and begins to provide information of value. The following techniques are to be used:

1. Depriving the prisoners of sleep, for example, by questioning them nonstop for twenty-four hours.
2. Removing religious and other comfort items from them.
3. Shaving their hair and beards against their will.
4. Keeping them hooded.
5. Putting them in solitary confinement, completely isolated from other prisoners.
6. Confining them in small, dark, and sound-proofed cells to create sensory deprivation.
7. Shining bright lights on them.
8. Blasting them with loud and offensive music or other sounds.
9. Introducing noxious odors into their cells.
10. Serving them repugnant or poor-tasting food.
11. Putting them on reduced rations.
12. Exposing them to extreme temperatures, either cold or hot.
13. Keeping them in handcuffs, leg irons, or other restraints.
14. Requiring them to stand or to assume stress positions for lengthy periods.
15. Stripping them.
16. Using dogs to frighten them.
17. Slapping them in the face.
18. Wrapping their faces in wet towels to produce a sensation of suffocation.
19. Threatening them with death or severe torture.
20. Tricking them into thinking they will be transferred to a particularly

hated third country for harsh treatment.
21. Conducting mock executions.

————

Would it be morally acceptable to use the above techniques progressively, from mild to harsh, to assist in the interrogation of the terrorist suspects at Diego Garcia?

Graduate student Roxana Botea of the Maxwell School at Syracuse University:

It depends. While some of the interrogation techniques seem perfectly acceptable (1, 2, 3, 5, 8, 15, 19, and 20), others are problematic. Methods that cause permanent physical or psychological damage are not ethical under most circumstances. Several of the techniques (4, 6, 13, 14, 16, 17, and 18) may fall in this category. Not being a physician or psychiatrist, however, I do not feel qualified to make this determination. Only in a situation of emergency (imminent and horrific threat) do these methods become tolerable. If the CIA has firm reason to believe there is an impending attack that endangers the lives of large numbers of Americans, then it should use any and all of the twenty-one techniques. In the absence of such threat, the ends do not justify the means.

Randy Everett, M.D., of Fort Collins, Colorado:

Techniques 1–18: yes. Techniques 19–21: it depends. Many of these techniques, or variations of them, have been practiced around the world for centuries. Activities that include physical discomfort with coercion or threat have been routinely used in college initiations and military and athletic training. I am ambivalent about the acceptability of steps 19–21 because the emotional distress seems to me considerably more severe and hence closer to torture. But when one considers what here is only threatened or pretended and what terrorists without hesitation actually carry out, it is understandable why even steps 19–21 might be palatable to prevent further mayhem and death.

Ph.D. student Margaretta Mathis:

No. These methods appear to me to be no different from torture, and I think torture is always morally unacceptable.

Ph.D. student Margaret Meacham:

Techniques 1–10: yes. Techniques 11–21: no. Methods 1–10 are psychological, so are morally acceptable. Methods 11–21 are physical and therefore are not morally acceptable. We cannot set the precedent for other countries that it is O.K. for them to do this to our people, nor can we be hypocritical about doing it to them but opposing having them do it to us.

Colonel Cindy R. Jebb of the United States Military Academy:

[The opinions expressed by Colonel Jebb are her own and do not necessarily reflect the views of the United States Military Academy, the Department of the Army, or the Department of Defense.]

No, with a possible exception. The above techniques are not morally justifiable. First, the captives are "suspects" and therefore may be innocent. Second, this is torture, and torture is not morally acceptable. What if the CIA is wrong and the captive is innocent? If we corrupt our own morals, then how do we, as a nation, continue to stand for bedrock values? The problem is that even if it is done covertly, the assumption has to be that the use of torture will be exposed. This will bring great discredit on the United States. Moreover, we must consider the effect not only on the tortured victim, but also on the torturer. Is it not just as dehumanizing for the torturer to engage in such activity? In addition, from a practical side, how reliable is intelligence obtained by the above methods?

However, if the information derived from torture prevents a horrific act, then it may be justifiable. Several points must be taken into account for each case, and it seems that moving beyond number one on the scale of interrogation techniques would require "knowing" that the suspect has information related to an imminent catastrophic act. Only if the U.S. government had that absolute knowledge, which I believe would be extremely rare, would moving down the interrogation scale be morally permissible. It seems to me that the morality involved in keeping citizens safe at that point would be the overriding consideration.

Former FBI senior official Oliver "Buck" Revell:

It depends. I believe the use of nonphysical coercive and deceptive interrogation techniques in situations where vital information is at stake and those being interrogated are not American citizens, protected resident aliens, or combatants operating as regular military (and thus covered by the Geneva Convention) to be morally acceptable. There should be a high level of certainty that the detainee to be interrogated under the expanded authority is in fact a terrorist and is likely to be withholding vital information. We are under no legal authority or moral obligation to give all the rights and privileges of our society to those whose intent it is to destroy our society and who do not recognize any limits on the violence and terrorism they carry out against us.

Author's comment:

The U.S. government has had a hard time trying to formulate and implement interrogation guidelines for prisoners detained outside the United States. The starting point is the U.N. Convention Against Torture and Other Cruel, Inhuman, or Degrading Treatment or Punishment, which the United States ratified in 1994. Article 1 of the Convention defines torture as "any act by which severe pain or suffering, whether physical or mental, is intentionally inflicted on a person." Article 16 prohibits "other acts of cruel, inhuman or degrading treatment or punishment which do not amount to torture as defined in Article 1."

But what constitutes "severe pain or suffering" and "cruel, inhuman or degrading treatment"? Correctly interpreting these concepts became a pressing issue when the United States began detaining and interrogating large numbers of Taliban and al Qaida suspects in late 2001 and early 2002. In response to a CIA request for legal guidance, the Office of Legal Counsel of the U.S. Department of Justice sent a memorandum to Alberto R. Gonzales, counsel to the president, on August 1, 2002. This now disavowed memorandum gave considerable latitude to field interrogators:

> Physical pain amounting to torture must be equivalent in intensity to the pain accompanying serious physical injury, such as organ failure, impairment of bodily function, or even death. For purely mental pain or suffering to amount to torture . . . it must result in significant psychological harm of significant duration, e.g., lasting for months or even years.
>
> We conclude that the treaty's text prohibits only the most extreme acts . . .
>
> . . . while many of these techniques may amount to cruel, inhuman or degrading treatment, they do not produce pain or suffering of the necessary intensity to meet the definition of torture . . .
>
> . . . we conclude that there is a wide range of such techniques that will not rise to the level of torture.

In an earlier memorandum to the president in January 2002, Gonzales stated that in his legal opinion the value of the intelligence to be obtained from the Guantanamo detainees might be such that the Geneva Convention restrictions on interrogating detainees would be "obsolete."

On April 16, 2003, Secretary of Defense Donald Rumsfeld approved twenty-four specific techniques for use in the interrogation of suspected terrorist detainees at Guantanamo. Even though the Department of Defense emphasized that none of the authorized procedures "authorized, permitted, or tolerated torture," Rumsfeld was criticized widely for the severity of the measures. Among the most controversial were

> Dietary Manipulation: Changing the diet of a detainee; no intended deprivation of food or water; no adverse medical or cultural effect and without intent to deprive subject of food or water, e.g., hot rations to MREs.
>
> Environmental Manipulation: Altering the environment to create moderate discomfort (e.g., adjusting temperature or introducing an unpleasant smell). Conditions would not be such that they would injure the detainee . . .
>
> Sleep Adjustment: Adjusting the sleeping times of the detainee (e.g., reversing sleep cycles from night to day). This technique is NOT sleep deprivation.
>
> False Flag: Convincing the detainee that individuals from a country other than the United States are interrogating him.
>
> Isolation: Isolating the detainee from other detainees while still complying with basic standards of treatment. (Caution: The use of isolation as an interrogation technique requires detailed implementation instructions, including specific guidelines regarding the length of isolation, medical and psychological review, and approval for extensions of the length of isolation by the appropriate level in the chain of command. This technique is not known to have been generally used for interrogation purposes for longer than 30 days.)

The abuses of detainees at Abu Ghraib prison and elsewhere, including at least two deaths of detainees under interrogation, have been well documented. The U.S. government insists that these actions were unauthorized excesses and the guilty parties were held criminally liable. U.S. officials have consistently asserted that the United States does not engage in torture and strictly abides by U.S. laws and international treaty obligations.

The fact remains that interrogation guidelines for U.S. personnel serving in Afghanistan, Iraq, and Guantanamo remain vague and controversial. Methods of causing even relatively mild discomfort, such as cold food or hot quarters, have been denounced by some as excessive. In 2005, Senator Richard Durbin compared U.S. treatment of the detainees at Guantanamo to the atrocities committed by the Nazis and Pol Pot. Amnesty International issued a series of scathing denunciations of U.S. detention and interrogation practices.

Harvard University's John F. Kennedy School of Government and

Harvard Law School conducted a joint project in 2004 to examine how democratic freedoms and national security could be balanced in the war on terrorism. The Harvard Project brought together a wide variety of legal experts and former government officials representing diverse points of view. One of the areas considered by the panel was the question of "highly coercive interrogation" techniques. In their final recommendations, the Harvard Project participants took a somewhat surprising middle ground. They started out by categorically rejecting torture, as expected, but then left the door open for aggressive interrogation in some instances:

> For all but the rarest of cases, authorized highly coercive interrogation techniques should also comply with our additional treaty obligations not to engage in "cruel, inhuman, or degrading treatment."
>
> A list of permissible highly coercive interrogation techniques consistent with the Convention Against Torture should be promulgated by the President and provided to a number of relevant committees of both congressional chambers. Even then, such techniques should be used in an individual case only when the factual basis for the need, the exceptional importance of information sought and the likelihood that the individual has that information is [*sic*] certified in writing by a senior government official and made available to the Attorney General and both the Senate and House Intelligence Committees.
>
> For the extremely rare case of an immediate threat to U.S. lives, unavoidable in any other way, we would allow the President to personally authorize an exception to the U.S. obligation under the Convention Against Torture and the U.S. Constitution not to engage in "cruel, inhuman, or degrading treatment," short of torture, so long as the decision by the President is based on written findings documenting his reasons and is promptly submitted to the appropriate congressional committees.

It is hard to imagine that any president would risk the political heat that would result from preparing a "list of permissible highly coercive interrogation techniques." In fact, I am convinced it would be hard to find any U.S. politician who would be willing to draft or to endorse such a list. Doing so would be a political loser for any politician. And that's precisely our problem; interrogations of terrorists can produce extremely valuable actionable intelligence, but even now, after all this time, we have no clear-cut rules.

AFTERWORD

When the Cold War ended in 1991, those of us who had fought in it hoped we could bequeath to our children and grandchildren a new era of peace. But that was not to be. The world forced upon us by the events of September 11, 2001, is not the world we would have chosen to live in, but it's the world we have. Today, we find ourselves mired in an ugly war and hard hit by escalating international violence. The war on terror, many experts fear, could turn out to be even longer, bloodier, and deadlier than the Cold War was. I'm convinced it will be.

Intelligence is essential to winning the war on terror. There seems to be general agreement on that point on both sides of the political aisle, but there are widely divergent views on how that intelligence should be obtained. We have seen disagreements on the appropriateness of various spying techniques throughout U.S. history, but perhaps the debate is more strident and politicized now than ever before. The fifty scenarios in this book are an attempt to encapsulate some of the most important moral dilemmas facing the world of intelligence today. They are not academic; they need to be addressed. Almost everyone agrees that we need to fight tough if we're going to defeat terrorism, but where exactly do we draw the line when it comes to assassinations, torture, renditions, blackmail, sex, drugs, kidnappings, electronic eavesdropping, and the other moral issues raised in these scenarios?

If you pick the right theologian or philosopher, you can defend almost any position, from moral absolutism to unconstrained utilitarianism to everything in between. In fact, one of the realities that makes this debate so damnably difficult is that there are good, conscientious, and patriotic people on both sides of it. Even in the unscientific sampling of the commentators, we saw a surprising lack of predictability. We could not, for example, assume all former CIA officers would see things the same way. The same was true of State Department officers, academics, journalists, students, religious figures, and military officers. In the same individual we sometimes saw apparent inconsistencies from one moral issue to another. I suspect the results would be similar for the population as a whole. With the exception of un-compromising civil libertarians on one end of the spectrum and equally uncompromising Rambo-types on the other, most people seem conflicted when analyzing these moral issues.

I believe it is imperative for us, as a nation, to work through these con-flicts. If we are to prevail over vicious and rampant international terrorism, we cannot afford to hobble or underutilize our vast intelligence capabilities. Just as importantly, we cannot trample our civil liberties in the process. It will take strong national leadership to get beyond our current *ad hoc* ap-proach to the morality of spying, to reach across the political divisions, to find some measure of consensus, and to articulate clear rules of engage-ment for our intelligence personnel. We don't have clear rules now, but we desperately need them. And there isn't much time left.

─── Notes: Spying 101 ───

As I began writing the main body of this book, I realized that many of the intelligence terms, concepts, and methods to which I would be referring would not be familiar to all readers. I therefore thought it would be helpful to add this section to the book to provide background, clarification, and context where necessary.

Introduction: A Career Under Cover

1. It is very important to use the right terminology to describe those who spy. "Spy" is a generic term that refers accurately to either a professional intelligence officer who works for an intelligence service, or to a foreign source or asset who steals secrets on behalf of that intelligence service. I was a spy. So were the many courageous Russians and others I handled during my career in the CIA. A professional clandestine service officer, however, as I was with the CIA, is more properly referred to as an "operations officer," an "operator," an "operative," or, even better, a "case officer." "Case officer" is the term most of us prefer. A case officer can work for any service. Thus, there are American case officers working for the CIA, Russian case officers working for the SVRR, Israeli case officers working for the Mossad, and British case officers working for MI6. The people that case officers recruit as penetrations of foreign governments and organizations are their "agents." Agents have access to important information and pass that information secretly to their case officers. A case officer handles an agent. It is totally incorrect to refer to a professional CIA officer as an "agent." The media make this mistake constantly: "CIA agent Valery Plame," "former CIA agent Aldrich Ames," "former CIA agent Porter Goss," etc. We are not agents; we are case officers. In fact, I inform my students in my intelligence classes at the Bush School that it is a "flunkable offense" for them to refer to me or to my colleagues at the CIA as "agents." And I mean it. U.S. law enforcement agencies, including the FBI, call their employees "agents," or "special agents," and their recruited sources "informants" or "confidential

informants," and that's fine. But if we are referring to an intelligence service, the correct terms are "case officer" and "agent."

2. Recruitment at the CIA has changed a great deal since I joined. The CIA still uses friendly "spotters" around the country, mostly retired CIA officers, to identify outstanding candidates, but that happens less often today. The process is much more open now than it was before. The CIA sends recruiters to campuses across the country unless, as sometimes happens, they are told they are not welcome. Most college placement offices, however, are cooperative and support the CIA's recruitment efforts by providing space for information sessions and interviews. For the first twenty years of its existence, the CIA recruited predominantly in the Northeast, but today it recruits nationwide. CIA recruiters also attend job fairs and conferences, where they set up information booths and pass out literature to interested young people. (As a general rule, the CIA does not recruit anyone over the age of thirty-five, but there are occasional exceptions for individuals with highly valued skills, such as knowledge of rare languages.) The CIA also advertises in newspapers and specialized publications. It even has a website, cia.gov, where job openings and requirements are listed. As a matter of fact, the CIA requires today that all initial applications be made electronically via the website; a candidate does not exist in the CIA's recruitment system until he or she has an electronic identity. Each major career field in the CIA recruits separately, so there is a department for hiring analysts, another for scientists and engineers, one for administrative personnel, one for operators, etc. The hiring of analysts, scientists, engineers, administrators, and personnel for most other job categories is done overtly; these applicants will not be under cover and can discuss their CIA employment processing with family and friends. Applicants on the operational side are instructed from their very first contacts to be discreet about the process and, in fact, to downplay the fact they are pursuing employment with the CIA. This will make life much easier for them when they are hired and go immediately under cover. The entire process, from application through interviews, testing, psychological screening, medical exams, polygraphs, an extensive background investigation, and entry on duty, usually takes nine months to a year. The recruitment process for other U.S. intelligence and law enforcement agencies is similar.

3. CIA officers are on the same GS pay scale as other civilian employees of the U.S. government. I entered on duty as a GS-9, step 1. Today, an applicant with an advanced degree and/or military service would probably start somewhere in the GS-11, step 5, range, which would be roughly $59,000 a year.

4. This elite training program for future CIA case officers is now called the Clandestine Service Training Program, or CSTP. A sister program, the Professional Trainee Program, recruits younger and less-experienced applicants for up to two years of formal and on-the-job training in the Directorate of Operations. If PTs (professional trainees) do well, they are rolled into the CSTP.

5. Anatoly Golitsyn provided some valuable information on penetrations of Western countries by the Soviet KGB, but soon fell into an elaborate conspiratorial mindset. He developed a close relationship with James Jesus Angleton, the CIA's chief of counterintelligence, and the two of them fed on each other's paranoia. To them, nothing apparent was real; the West was being duped by diabolical Communist plots; the Sino-Soviet split was a fraud; and the Soviet KGB controlled everything. Angleton bought into everything Golitsyn said and rejected all evidence to the contrary. As a result, Angleton virtually destroyed the CIA's Soviet operational and counterintelligence programs for twenty years. Sadly, there are still some "Golitsynites" out there today, aggressively peddling the same outlandish conspiracy theories first espoused by Angleton and Golitsyn. The best book on the Angleton era is *Cold Warrior* by Thomas Mangold.

6. For years, the true nature of the Farm and its location were classified, but in the last ten years there have been multiple revelations in books, documentary films, and the press. The setting is beautiful, with pine forests, trails, deer, creeks, and the river. I always considered my visits to the Farm for training courses or conferences a nice respite from the fast pace of Washington. The facilities, accommodations, and food were all, in my opinion, first class. I hoped to have an assignment at the Farm as an instructor one day, but the timing never worked out. The recent movie *The Recruit* has a somewhat "Hollywoodized" version of CIA training at the Farm, but it is not too far off. The CIA has even acknowledged publicly that the movie gets it right in most ways.

7. Pyotr Popov was the CIA's first significant penetration of Soviet intelligence. Although the Soviets had recruited more than 200 Americans as spies in the 1930s, 1940s, and 1950s, the United States had done essentially nothing in return. Popov, a lieutenant colonel in Soviet military intelligence, volunteered his services to the CIA in Vienna in 1953. George Kisevalter was Popov's case officer in Vienna and, later, in Berlin. Popov was arrested and executed by the KGB in 1958. The best account of this historic case is William Hood's *Mole*. Oleg Penkovsky, a colonel in Soviet military intelligence, was possibly the most valuable spy the CIA has ever had. He volunteered to the CIA and to British MI6 in Moscow in

1961. Colonel Penkovsky had access to high-level information on Soviet missile forces and military doctrine. His intelligence was absolutely critical to President Kennedy during the Berlin crisis of 1961 and the Cuban Missile Crisis of 1962. The CIA and MI6 broke new ground by running Penkovsky as an in-place agent in Moscow, but, in retrospect, much of the tradecraft used in the operation was seriously flawed by today's standards. Kisevalter was part of a four-person team (two CIA case officers and two MI6 case officers) who handled Penkovsky. Penkovsky was arrested by the KGB in 1962 and executed in 1963. His story is told in the superb book *The Spy Who Saved the World* by Jerrold Schecter and Peter Deriabin. I heard Kisevalter do presentations on the Popov and Penkovsky cases three or four different times at the Farm and elsewhere, and, each time, he broke down. It was obvious to me that he was deeply attached emotionally to his two agents and had never gotten over their tragic ends.

8. When I went to the Farm for basic training, I was part of an entering class of ███████ students. All of us but one were male. Sally, the only woman, did exceptionally well in training, including the paramilitary aspects, and later had a successful career as a case officer in East Asian operations. She was also a fierce competitor on the racquetball court and was one of my regular playing partners at the Farm (I prefer not to comment on how our matches turned out). By the early 1980s women case officers were fairly common at the CIA. Today, roughly one-third of entering CSTP and PT classes are female, and many women occupy senior positions in the CIA's Directorate of Operations, both at home and abroad.

9. CIA officers serving overseas often have what is known as "official cover," ███ ████████████████████████ They have diplomatic immunity and, if caught in the act of spying, will generally be declared *persona non grata* and expelled from the country. Other CIA officers, however, serve overseas under what we refer to as "nonofficial cover," where they have no visible affiliation with the U.S. government. NOCs, as they are called, might typically operate as business executives, students, writers, or in some other nongovernmental capacity. They perform those jobs in addition to doing their espionage. If they are caught in the act of spying, they do not have diplomatic immunity and are subject to the full force of the local law, including prosecution for espionage and imprisonment. NOCs usually receive less scrutiny and surveillance from the local authorities than their official colleagues. They might also, depending on their cover, be able to move in circles that would ordinarily be closed to U.S. government

officials. Working as a NOC is exciting business. It's pure classical espionage, living by your wits, and burying yourself in the local scene. The downside is that you generally operate as a singleton and do not have the professional camaraderie and support that "inside," officially covered officers enjoy. It's lonely and cold as a NOC—but also indescribably exhilarating for those who love the art of spying.

10. CIA code names for agents and operations usually consist of a two-letter digraph, e.g., GT, followed by a randomly generated word, e.g., TAW. The digraph indicates a specific country or, sometimes, a specialized office, such as counterintelligence. The digraphs are changed periodically for security reasons.

11. It is an indispensable skill for a CIA case officer to be able to spot, manipulate, and defeat hostile surveillance. There was nothing that Meredith and I spent more time on during our denied-area tradecraft training than how to do just that. We trained for days on end against professional CIA and FBI surveillance teams in the United States, until we got to the point we could routinely beat them. Professional case officers, of all services, conduct lengthy "surveillance detection runs" or SDRs before engaging in operational acts. A good SDR gives a case officer the opportunity to flush out surveillance if it is there and to make an absolute determination of his or her surveillance status. The CIA jargon for completing an SDR and verifying without any doubt that surveillance is not there is "getting black." A case officer's worst nightmare is being wrong about getting black. I don't know how I could live with myself today if I had ever gone to an operational act and had inadvertently taken hostile surveillance with me. A failure like that could easily mean execution or years in prison for the agent. Hostile surveillance teams range from superb professionals to Keystone Kops. Meredith and I, along with our colleagues, were subjected to some of the world's best surveillance when we served in Moscow. I have also seen surveillance teams from other countries that operated in a discreet and hard-to-beat mode. On the other extreme, I once operated against a Bulgarian team that was just unbelievably amateurish and clumsy; they could not have been more obvious if they had been wearing signs. I was insulted by how bad they were. Putting that kind of team on me wasn't showing me any professional respect!

12. Lonetree was by no means unique. U.S. counterintelligence annals are filled with cases of U.S. personnel enticed into espionage by sexual entrapment. The Soviet KGB was particularly skilled at using attractive young Russian women, called "swallows" by the KGB, to seduce Western diplomats and other officials. Violetta was one of the approximately

three hundred Soviets employed by the U.S. embassy in Moscow to do clerical, housekeeping, and other supposedly nonsensitive jobs. All of these Soviet employees at the U.S. embassy, a large proportion of whom were attractive young women, were cleared by the KGB and had to co-operate in order to keep their jobs. It also worked the other way. Meredith found it amusing that whenever she traveled around the USSR with Western women's groups there were always handsome young Russian men hanging around the hotel offering to buy them drinks and asking them to dance. Other countries' intelligence services do exactly the same thing. Sharon Scranage, a CIA employee in Ghana, was lured into espionage by her Ghanaian lover in 1983. Her spying compromised several CIA operations in Ghana, including the arrests of at least eight Ghanaian agents. It is hard for me to believe that U.S. government officials, who are thoroughly briefed on the dangers of unauthorized romantic relationships overseas, can still fall for this obvious ploy, but they do.

13. Double agent operations are the caviar of the intelligence business. There is nothing, in my opinion, more exquisite or delicious in the world of spying than a good, well-run double agent operation. The term "double agent," however, is frequently misunderstood and misused. A double agent is an agent who has been recruited by one service but who is actually loyal to and responsive to another service. Lonetree, for example, was an agent of the KGB. He would become a U.S. double agent if he agreed to work for the CIA in the future against the Soviets. In other words, Lonetree would pretend to be working for the KGB, but would actually be taking all his orders from the CIA and would be reporting everything that happened to his CIA case officer. Double agent operations require a fine touch, excellent acting ability on the part of the double agent, and a willingness to give up something to get something more valuable in return. The opposition case officer has to be manipulated into believing that the operation is genuine and that the intelligence it is producing is legitimate and worthwhile. This is no small feat, because all case officers, regardless of nationality or service, are trained to be constantly on the lookout for doubled operations. The information given up to make the case look good is called "feed material." A good double agent operation can produce several positive results: (1) reveal the opposition's *modus operandi*, i.e., tradecraft, payment mechanisms, technology, locations, etc.; (2) provide identification and assessment of the opposition's case officers; (3) serve as a channel for disinformation; (4) disclose the opposition's collection requirements, i.e., what information gaps it is trying to fill; (5) tie up the opposition in useless activity; and (6) take the opposition's money, i.e., the salary and

bonuses paid to the double agent. Two case studies I use in my classes at the Bush School are based on two of the most brilliant double agent cases in U.S. intelligence history, one run by the FBI (SOLO) and the other by the U.S. Army (SHOCKER). I strongly recommend to interested readers *Operation Solo* by John Barron and *Cassidy's Run* by David Wise for detailed accounts of these two spectacular double agent operations.

14. The CIA's Officer-in-Residence Program sends experienced CIA officers to colleges and universities around the country, at the schools' request, to teach courses on intelligence. The CIA continues to pay the salaries and benefits of these officers while they are on campus, usually for two years; the universities agree to provide the CIA officers-in-residence with office space and other basic support offered to all faculty members. The CIA hopes the OIR program will encourage the study of intelligence as an academic discipline and strengthen CIA ties to the U.S. academic community. All OIRs are overt and are prohibited from engaging in any clandestine activity on campus. They do not recruit for the CIA, but are available to interested students as a source of information on intelligence careers and can refer them, if requested, to the appropriate CIA recruitment channels. The program is small, with only five to ten OIRs assigned at any one time. The demand for OIRs from U.S. colleges and universities far exceeds the supply; several schools have been waiting for years and have still not been assigned an OIR. The OIRs come from various backgrounds, but are usually analysts or operators. Most OIRs have been well received, but there have been occasional instances of student protests, faculty senate resolutions, boycotts of classes, and other negative reactions to their presence on campus. Since OIRs are required to be overt, Meredith and I had to make the difficult decision to come out from under cover for me to accept the OIR position at Texas A&M. Even after we came out, it was a long time before we were comfortable uttering in public the three magic letters we had hidden for so long.

Philosophical and Historical Arguments

1. General Reinhard Gehlen was head of the German General Staff's Foreign Armies East branch during World War II. In that position, he was responsible for all military intelligence on the Soviet Union. As WWII was about to end, Gehlen and several of his senior officers surrendered to U.S. forces. After protracted discussions, Gehlen agreed to resurrect his organization on behalf of U.S. intelligence, to reactivate his agents, to dig up his buried files, and, in short, to do everything possible to

assist U.S. intelligence operations against the USSR Gehlen built up a large and powerful organization that was of great service to the United States, eventually becoming the core of the West German Federal Intelligence Service, the BND. Nevertheless, the CIA and the U.S. government as a whole were widely criticized for "collaborating with Nazis."

2. The age-old process by which intelligence services recruit agents is known as the "agent acquisition process" or, more commonly, as the "recruitment cycle." Every intelligence service does it the same way—and it will always be done the same way. The recruitment cycle is the essence of spying. It is what case officers do for a living. Just as in academia the workplace imperative is "publish or perish," in the world of intelligence it is "recruit or perish." Case officers' careers are made or broken on the basis of how successful they are in recruiting agents. If a case officer cannot recruit, he or she is definitely in the wrong business. We jokingly say among ourselves, "What do you call a case officer who can't recruit?" Answer: "A former case officer." The recruitment cycle is described differently in different places, but it always boils down to the same multistep process. In my courses at the Bush School, I teach it as consisting of the following seven steps:

    1) Spotting. A good case officer is always "on the make," that is, constantly trolling for recruitment candidates. This means moving in wide circles around town and hanging out in places where foreign recruitment targets can be "spotted." Case officers, for example, might regularly attend diplomatic receptions, conferences, ceremonies, dinner parties, etc., in an effort to observe foreigners who have access to intelligence information of interest. They might also frequent tennis clubs, other sports groups, jogging trails, or anywhere potential targets can be found. An ambitious CIA case officer will not spend many evenings at home . . . because time at home means time not spotting.

    2) Assessing. Once a potential agent is spotted, the case officer proceeds with "assessing" the target. What do we know about this second secretary in the Libyan embassy? Has anyone met him before? Are they any traces on him? Where does he hang out? What are his interests? What do we know about his family, education, past assignments, etc.? What are his attitudes toward the United States? Is he materialistic? Does he appear to have any other vulnerabilities? Most importantly, does he have access to classified information we need? Assessment information can be gathered from the files, from casual observation or conversation, from directories, and from other sources. Sometimes, case officers

have "access agents," people they have recruited who can mix naturally in the desired circles and report assessment information back to them. Assessment information might also be obtained through surveillance, telephone taps, or audio devices.

3) Developing. If the assessment data is positive, the case officer attempts to begin "developing" his or her prospective agent. Development is the establishment of some form of direct contact between the case officer and the target. It might at first be nothing more than occasional chitchat at diplomatic functions. That might lead to lunches or dinners together to discuss international topics of mutual interest. Finally, and ideally, the relationship will become social and personal, perhaps even reaching the point of "friendship." The families can become involved, too, for example, through picnics, sports events, movie nights, or other outings together. Throughout the development phase, of course, assessment of the target is continuing.

4) Pitching. By this point, the case officer and the target have a close relationship—and the case officer has assessed the target as ready for "pitching" on the basis of some perceived vulnerability. It might be that the target is venal and will sell out for money or some other material consideration. It might be that the target is secretly pro-American and is willing to provide secrets on that basis. Maybe the target or a family member needs expensive American medical care or some other favor. In some cases, resettlement in the United States might be offered in return for the target's willingness to work in place for an agreed-upon period. There are many, many variations on what might possibly motivate a given individual to cooperate. Maybe the target is assessed as having no vulnerabilities at all, in which case he or she will be dropped, and the case officer will move on to other targets offering more promise.

The actual pitch, of course, is the moment of truth. By making the pitch, the case officer is breaking cover and acknowledging his or her intelligence affiliation. The assessment of the target had better be right or the consequences can be severe. A failed pitch can lead to a case officer's being denounced to the local authorities, to a diplomatic protest, to expulsion from the country, or, worst of all, to a doubled operation. For NOCs, who do not have diplomatic immunity, a failed pitch can mean arrest. Pitches are carefully crafted to maximize the probability of success and, in fact, are not usually approved unless the odds of acceptance are extremely high. Most pitches are "warm" (based on solid assessment and development), but from time to time an intelligence service might carry out a "cold pitch" against a high-priority target for whom there has been no opportunity for extensive assessment and development. Cold pitches, since the chances of success are small, are usually "hit and run;" in other words, the case officer, most likely in alias and from out of country, makes the pitch and is prepared to exit the country immediately if it does not go well. In warm pitches, the hope is that the personal relationship between the case officer and target, established during the developmental phase, will offer some insulation against the most serious negative repercussions of a failed pitch. In other words, even if the target says no, his respect and "friendship" for the case officer may be enough to prevent him from reporting what happened to the local authorities.

5) Formalizing. Let's assume the pitch has been expertly delivered and the target (now our new "agent") has said yes. The case officer must then proceed to the important task of "formalizing" the clandestine relationship. The agent will sign a secrecy agreement and will be briefed in detail on security procedures. There will probably be a polygraph exam. The agent will be trained in tradecraft such as deaddrops, signal sites, electronic communications, secret writing, concealment devices, countersurveillance techniques, and whatever else is required for the operation. The agent's access to classified information will be examined carefully and collection requirements will be issued. The case officer and agent will cease as quickly as possible all visible personal contact.

6) Producing. The agent now begins "producing" intelligence under the direction of his or her case officer. This is the reason for the whole process; this is the payoff. The agent steals documents, diagrams, computer disks, and other classified information from his or her place of employment and delivers the data secretly to the case officer, using the tradecraft techniques established for this purpose. In most cases, the agent also submits to detailed debriefings by the case officer or by experts brought in specifically to provide more depth. These debriefing sessions take place in a safehouse or in some other secure location. If all goes well, the operation can continue in this manner for years.

7) Terminating. All good things must come to an end. At some point, the agent falls under suspicion by the local counterintelligence authorities, develops cold feet, loses access, retires, moves, becomes unresponsive, begins acting unreliably, or, for some other

reason, needs "terminating." The best terminations are by mutual agreement, a recognition by both parties that it is time to call a halt to the operation. Usually, a generous "termination bonus" is paid to the agent. A quitclaim is signed. Every effort is made to make the parting as amicable as possible (it is not in an intelligence service's interests to have a lot of disgruntled former agents running around). My experience in the CIA was that the termination of an agent was often emotional. The case officer–agent bond can become very close, based, as it often is, on several years of shared dangers, a common cause, mutual respect, and, yes, even genuine friendship. Termination can be a personal hardship for agents who have become dependent on their CIA salaries. I liked and admired many of the agents I worked with in my career and usually found it hard to say good-bye. Other terminations, of course, were less painful. It was not at all hard for me to terminate the sleazes who worked for us strictly for money and who possessed no particular redeeming qualities.

A successful case officer for the CIA or any other intelligence service should have several cases underway at any given time in various stages of the recruitment cycle. If, for example, I had a junior CIA case officer working for me overseas who was spotting aggressively and had three targets under assessment, two under development, and four in production, I would probably give him or her a high performance evaluation.

U.S. Attitudes Toward Spying

1. This is probably a good time to describe the four major categories of intelligence operations: SIGINT, HUMINT, IMINT, and covert action.

   1) SIGINT, or signals intelligence, is the interception and, if necessary, decryption of other countries' communications, radars, telemetry, and other electronic signals. The United States has always had a special knack for SIGINT, beginning with Herbert Yardley and his Black Chamber in WWI and continuing to the present. The bulk of U.S. SIGINT is done by the National Security Agency in Fort Meade, Maryland, but many other U.S. government agencies, including the CIA, the military, and law enforcement, are also heavily involved. Among foreign countries, the best SIGINT historically has been done by the British, Russians, and East Germans. The United States collects SIGINT around the world, using ground sites, ships, aircraft, and satellites to intercept the signals. Code breaking is an excruciatingly difficult and mysterious art. Not surprisingly, the National Security Agency (NSA) is one of

the world's leading employers of mathematicians and computer specialists. An excellent account of U.S. SIGINT is contained in James Bamford's book *Body of Secrets*.

2) HUMINT, or human intelligence, also called espionage, is the heart of the spy business. Nothing beats a human penetration inside a hostile foreign country, terrorist group, narcotics trafficking organization, or other high priority intelligence target.

3) IMINT, or imagery intelligence, is photo reconnaissance of foreign targets. In the United States, IMINT has evolved from balloons to aircraft to satellites. A major breakthrough was the development of the U-2 spy plane, which collected invaluable IMINT during overflights of the Soviet Union from 1956 to 1960. A successor spy plane, the SR-71, was capable of flying at an altitude of 85,000 feet and at a speed of Mach 3. The United States continues to use photo reconnaissance aircraft, but the mainstay of U.S. IMINT today is satellite technology. The first U.S. spy satellite was launched in 1960, and many, many more have followed. The precise details of U.S. IMINT capabilities are classified, but it is no exaggeration to say they are mind-boggling. A few other countries engage in rudimentary IMINT, but U.S. technological dominance in this field is unlikely ever to be challenged. U.S. spy satellites are built and operated by the National Reconnaissance Office, and the collected product is analyzed and disseminated by the National Geospatial-Intelligence Agency.

4) Covert action is often called the "dirty tricks" side of spying. It consists of sabotage, subversion, paramilitary operations, political action, psychological operations, and black propaganda. It is not always pretty. Covert action has historically been a relatively small part of the CIA's overall activity, but it is certainly the aspect of U.S. spying that has been the most controversial.

2. In 1975 and 1976 Senator Frank Church of Idaho and Representative Otis Pike of New York chaired special committees, in the Senate and House, respectively, to investigate allegations of widespread illegal activities by the CIA, NSA, FBI, and other U.S. government agencies. Their reports documented numerous instances of violations of the law and abuses of civil liberties by the U.S. government, including domestic spying, illegal drug tests, and the harassment of political opponents. The net result of the Church and Pike committees was a long overdue and much needed clean-up of the U.S. intelligence community, but some critics feel the committees went too far in undermining the effectiveness and morale of U.S. intelligence professionals. I personally deplore the

political grandstanding and vilification of the U.S. intelligence community that took place, but I'm glad the hearings were held. They served the very useful purposes of reasserting congressional oversight of intelligence operations and reminding all of us that U.S. spying *must* remain within the law. In law school, I particularly admired the legal opinions of Supreme Court Justice Louis Brandeis and have never forgotten the famous line from his dissent in Olmstead v. United States (1928): "If the government becomes a lawbreaker, it breeds contempt for law." Every U.S. spy should paste that quote on his or her mirror.

Scenarios

1. The DGI, Fidel Castro's notorious intelligence agency, has operated aggressively against the United States for over forty years. Although it received its training and other support from the Soviet KGB, the DGI, in my opinion, surpassed the KGB in tradecraft, discipline, and overall effectiveness. I consider the DGI the second-best service I worked against in my career (after the East German MfS). When DGI officer Florentino Aspillaga, code-named TOUCHDOWN, defected to me in Vienna in 1987, he revealed the shocking news that the DGI had controlled every CIA operation run against Cuba for over twenty years. In 2001, the FBI dismantled the so-called Wasp Network, a major DGI espionage and sabotage network in Florida targeted against anti-Castro groups and U.S. military installations. At about the same time, a U.S. Immigration and Naturalization Service official named Mariano Faget was convicted of passing classified information on Cuban asylum seekers and defectors to the DGI. Finally, on September 21, 2001, the FBI arrested Ana Belen Montes, a forty-four-year-old woman of Puerto Rican background, who was the senior analyst for Cuban affairs at the U.S. Defense Intelligence Agency. Using sophisticated radio and computer technology, Montes was able to pass massive quantities of intelligence to her DGI masters. In March 2002, she confessed to having been a spy for the Castro regime from 1985 to 2001. She was sentenced to twenty-five years in prison.

2. For most of its history the CIA excluded homosexuals from employment. Applicants to the CIA were required to fill out detailed questionnaires about their personal habits and preferences. In addition, they were subjected to interviews with psychologists and psychiatrists, who specifically asked them about their sexual experiences and preferences. These statements were then checked for veracity through an extensive polygraph examination and a background investigation. My CIA colleagues and I basically accepted, without question, the doctrine that homosexuals were susceptible to blackmail by foreign intelligence services and were

therefore security risks. By the late 1980s, we had begun to question those assumptions. In studies conducted by the CIA and the Defense Personnel Security Research Center (PERSEREC) in Monterey, California, it became clear that Americans betrayed their country for many reasons, mostly for money, but that homosexuality was rarely a factor. The long accepted view that homosexuality was a security risk proved to be wrong. In addition, wider acceptance of homosexuality in society began to remove the stigma of being homosexual and thereby reduced the likelihood that shame and secrecy could make a homosexual vulnerable to blackmail. In the early 1990s, the CIA changed its policy and no longer excluded applicants on the basis of homosexuality. In 1995, President Clinton signed an executive order barring the federal government from using homosexuality as grounds for denying a security clearance. For several years now, the CIA has had its own Gay, Lesbian, and Transgendered Support Group, and in 2000 it hosted its first Gay Pride Day at CIA headquarters in Langley, Virginia.

3. The MSS is the principal Chinese intelligence service. It was established in 1983, replacing and expanding on the Central Investigation Department of the Chinese Communist Party. The MSS makes use of diplomatic, journalistic, trade, and tourist covers for its operations overseas. It also uses the cover of Chinese students who are studying abroad, particularly graduate students, for espionage operations. The MSS has almost always played the ethnic card in its recruitment operations. It targets the millions of ethnic Chinese who live abroad in virtually every country around the world. The MSS is particularly interested in stealing secrets that can be used to advance Chinese technology, particularly military technology. There are over 2,600 Chinese diplomats and commercial representatives in the United States; probably 40 percent of them, or more than 1,000, are MSS officers under cover. Among the many Americans implicated in espionage for the MSS were Larry Wu-Tai Chin, a CIA employee; Peter Lee, a TRW employee; and James Smith, a special agent for the FBI.

4. In 1999, the House Select Committee on U.S. National Security and Military/Commercial Concerns with the People's Republic of China released its final report. This report—more commonly called the Cox Report after its chairman, Representative Christopher Cox of California—was a devastating exposé of China's massive acquisition of restricted U.S. technology. According to the report, "The PRC has mounted a widespread effort to obtain U.S. military technologies by any means— legal or illegal." The stolen technologies have enabled the Chinese military establishment to upgrade its nuclear weapons, missiles, high-performance

computers, submarines, information warfare, command and control procedures, and other capabilities.

5. When the Soviet Union collapsed in 1991, the monolithic Soviet intelligence service, the KGB (Komitet Gosudarstvennoy Bezopasnosti—Committee for State Security) was broken up into two new organizations: the SVRR (Sluzhba Vneshney Razvedki Rossii—Russian Foreign Intelligence Service) and the FSB (Federal'naya Sluzhba Bezopasnosti—Federal Security Service). The SVRR was put in charge of foreign intelligence operations, and the FSB was given responsibility for counterintelligence and internal security. For the most part, the personnel, targets, and operations of the KGB simply rolled over to the SVRR and the FSB. Although useful intelligence exchanges in areas of mutual concern, for example, terrorism and organized crime, have taken place between the United States and the new "democratic" Russia, the two countries have never ceased spying on each other. It was SVRR case officers who handled the notorious American spies Aldrich Ames (CIA), Harold James Nicholson (CIA), James Earl Pitts (FBI), Robert Hanssen (FBI), George Trofimoff (U.S. Army), and others. At a conference on counterintelligence in College Station in April 2005, cosponsored by the National Counterintelligence Executive (NCIX) and the George Bush School of Government and Public Service, counterintelligence experts from the CIA, FBI, and NCIX confirmed that Russian intelligence operations against the United States have continued unabated.

6. Our good friends the British have two principal intelligence services: MI5 and MI6. MI5 is responsible for counterintelligence and internal security. It is roughly the equivalent of the American FBI. The actual correct title for MI5 today is BSS, British Security Service, but old pros and others who want to be "in the know" still call it MI5. MI6 is responsible for foreign intelligence and is roughly the equivalent of the American CIA. The current official title of MI6 is SIS, Secret Intelligence Service, but, again, professionals prefer the older designation. British SIGINT is the responsibility of GCHQ, General Communications Headquarters, the direct counterpart of the American NSA.

7. Safehouses are secure locations used by intelligence services to meet with agents or for other clandestine purposes. The renter or purchaser of a safehouse is usually a cutout, someone who has no visible connection

with intelligence work or with any official organization. ~~The~~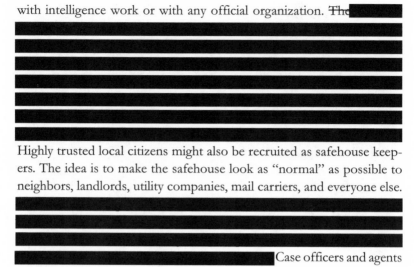

Highly trusted local citizens might also be recruited as safehouse keep-ers. The idea is to make the safehouse look as "normal" as possible to neighbors, landlords, utility companies, mail carriers, and everyone else.

Case officers and agents tend to like safehouse meetings because they provide a secure and re-laxed setting, usually with drinks and snacks, for debriefings and training sessions. Other uses of safehouses might include staging areas for sur-veillance teams, short-term stash sites for defectors, or overnight pads for transient CIA officers.

8. The CIA is divided into three primary directorates, the Directorate of Intelligence (analysis), the Directorate of Science and Technology, and the Directorate of Operations (HUMINT and covert action). The Di-rectorate of Operations, or the DO, where I spent my career, comprises divisions, centers, and staffs. Most of the divisions cover geographic areas, such as the Africa Division, the European Division, the Near East Division, the Latin America Division, and the East Asia Division. The centers and staffs are usually responsible for specific subject matters, such as counterintelligence, nonproliferation, or crime and narcotics. The organization of the DO, like the Agency as a whole, has been in con-stant flux, so the names, tasks, and acronyms have changed frequently, but the basic breakdown into geographic and substantive components has remained relatively constant. There is keen competition within the DO to sign up the newly minted case officers as they complete the CSTP. The divisions and centers send teams to the Farm to explain to the recruits the advantages of joining their components. It would not be unusual for a top CSTP graduate to receive offers from three or more divisions and centers. Some CSTP students are essentially predestined for specific components. An officer with an M.A. in Middle Eastern Studies and fluent in Arabic, for example, will most likely go to the Near East Division or to the Counterterrorism Center. The "needs of the

service" will ultimately prevail, but, in general, new case officers have a significant voice in where they end up going. The determining factors for most of them are how good the language training will be, how soon they can get overseas, what covers are available, and how important the target is. Most case officers want to be where the action is, so, not surprisingly, the high-demand areas today are the Middle East, counterterrorism, nonproliferation, and China. A new case officer will "home base" in one of the divisions or centers, and his or her career will be managed by that component up through grade 15. This does not mean, however, that this officer will spend an entire career in that area. The DO encourages rotational assignments to different components and even, at times, outside the DO, for career development purposes. A typical DO career might easily consist of assignments in three or more geographical or substantive areas and three or four different foreign languages (the CIA taught Meredith and me French, Russian, German, and Spanish—not unusual for a DO career).

9. A crucial but often overlooked part of U.S. intelligence efforts is liaison with foreign intelligence services. The CIA, FBI, military, Drug Enforcement Administration, Customs, and other U.S. government agencies work closely with their counterparts in many countries, usually discreetly, in areas of common interest. Even when the bilateral political relationship has been strained, quiet cooperation in areas like terrorism, organized crime, immigrant smuggling, and money laundering often continues. These exchanges are mutually advantageous. The United States, with its vastly superior capabilities in SIGINT and IMINT, is often in a position to provide its liaison partners with vital and actionable intelligence. In return, the United States receives intelligence and other forms of local support from those countries. The United States also provides training, equipment, and other assistance to friendly foreign intelligence services. A productive liaison relationship does not necessarily preclude spying on each other—but it does mean both sides try to be especially careful not to get caught at it.

10. A CIA operational center overseas is known as a "station." A station is usually, but not always, located under cover in a U.S. official installation. The senior officer in charge of a station is known as the chief of station, or COS. The number two in that station is the deputy chief of station, or DCOS. If the CIA has an operational presence in another city of the same country, that secondary location is known as a "base," with a chief of base (COB) and a deputy chief of base (DCOB) in charge. The COS is responsible for all U.S. intelligence activity that takes place in a given country. COBs, if they exist, report to the COS. The

British equivalent term for a COS is "head of station." The Russian term for a station is "residency," or *rezidentura*, and the senior officer in charge is known as the *rezident*.

11. Applicants for the CIA's Directorate of Operations are instructed from their first contacts with the Agency to be discreet about the process. They should not, for example, gratuitously broadcast to friends and acquaintances that they have applied to the CIA. What they tell their families is up to them. Many DO applicants choose not to inform their parents, brothers, sisters, or other close relatives. They may decide to do so later, but, at least initially, they prefer to keep the number of witting persons to the absolute minimum. Meredith and I chose not to tell our parents we were in the CIA because of our concern they would worry too much if they knew the truth, especially when we were posted overseas. This was probably the right call for us. Several years later, in fact, when Meredith and I did tell our parents we were in the CIA, both sets of parents reacted the same way: "Thanks for not telling us sooner!" The CIA insists that all DO officers tell their spouses the truth. It would be totally unworkable and, we believe, immoral for one of our officers to conceal such an important fact from a spouse. CIA recruiters work with DO applicants from the beginning to formulate cover stories they can use to hide the fact they are in processing for CIA employment. DO officers are asked about their "disclosures" in their polygraph sessions and must be prepared to justify whom they have told and why. Other applicants for CIA employment, for example, analysts, scientists, engineers, and administrators, etc., are totally "overt" (with only a few exceptions) and are not required to conceal their CIA employment.

12. Compartmentation is the process of strictly limiting the number of people who are aware of a given intelligence operation. Some writers use the term "compartmentalization" to describe this principle, but the correct term of art inside the U.S. intelligence community is "compartmentation." Only personnel with an absolute "need to know" should be admitted into the compartment. Simply having the requisite clearances is not enough; the individual in question must have a legitimate work-related reason to know about the operation.

For the most sensitive operations, the CIA maintains what it calls "bigot lists" to document precisely who is witting of a particular operation. Keeping the bigot list as small as possible is the goal, but in practice it is easier said than done. Case officers, their supervisors (both in the field and at headquarters), operational support personnel, communicators, analysts, senior managers in the Agency, congressional oversight committees, and others have valid claims to be included on bigot lists. These people, moreover, frequently turn over and move on to other assignments, so their replacements have to be briefed. An operation that continues for many years almost inevitably develops a much larger than desired compartment. When CIA counterintelligence officers tried to reconstruct who knew about the dozen or more sensitive Soviet agents compromised in 1985 (by Aldrich Ames, as we later learned), the number of CIA officers on the bigot list was approximately 200! That was probably excessive, but, in practice, it would have been difficult to keep the list much smaller than that.

An intelligence service that is careless about compartmentation pays the price. An example I use in my classes at the Bush School relates to the atomic espionage operation run by the NKVD (Narodnyy Komisariat Vnutrennikh Del—People's Commissariat for Internal Affairs, predecessor to the KGB) in the United States before and during World War II. To save a few dollars, the Soviets used the same courier to service the Soviet spies Klaus Fuchs and David Greenglass in Los Alamos, New Mexico, even though Greenglass had been recruited by Julius and Ethel Rosenberg (his brother-in-law and sister), who were active Soviet spies in another compartment. When Fuchs, under interrogation by the FBI and the British security service MI5, confessed to espionage in 1950, he gave up the courier (Harry Gold), who gave up Greenglass, who gave up the Rosenbergs. If the Soviets had practiced good compartmentation, their losses could have stopped at Gold. As an intelligence professional, I can't resist saying "shame on the NKVD" for having violated such a fundamental intelligence principle.

13. One of the first decisions that has to be made when an agent is recruited is whether his or her handling will be "personal" or "impersonal." Personal handling means direct human contact between the agent and the case officer, for example, in safehouses, out-of-the-way cafés, parks, alias-rented hotel rooms, or cars. Many agents prefer personal handling because of the efficiency, the moral support, and the certainty that all sensitive documents and other materials are safely exchanged hand-to-hand. Needless to say, both the agent and the case officer must do thorough surveillance detection runs before making personal contact. A sloppy SDR by either of them could be disastrous. The case officer determines in each case whether personal handling is suitable for a given agent in a particular operational environment. Some operational environments are so hostile and tight that personal handling is not possible. It may also be that the CIA does not have a permanent operational presence in the city where the agent resides, thereby necessitating impersonal handling. Impersonal handling is a combination of deaddrops, caches, signals, secret

writing, brush passes, and electronic exchanges. A case officer and agent who are operating impersonally rarely, if ever, see each other. CIA case officers are expected to "case" constantly for suitable operational "sites" and to write them up so they are available for issue to future agents. Since, as a rule, deaddrop, cache, and other operational sites are not used more than once, it is extremely important for stations to maintain a well-stocked "site inventory."

14. The FBI aggressively recruits diplomats and other foreign officials assigned to the United States. This is in keeping with the FBI's responsibility for counterintelligence inside the United States, namely, preventing espionage and covert action by foreign countries against the United States. It is axiomatic in intelligence work that "there is no better counterintelligence than recruiting the other side's intelligence officers." The FBI has been very successful in doing this; it has also recruited non–intelligence officers. The FBI handles these recruited sources while they are in the United States, but usually turns them over to the CIA for handling when they return to their home countries. The CIA returns the favor by bringing the FBI into the operation whenever a CIA-recruited source overseas receives an assignment to the United States. This is not just service-to-service comity; it is the *law* that the CIA does not "operate" in the United States and the FBI does not "operate" overseas.

15. Denied area tradecraft is the specialized clandestine methodology used in handling agents in particularly difficult and hostile environments. Officers (and their spouses) being assigned to one of these locations go through rigorous "denied area" training, during which the hostile operating conditions of the country in question are duplicated to the extent possible. This could mean around-the-clock surveillance, harassment, arrests and interrogation (simulated), and listening devices everywhere. Not only must the officer and his or her spouse conduct operations with "agents" (role-playing CIA personnel), case for operational sites, and do everything else expected of overseas cases officers, but they must also demonstrate they can withstand the constant stress, make good operational decisions while under surveillance, and function effectively as a team. In some cases, both the husband and wife are full-fledged DO case officers, forming what we call a "tandem couple." In other cases, the non-CIA spouse is put under contract and trained in all the necessary denied area skills. Denied area operations are not for everyone—and definitely not for every marriage. Couples selected for denied area assignments are subjected to intensive psychological screening.

16. Markus Wolf was one of the best spy chiefs ever. From 1958 until 1987, he headed the HVA (Hauptverwaltung Aufklärung—Main Intelligence

Directorate), the external intelligence arm of the East German MfS (Ministerium für Staatssicherheit or "Stasi"—Ministry for State Security). Wolf was successful in placing HVA spies throughout the West German government, including at the highest levels of the chancellor's office and inside the West German BND (Bundesnachrichtendienst—Federal Intelligence Service). Although the HVA's main target was West Germany, Wolf also recruited several Americans as agents and "doubled" many of the CIA's operations in East Germany. Wolf was totally dedicated to the Communist cause and ruthless in his defense of East Germany's security. His autobiography, *Man Without a Face*, is well worth reading.

17. It is standard practice, whenever a defector comes forward, for an intelligence service to explore whether that defector can "stay in place." In most cases, it would be highly advantageous for the service to have a source with high-level access remain in his or her position as a producing agent. Several variables have to be considered first. Is the defector *willing* to stay in place? (Sometimes financial incentives are helpful here). Has the defector burned his or her bridges, in other words, is he or she in serious trouble, under suspicion, known to be missing, etc.? Is the defector psychologically suited for such a high-stress role? Many defectors are emotionally distraught when they appear (defection is psychologically akin to suicide; the defector is in a desperate work or family situation and sees no other escape but to "jump"). Other defectors have drinking problems. For whatever reason, the reality is that some defectors simply cannot be "turned back." Finally, acceptance and resettlement of defectors is expensive for the receiving service, and some potential defectors do not qualify because of insufficient immediate intelligence value. These volunteers might, however, be able to earn their way to defection and resettlement by agreeing to work in place for a specified period before defecting.

18. Some agents are met only when they travel outside their home countries. Handling them inside their countries is either deemed too dangerous (some agents categorically refuse to be handled in their own countries) or the handling service does not have an operational presence there. In such cases, the communications arrangement with the agent will include a "universal contact plan," a way of establishing contact wherever the agent shows up. The agent might call a sterile phone number (not traceable to any U.S. government facility), for example, and, without using a name, indicate the city and date where the meeting will take place. The place and time for the meeting are often agreed upon in advance, so they do not have to be mentioned during the phone call. What does every

city have that can be used as an initial contact point? The main post office? The city hall? The first hotel listed in the yellow pages? The central train station? Whatever it is, the designated place must be unique and easily locatable. Universal contact plans are therefore tricky, and the potential for confusion is great. If the phone line (or other means of communication used to signal the agent's travel) is secure enough, the agent can be more explicit in making the meeting arrangements, but only if security allows. The regular case officer for the operation will usually travel to the indicated city for the meeting with the agent. Since this is not always possible, the communications plan must also allow for the possibility of having the meeting handled by a previously unknown case officer, who will identify himself or herself to the agent through an agreed upon "parole," or distinctive word or phrase.

19. A common tradecraft technique used by many intelligence services for personal meetings is the car pickup. The agent waits in a doorway, between two buildings, in a parking area, or at some other appropriate location. At the agreed upon time, the case officer drives up, stops briefly, and the agent climbs in. The meeting is then conducted as the two drive around. It is usually not a good idea to park, because two people sitting together in a parked car can attract attention. Car pickups are particularly good at night, when other motorists and pedestrians cannot see who is in the car. There are obvious risks to car pickups, such as accidents, breakdowns, roadblocks, or being stopped by the police. A good case officer works out a cover story with the agent in advance to explain why they are together and will also have a contingency plan ready for each of the above incidents. Car meetings are limited and, to some extent, inefficient, because the case officer needs to concentrate on driving. There is little personal interaction with the agent, as there is in a safehouse meeting. Likewise, car meetings do not lend themselves to training, examining documents, or taking notes. The case officer may record the meeting, but the audio quality in a moving car tends to be poor. Case officers under official cover often have cars with diplomatic license plates, making them conspicuous and susceptible to bugging by the local counterintelligence service. Sterile, locally plated vehicles are preferable.

20. The approval process for CIA covert action operations is very strict. The exact procedures are described in National Security Decision Directive 286 of October 15, 1987. NSDD 286 starts off by explaining the "policy context":

In discharging his constitutional responsibility for the conduct of foreign relations and for ensuring the security of the United States, the President may find it necessary that activities conducted in support of national foreign policy objectives abroad be planned and executed so that the role of the United States Government is not apparent or acknowledged publicly. Such activities, the failure or exposure of which may entail high costs, must be conducted only after the President reaches an informed judgment regarding their utility in particular circumstances. To the extent possible, they should be conducted only when we are confident that, if they are revealed, the American public would find them sensible.

NSDD 286 designates the assistant to the president for national security affairs as the "manager" of this process and as the president's "principal adviser" with respect to all "special activities" (covert action). The president's role in covert action is clearly laid out:

In all cases, special activities of the Central Intelligence Agency in foreign countries require . . . Findings by the President that such activities are important to the national security of the United States. Presidential Findings shall be obtained with respect to all CIA activities abroad, other than those activities that are intended solely for obtaining necessary intelligence.

Routine HUMINT is therefore specifically excluded from the requirement for a presidential finding; only CIA "covert action" comes under the directive. NSDD 286 specifies that the presidential finding must be in writing and the appropriate oversight committees of Congress must be notified. It is certainly fair to criticize the CIA for its failed or improper covert actions of the past, but critics of the CIA should keep in mind that the Agency does not act on its own. In each case, the NSC endorses the covert action and the president approves it . . . in writing.

21. Assessment and development are inherently dishonest. A target is led to believe the case officer's interest in him or her is sincere, whereas, in fact, it is entirely ulterior. Most case officers have no problem in rationalizing this deception as a necessary part of the process, but a few have moral qualms. During one of my overseas assignments, a young tandem couple reported for duty as brand-new case officers. She had a law degree; he was an engineer. They were bright and socially facile. They looked like natural recruiters to me, and I had high hopes for them. After less than a week at the CIA office, however, they asked to see me to discuss an important personal issue. It turns out that both the husband and wife

had serious ethical problems with developing targets under false pretenses. They said they simply could not bring themselves to mislead and to manipulate innocent people that way. My deputy and I had lengthy discussions with them and, at the end, concluded they could not be salvaged. I was very curious why their moral reservations had not shown up during training at the Farm. They said they had expressed serious doubts to their instructors, but had been told "everything would be fine" once they got to their first assignment. Everything was not fine. The couple resigned from the CIA and, the last I heard, they were driving a long-haul truck together in California.

22. As a Latin American diplomat assigned to Mexico City, Rosario would presumably have had easy social and professional access to other Latin American diplomats there, including Cubans, something American "diplomats" might have had trouble doing. Good access agents can significantly extend a case officer's assessment reach.

23. The French have a long tradition of tough and professional intelligence services. The foreign intelligence service is the DGSE (Direction Générale de la Sécurité Extérieure—General Direcorate for External Security), which replaced the infamous SDECE (Service de Documentation Extérieure et de Contreespionnage—Service for External Documentation and Counterespionage) in 1981. The SDECE (pronounced "zdeck") was known for its ruthlessness. It has been well documented that the SDECE engaged in assassinations, kidnappings, torture, hijackings, bombings, and other illegal activities, most notably in connection with France's colonial wars in Indochina and Algeria.

    The DGSE, which was supposed to be a cleaned up version of the SDECE, turned out to be not much different from its predecessor. In 1985, DGSE operatives blew up the Greenpeace ship *Rainbow Warrior* while it was in port in New Zealand. The *Rainbow Warrior* had aroused the ire of the French government because of its interference with French nuclear weapons tests in the South Pacific. More recently, the DGSE has specialized in industrial espionage, with the United States as its number one target. U.S. high-tech firms have been aggressively targeted by the DGSE, and there have been numerous reports of DGSE buggings, surreptitious entries, and other forms of espionage against American companies. The French internal security service is the DST (Direction de la Surveillance du Territoire—Directorate for Surveillance of the Territory). The DST has been especially adept at counterintelligence, not only against the former Soviet Union, which was hit hard by the DST, but also against any other country that dares to spy inside France. The DST has also established a reputation for effective counterterrorism operations.

24. The GRU is Russia's military intelligence service. The GRU has been in existence since 1918 and is as active today as it has ever been. Although primarily responsible for military, strategic, and scientific intelligence, the GRU has often overlapped with its civilian counterpart (KGB before 1991, SVRR since then) in its targeting and operations. Just like the SVRR, the GRU has *rezidenturas* in Russian embassies around the world. Russian military attachés are almost always GRU officers under cover. The GRU also makes extensive use of other official covers, such as trade representatives, Aeroflot employees, journalists, and others. Finally, it sends out some of its officers as "illegals," with false identities, "legends" (documented life stories), and, usually, non-Russian nationalities. Illegals can pose as students, business representatives, or persons of practically any other profession. (Most major intelligence services dispatch illegals, including the Russian SVRR, the Chinese MSS, the Cuban DGI, the Israeli Mossad, and many others.) The rough U.S. equivalent of an illegal is a NOC. The GRU has been penetrated by the CIA on several occasions, with the best known spies being Pyotr Popov and Oleg Penkovsky (see note 7 to the introduction) and General Dimitri Polyakov (initially recruited by the FBI), all GRU officers. The GRU can run good, solid operations, but it was my experience in counterintelligence that the GRU, as a rule, lagged behind the KGB/SVRR in professionalism, discipline, and tradecraft.

25. Establishing an agent's bona fides is a tricky process. There is always the danger that an agent is doubled by the other side or is peddling fabricated information. The best indicator of bona fides is usually production. If the agent is providing verifiable intelligence that is demonstrably damaging to the other side, he or she is most likely a valid agent. Polygraphs are also used to test an agent's bona fides (polygraphs are not infallible, but more often than not a skilled CIA polygraph operator can detect deception). With experience, a good case officer develops a sixth sense about an agent's bona fides. Some agents just don't "smell right," and an alert case officer can pick up subtle indications of doubling or fabrication. The CIA was badly burned by double agents run by the Cubans, East Germans, and Russians in the 1980s. As a result, the Agency instituted a formalized counterintelligence review process, known as the Agent Validation System, to test each case for possible hostile control.

26. CIA employees, both at home and abroad, are required to report any "close and continuing" relationships with foreign nationals that are not already officially sanctioned, for example, job-related relationships. Any kind of dating relationship, business dealing, or regular social interaction would clearly fall within the reporting parameters. The purpose of

the regulation, of course, is to provide the CIA with early counterintelligence monitoring of what might be a foreign intelligence service's effort to assess and develop CIA personnel. In most cases, the relationship is innocent and the employee is allowed to maintain the contact—as long as regular reporting continues. Requests by CIA employees to marry foreign nationals will often be approved, depending on the nationality and other circumstances, but might also lead to resignation or termination on security grounds.

27. The Mossad, the Israeli foreign intelligence service, is of world-class quality. Established in 1951, the Mossad has compiled a remarkable record of espionage and covert action successes. Mossad officers are tough and unbelievably dedicated. I had the opportunity to work with several of them during my career and developed the highest professional respect for them. They are absolutely ruthless in defending Israel's security interests and do not hesitate to engage in kidnappings and assassinations. In what can only be described as a "beautiful" operation, the Mossad tracked down in Argentina in 1960 Adolf Eichmann, the Nazi functionary responsible for the killing of millions of Jews in World War II, kidnapped him, and took him back to Israel to stand trial. Two Mossad illegals, Eliahu Cohen and Wolfgang Lotz, brilliantly penetrated the top leadership circles of Syria and Egypt respectively. In 1968, the Mossad hijacked a ship on the high seas and stole the two hundred tons of uranium on board, uranium that Israel needed for its secret nuclear weapons program. The list goes on and on.

The main focus of the Mossad today is fighting terrorism, which it does with a vengeance. The Mossad has made frequent raids into Beirut and elsewhere to assassinate terrorists and radical Arab leaders. Israel's internal security force is called Shin Bet. Shin Bet has been just as single-minded as the Mossad in defending Israel, particularly against sedition by the Arab population and espionage. Shin Bet has had its share of scandals, specifically revelations of assassinations, torture, false testimony, planting evidence, and other illegal acts. These "excesses of zeal" must be condemned, of course, but a large number of Israelis, perhaps a majority, accept the principle that violence is necessary to defeat violence. Israel is apparently a believer in Cicero's maxim, "The good (safety) of the people is the supreme law."

The United States and Israel are, of course, the "best of friends" and work together closely in the intelligence and counterterrorism arenas. That has not stopped them, however, from spying on each other. Major Yossi Amit, an Israeli military intelligence officer, was arrested by Shin Bet in 1986, tried in secret, and convicted of spying for the United

States. He was sentenced to twelve years in prison. In the same year, Jonathan Pollard, a U.S. Navy intelligence analyst, was convicted of spying for Israel and was sentenced to life in prison.

28. Agee runs a company in Havana called Cubalinda. Its mission is to promote tourism to Cuba and, more specifically, to help American tourists evade the U.S. government embargo on travel to Cuba.

29. I am a big fan of John Le Carré's spy fiction. *The Spy Who Came in from the Cold* is, in my opinion, one of the best-crafted spy novels ever written. Also outstanding are the books of his so-called Karla Trilogy: *Tinker, Tailor, Soldier, Spy*; *The Honourable Schoolboy*; and *Smiley's People*. The only other Le Carré spy novel I can strongly recommend is *A Perfect Spy*. Le Carré's more recent work has been of lower quality, I think, and of less interest to me. There are a few other authors of the genre that I particularly admire. Somerset Maugham's *Ashenden* stories, although published in 1928, still ring true to intelligence professionals. They are among my favorites. Graham Greene's espionage novels are also worth reading, especially *Our Man in Havana*, *The Quiet American*, and *The Human Factor*. Le Carré, Maugham, and Greene all served as British intelligence officers and have a good grasp of the psychology, terminology, and subtleties of the business. On the American side, I think the best author of spy fiction is Charles McCarry. He "gets it right." I have really enjoyed McCarry's Paul Christopher novels: *The Miernik Dossier*, *The Tears of Autumn*, *The Secret Lovers*, *The Last Supper*, *Second Sight*, and *Old Boys*. Tom Clancy's "Jack Ryan" series is okay, too, although I find some of his plot lines implausible. *The Hunt for Red October*, *The Bear and the Dragon*, and *Red Rabbit* are excellent. There is a tremendous amount of junk out there posing as spy fiction, and the informed reader should stay away. Just to give one particularly egregious example, I tell my intelligence students at the Bush School that I never want to catch them reading anything by Robert Ludlum. I don't want them wasting their time.

30. Deaddrops are pre-cased hiding places used by intelligence services to conduct exchanges with agents. The deaddrop site must be easily accessible to both case officer and agent; there must be cover for action in the area, an ostensible reason for being there; the site must be clearly describable so there will be no confusion about the precise location; and the "package" must be safe from disturbance by maintenance crews or casual pedestrians. The contents of the deaddrop are concealed inside an innocuous-looking item ("concealment device"), such as a crumpled up soft drink can, a hollowed out rock, a fake tree branch, or something similar. Deaddrops can work in both directions: case officer to agent or agent to case officer. A case officer might use a deaddrop to deliver

money, spy gear, instructions, or medicine to an agent; an agent would probably deliver documents, film, or computer disks to his or her case officer. Deaddrops are generally used in conjunction with signals—for example, a chalk mark on a post—to indicate "have loaded" and "have unloaded." One of the most shocking aspects of the Robert Hanssen spy case was that the deaddrop sites he loaded and unloaded for the KGB (and later for the SVRR) were close to his home (a very bad idea) and were used over and over again (a terrible idea). A pro like Hanssen should have known better.

31. The "pipeline" is CIA jargon for the lengthy screening, testing, training, and processing period that precedes a specific operational assignment, usually a denied area assignment.

32. An exfiltration is an operation to get an individual secretly and illegally out of a hostile area. Intelligence services study closely the border crossing and airport procedures in countries where exfiltrations might one day be necessary. The actual operation might involve a helicopter or boat pickup, a dash across the border in a remote area, disguise, false documents, or a whole range of ingenious techniques that are still classified. Two sensational examples of exfiltration operations were the escapes of KGB officer Oleg Gordievsky from the Soviet Union in 1985, orchestrated by MI6, and KGB officer Victor Sheymov, his wife, and daughter from the Soviet Union in 1980, carried out by the CIA.

33. During World War II, the U.S. Office of Strategic Services and the British Special Operations Executive parachuted what were called "Jedburgh teams" into Nazi-occupied France, Holland, Belgium, and Norway. Their purpose was to collect intelligence, conduct sabotage, and link up with local resistance forces. Each team usually consisted of one OSS officer, one SOE officer, and one national from the country involved. The SOE was established by Winston Churchill in 1940 to carry out guerilla and sabotage operations behind German lines or, as Churchill put it, "to set Europe ablaze." William Colby, an OSS veteran and the director of the CIA from 1973 to 1976, jumped into France and Norway as a Jedburgh during World War II.

34. Harold "Kim" Philby is one of history's most notorious spies. He became a Communist when he was a student at Cambridge in the early 1930s. He was recruited by the Soviet NKVD (predecessor of the KGB) and instructed to penetrate British intelligence. Bright and socially well-connected, Philby was able to join MI6 at the beginning of World War II, despite his Communist history. Thus began Philby's long dual career as a rapidly-rising MI6 officer and Soviet spy. Philby was in a position to betray virtually all British intelligence operations against the USSR—

and also many U.S. operations because of his close relationship with senior CIA officials, especially James Angleton, head of counterintelligence. Philby was under suspicion as a spy as early as 1951, but was able to survive and eventually escaped to the Soviet Union in 1963. He died there in 1988. It was later revealed that Philby was part of a large Soviet spy ring that the KGB called "the Cambridge Five." The other four members were Donald Maclean, Guy Burgess, Anthony Blunt, and John Cairncross.

35. All good intelligence services have sophisticated surreptitious entry capabilities. It is often useful to be able to break into a target's office or residence, to get done whatever needs to be done, and to exit without leaving a trace. A counterintelligence service, for example, might enter a suspect's home surreptitiously (with or without a warrant, depending on the country) in search of incriminating spy gear. Another target of a surreptitious entry might be a foreign embassy or consulate for the purpose of copying code books, implanting listening devices, or examining code machines. Specialists in this stealthy art obviously have to be skilled at picking locks, bypassing alarms, and cracking safes. The FBI refers to surreptitious entries as "black bag jobs."

36. Just like its civilian counterpart, the MSS, the Military Intelligence Department of the Chinese People's Liberation Army conducts large-scale intelligence operations in the U.S. The PLA/MID, or 2 PLA, as it is commonly called, has been particularly successful at stealing U.S. military technology. In October 2005, two Chinese-Americans and two Chinese resident aliens were arrested in California and charged with passing highly sensitive information on U.S. Navy technology to the Chinese, most likely to 2 PLA. One of the Chinese-Americans, who held a secret U.S. government security clearance, worked as an electrical engineer for a defense contractor firm in Anaheim, California, and admitted to passing substantial amounts of proprietary defense information to the Chinese for over twenty years. His wife, brother, and sister-in-law, who were also arrested, were involved in the operation as accomplices and couriers. The information passed illegally to the Chinese included sensitive technical data on U.S. submarines, propulsion systems for Navy warships, the Aegis weapons system, and a new catapult system for aircraft carriers. Federal investigators said the case could turn out to be one of the most damaging spy cases in the United States in the last twenty years. I believe the American people would be shocked and outraged if they knew the full extent of Chinese MSS and 2 PLA spying inside the United States.

37. Polygraphs for U.S. personnel in intelligence and other sensitive national

security positions are an awful but necessary ordeal. We all hate them. Every applicant to the CIA, FBI, and NSA is required to go through what is called a "full lifestyle" polygraph before being approved for employment. Other government agencies administer less invasive "counterintelligence only" polygraphs, limited to questions about possible involvement with foreign intelligence services. Full lifestyle polygraphs go into every aspect of an individual's background, even into the nooks and crannies. A polygraph examination—which can extend over several lengthy sessions—is rude, intrusive, and sometimes humiliating. Examiners are trained to be aggressive and confrontational when necessary. As a rule, single stupid events are not disqualifying (we have all done them), but events that indicate a pattern of criminal conduct, dishonesty, or disloyalty are.

When Meredith and I joined the CIA, even a single experimental use of a controlled substance was an absolute bar to employment. Today, with societal changes, that is no longer the case. The examiner looks instead at what kinds of drugs, how recently, under what circumstances, and whether the applicant ever dealt (that's bad). Other areas explored in great detail are alcohol use, foreign contacts, stealing, fraud, financial responsibility, abusive or other antisocial behaviors, disclosure of classified information (if relevant), and so on. It's a grueling process.

There is, of course, the problem of false positives, in other words, reactions to certain questions even though the individual is concealing nothing. The examiner and the subject can usually work through these problem areas and produce clean charts, but not always. Unfortunately, some well-qualified and upright applicants, especially those with a heightened sense of right and wrong, sometimes fail. Another problem is that certain sociopaths and born liars can occasionally squeak through; the CIA traitors Aldrich Ames and Larry Wu-Tai Chin are noteworthy examples. The CIA and other intelligence agencies conduct periodic repolygraphs of their employees on a random basis as part of the security reinvestigation process. (You know it's going to be a bad day at the CIA when you arrive at your office in the morning and find a green slip on your desk saying "report to Security immediately.") Much has been made of the so-called counter-polygraph measures—tranquilizers, concentration techniques, pain distractions (the old tack-in-the-shoe trick), etc. They don't work. I know all of them because of my work in counterintelligence—but I couldn't beat the blasted thing, even if I wanted to.

38. It's amazing what you can find in people's trash. When Aldrich Ames was under investigation, one of the FBI special agents working the case proposed a "trash cover" on him. This entailed some risk, because the

FBI would have to steal Ames's trash can at night, replace it temporarily with a look-alike, sort through it at a separate location, and then replace it exactly as it was before morning. The prospects of actually finding anything of value were low, but FBI management authorized the trash cover and obtained the necessary court approval. Incredibly, the FBI found drafts of notes Ames had prepared for his SVRR handlers and discarded printer ribbons with recoverable compromising text. Thank you, Rick, for being so stupid.

39. The Foreign Intelligence Surveillance Act (FISA) of 1978 established a special court, known as the Foreign Intelligence Surveillance Court (FISC), to authorize "warrantless" wiretaps and electronic eavesdropping against individuals and establishments suspected of involvement in espionage, sabotage, or terrorism in the United States on behalf of a foreign power or organization. The Act was later amended to allow the FISC to approve surreptitious entries (black bag jobs) in addition to electronic surveillance. The FISC is comprised of seven U.S. district judges from around the country, who serve on a rotating basis. All deliberations and decisions of the FISC are secret. The U.S. Department of Justice submits requests for electronic surveillance or surreptitious entry to the FISC on behalf of the FBI, NSA, and other U.S. government agencies and explains to the court why the requested action is necessary for U.S. national security. Few, if any, requests are turned down.

    FISA does not apply to U.S. counterintelligence activities overseas. A "spy scandal" broke out in late 2005 when the *New York Times* revealed that NSA had been intercepting communications between U.S. citizens in the United States and known or suspected terrorists outside the United States since shortly after the 9/11 attacks, without FISC approval. The secret program, according to a follow-up article in the *Washington Post*, was initiated by NSA on its own "authority" immediately after the attacks, but was made official by a presidential order in early 2002. Bush administration officials defended the president's actions by stating they clearly come under his constitutional duty to preserve and protect the nation, specifically under his presidential war power as formalized in the 2001 Authorization for Use of Military Force. Vice President Cheney said the intercepts were "a vital step" in ensuring America's security. He added that if the program had been in effect before 9/11, it might have picked up key conversations between the hijackers in the U.S. and their masters overseas. Critics of the program insist the president violated the law by bypassing the FISC and ordering electronic surveillance of U.S. citizens inside the United States without a warrant.

40. The largest and, in my opinion, the best of the U.S. government programs

to help U.S. companies defend themselves against foreign espionage is the FBI's DECA (Development of Espionage, Counterintelligence, and Counterterrorism Awareness) program. The FBI maintains regular contact with U.S. firms involved in "national critical technologies" and provides them with briefings, videotapes, and other materials on the nature of the foreign threats. Each FBI field office has a designated DECA coordinator. Tens of thousands of U.S. firms have received counterintelligence support from the FBI's DECA program.

41. Almost every spy service in the world, including the CIA, uses one-time pads for secret communications. One-time pads are sheets of randomly generated numbers, usually formatted into four- or five-digit groups. Each party to the secret communication—for example, the center and the *rezidentura*, or a case officer and an agent—uses the same one-time pad. By a simple process of alphabetic substitution, along with "false subtraction" and "false addition," the two sides can securely communicate with each other. Once a message is encrypted using a one-time pad, it can be passed to the other party in a deaddrop, transmitted by radio, sent by secret writing, or delivered by some other means. One-time pad systems are *absolutely* secure and unbreakable if the generated numbers are truly random (not a trivial problem), the same pad is never used for more than one message, and the pads have never fallen into the wrong hands.

42. ULTRA, one of the biggest secrets of World War II, was the British ability (shared with the Americans) to break enciphered German military communications, as well as some intelligence and diplomatic traffic, throughout the war. The German messages were encrypted using a machine called ENIGMA, which the Germans incorrectly considered unbreakable. ULTRA allowed the Allies to anticipate German military operations, including U-boat attacks on transatlantic shipping and bombing raids on Allied forces, saving countless lives in the process. The code name MAGIC refers to the U.S. ability (shared with the British) to break Japanese codes, enciphered on a machine called PURPLE, during World War II. F. W. Winterbotham's wonderful book, *The Ultra Secret*, published in 1974, was the first detailed account of British code breaking during the war.

43. When intelligence services conduct high-risk operations, such as meetings with unproven volunteers, narcotics traffickers, or terrorists, they frequently deploy a "countersurveillance" team to the meeting site to ensure that there is no hostile surveillance or other threatening presence in the area. The purpose of the team can be to protect the case officer in the event of an ambush or simply to verify that the person being met is

not under surveillance. The case officer does not go to the meeting site until he or she has been signaled by the countersurveillance team that it is safe to approach. Countersurveillance is a cat-and-mouse game, because the countersurveillance team is trying to spot the surveillance team without being spotted in return, and that's not always easy.

44. Some highly paid agents cannot safely absorb a large amount of extra income without attracting attention, particularly from the local counterintelligence authorities. To avoid this risk, agents often ask their handling services to keep all or part of their money for them in an "escrow account," usually interest bearing, which they can claim later, generally when they resettle or retire. The U.S. spy Jonathan Pollard had a generous escrow account with the Israelis. Several American spies had escrow accounts with the Russians. Escrow accounts require a great deal of trust, of course, but as a matter of honor (yes, honor) and reputation, all the intelligence services I'm aware of pay up when the time comes.

I can think of one really nasty violation of trust, however. During World War II, the Germans had a valuable agent, code-named "Cicero," who was the valet to the British ambassador in Turkey. The ambassador carelessly kept highly classified documents in his residence, which Cicero photographed for the Germans. The Germans showed their gratitude to Cicero—by paying him in counterfeit money.

45. One of the toughest and most thankless jobs in the world of spying is defector resettlement. The objective, of course, is to help the defector adjust to his or her new life in the new country and eventually become self-sufficient. Most defectors during the Cold War were from East to West. Only a handful of American traitors (Noel Field, Jeffrey Carney, William Martin, Bernon Mitchell, Edward Lee Howard, Glenn Souther, and a few others) resettled in Communist countries. There was, on the other hand, a flood of defectors in the other direction, mostly to the U.S. and U.K. Guilt, separation from loved ones, drinking problems, and other emotional difficulties are common with defectors. They are also, in many cases, frustrated and disoriented by the new culture and language. Some of the defectors to the United States, for example, had never been to the West before and spoke only their native language. They were totally unprepared for the reality of living in the United States.

I remember one Russian defector who, shortly after his arrival, was taken to a typical American grocery store. Afterwards, he told us, "That was nice, but I know it wasn't real; you just set that up to impress me." Another Russian defector seemed to be progressing well with his resettlement, and we thought he was ready to venture out a bit on his own. We gave him $200 in cash and told him to go, by himself, to a nearby shopping center to buy some clothes. He proudly set off. A short time later, he returned with a sack containing five pairs of shoes, nothing else. We said, "That's great, Yuri, but we thought you would buy a complete set of clothes." He answered, "Well, I was going to do that, but the first store I went into was a shoe store—and they had shoes!" (In the USSR, if consumer goods ever showed up on the shelf of a store, a rare occurrence, a Soviet shopper bought them immediately). Yet another defector, who had just been given his own apartment, excitedly called his resettlement officer one day and said, "You've got to come over here right away; something wonderful has happened!" When our officer arrived, the defector screamed, "I have just won five million dollars," as he held up his letter from Ed McMahon and Publisher's Clearing House.

Defector resettlement is a slow and painful process, and I take my hat off to the kind and patient people who do this important work for us. They do a good job. There are, unfortunately, occasional resettlement failures—even "redefections" and suicides—but most defectors to the United States have become happy and productive citizens.

46. Plausible deniability is the concept that allows the United States government, specifically the U.S. president himself, to claim no knowledge of or involvement in a covert action that goes public, particularly if it has gone badly.

47. "Psyops," or psychological operations, are operations that send carefully selected and tailored information, whether true or false, to foreign targets in an attempt to influence their judgments, actions, and morale. They are often distinguished from "propaganda" operations in that psyops are meant to influence behavior, whereas propaganda operations are meant to change beliefs. Psyops usually have short-term tactical objectives, often in battlefield situations, and are therefore, in the U.S. intelligence community, primarily the responsibility of the U.S. military.

──THE ESSENTIAL── INTELLIGENCE LIBRARY

If I were to start all over again to build a personal intelligence library, these are the first fifty books I would acquire. Limiting the list to fifty was quite an undertaking, because the intelligence literature is so incredibly rich and is expanding every day. For me, however, these books have made a lasting impression and have contributed significantly to my professional knowledge. Anyone who reads all fifty of these books will have the equivalent of a master's degree in advanced intelligence studies.

Aldouby, Zwy, and Jerrold Ballinger. *The Shattered Silence: The Eli Cohen Affair*. New York: Lancer Books, 1971.
> An absolutely riveting account of how the Mossad inserted an illegal into Syria in the 1960s.

Ambrose, Stephen E. *Ike's Spies: Eisenhower and the Espionage Establishment*. Garden City, NY: Doubleday, 1981.
> The best short history of how Eisenhower used intelligence during World War II and revolutionized it during his presidency.

Andrew, Christopher, and Vasili Mitrokhin. *The Sword and the Shield: The Mitrokhin Archive and the Secret History of the KGB*. New York: Basic Books, 1999.
> The sensational book that used actual KGB archival material to describe in detail KGB espionage operations against the West.

Andrew, Christopher, and Oleg Gordievsky. *KGB: The Inside Story*. New York: HarperCollins, 1990.
> The bible on the KGB, indispensable reading, cowritten by the best contemporary British intelligence historian and a KGB defector.

Baer, Robert. *See No Evil: The True Story of a Ground Soldier in the CIA's War on Terrorism*. New York: Crown Publishers, 2002.
> Middle Eastern intrigue, as lived by a brave frontline CIA case officer, and his stinging indictment of what he believes the CIA has become today.

Bamford, James. *Body of Secrets: Anatomy of the Ultra-Secret National Security Agency from the Cold War Through the Dawn of a New Era*. New York: Anchor Books, 2001.

A valuable primer on the history of U.S. SIGINT, as practiced by one of America's largest but least-known intelligence services.

Barron, John. *Operation Solo: The FBI's Man in the Kremlin.* Washington, DC: Regnery Publishing, 1996.

The incredible story of the FBI's brilliant twenty-seven-year penetration of the top leadership circles of the USSR, must reading for students of double-agent operations.

Bearden, Milt, and James Risen. *The Main Enemy: The Inside Story of the CIA's Final Showdown with the KGB.* New York: Random House, 2003.

A detailed chronicle of the end game in the historic confrontation between two great intelligence services, a rare glimpse into what was really going on in Washington, Moscow, and Afghanistan from 1985 to 1991.

Blitzer, Wolf. *Territory of Lies: The Exclusive Story of Jonathan Jay Pollard: The American Who Spied on His Country for Israel and How He Was Betrayed.* New York: Harper & Row, 1989.

The treasonous journey of a young American Jew who traded a career in U.S. Navy intelligence for life behind bars as a convicted spy.

Blum, Howard. *I Pledge Allegiance: The True Story of the Walkers: An American Spy Family.* New York: Simon & Schuster, 1987.

A well-written analysis of the long and devastating spy career of Navy warrant officer John Walker, especially valuable for its keen psychological insights into the spy and his dysfunctional family.

Brown, Anthony Cave. *Bodyguard of Lies.* New York: Harper & Row, 1975.

An intelligence classic, the remarkable story of British intelligence operations in Europe before and during World War II, a masterpiece of denial and deception.

————. *The Last Hero: Wild Bill Donovan.* New York: Times Books, 1982.

A superb biography of an intelligence hero, the man more responsible than anyone else for making America a spying superpower.

Clarridge, Duane R. *A Spy for All Seasons: My Life in the CIA.* New York: Scribner's, 1997.

The colorful and readable book that broke new ground in how much a case officer could say about past operations.

Colby, William E. *Honorable Men: My Life in the CIA.* New York: Simon & Schuster, 1978.

The autobiography of the OSS officer who went on to become the director of the CIA during a period of unprecedented turmoil and crisis in the U.S. intelligence community.

Early, Pete. *Confessions of a Spy: The Real Story of Aldrich Ames.* New York: Putnam, 1997.

A skillful use of Ames's own words to penetrate his arrogant and glib façade—and to expose him for what he is, the CIA's worst traitor ever.

Farago, Ladislas. *The Game of the Foxes: The Untold Story of German Espionage in the United States and Great Britain During World War II.* New York: McKay, 1971.

One of the first intelligence books I read, still one of my favorites, a meticulous recreation of how Abwehr spies operated inside enemy territory during the war.

Frenay, Henri. *The Night Will End.* London: Hodder & Stoughton, 1977.

A book that made a strong impression on me, the memoirs of the brilliant, driven, and fearless leader of the French Resistance during World War II.

Gates, Robert M. *From the Shadows: The Ultimate Insider's Story of Five Presidents and How They Won the Cold War.* New York: Simon & Schuster, 1996.

The exemplary career of the only person ever to rise from entry-level analyst to director of the CIA.

Gup, Ted. *The Book of Honor: Covert Lives and Classified Deaths at the CIA.* New York: Doubleday, 2000.

A book that is extremely valuable for its portrayal of who CIA officers are and why they do what they do.

Helms, Richard, and William Hood. *A Look Over My Shoulder: A Life in the Central Intelligence Agency.*

The autobiography of the spy's spy, a man I was privileged to know, the professional intelligence officer I admired and respected above all others.

Höhne, Heinz. *Canaris: Hitler's Master Spy.* Garden City, NY: Doubleday, 1979.

The balanced and well-researched life story of the head of German military intelligence during World War II, a courageous patriot who opposed Hitler and paid with his life.

Holm, Richard L. *The American Agent: My Life in the CIA.* London: St. Ermin's Press, 2003. Reprinted, 2005.

Perhaps the best of the case officer books, written by an accomplished spy and true hero.

Hood, William. *Mole: The True Story of the First Russian Intelligence Officer Recruited by the CIA.* New York: Norton, 1982.

The fascinating story of Soviet spy Pyotr Popov, with an excellent analysis of the complex tradecraft and counterintelligence issues that arose in his handling.

John, Otto. *Twice Through the Lines: The Autobiography of Otto John.* New York: Harper & Row, 1972.

The self-serving and ultimately unconvincing explanation of what really happened to this high-ranking West German intelligence officer in 1954, a book to be read as a study of amorality, betrayal, and conflicted loyalties.

Levchenko, Stanislav. *On the Wrong Side: My Life in the KGB*. New York: Dell, 1989.

An honest and well-written account of what it was like to serve in a KGB *rezidentura* overseas.

Lindsey, Robert. *The Falcon and the Snowman: A True Story of Friendship and Espionage*. London: Jonathan Cape, 1980.

The tragic tale of how two middle-class American boys thought they could make big money by selling U.S. satellite secrets to the KGB.

Mangold, Tom. *Cold Warrior: James Jesus Angleton: The CIA's Master Spy Hunter.* New York: Simon & Schuster, 1991.

The first book that anyone considering a career in the arcane world of counterintelligence should read.

Martin, David C. *Wilderness of Mirrors*. New York: Harper & Row, 1980. Reprinted, 2003.

A troubling descent into the Stygian Angletonian nightmare of the '50s and '60s. *Caveat lector.*

Masterman, Sir John C. *The Double-Cross System in the War of 1939 to 1945.* New Haven, CT: Yale University Press, 1972.

The classic textbook on how to run fiendishly clever and meticulously planned deception operations during wartime.

Moyar, Mark. *Phoenix and the Birds of Prey: The CIA's Secret Campaign to Destroy the Viet Cong*. Annapolis, MD: Naval Institute Press, 1997.

The authoritative elucidation of what the Phoenix program really was, a long overdue correction of the historical record.

Persico, Joseph E. *Piercing the Reich: The Penetration of Nazi Germany by American Secret Agents during World War II*. New York: Viking Press, 1979.

Still the best and most accurate account of the brilliant OSS penetration operations into Germany and Austria during World War II.

Philby, Kim. *My Silent War.* New York: Grove Press, 1968.

The British traitor's beguilingly dishonest attempt to justify his life of betrayal.

Richelson, Jeffrey T. *The Wizards of Langley: Inside the CIA's Directorate of Science and Technology*. Boulder, CO: Westview Press, 2002.

An amazingly detailed look at how CIA scientists and engineers reshaped the world of spying.

Riebling, Mark. *Wedge: The Secret War Between the FBI and the CIA*. New York: Knopf, 1994.

The infuriating story of how two fine organizations failed the American people by bogging themselves down in petty squabbling and turf wars.

Saunders, Frances Stonor. *The Cultural Cold War: The CIA and the World of Arts and Letters.* New York: New Press, 1999.

A well-researched study of the CIA's elaborate propaganda and cultural programs of the Cold War, worth reading even though the author's anti-CIA bias sometimes goes over the top.

Schecter, Jerrold L., and Peter Deriabin. *The Spy Who Saved the World: How a Soviet Colonel Changed the Course of the Cold War.* New York: Scribner's, 1992.

The definitive account of the espionage career of Colonel Oleg Penkovsky, probably the best spy the CIA has ever had.

Schroen, Gary C. *First In: An Insider's Account of How the CIA Spearheaded the War on Terror in Afghanistan.* New York: Ballantine Books, 2005.

Indispensable reading for anyone who wants to understand the role of covert action in fighting terrorism.

Shevchenko, Arkady N. *Breaking with Moscow.* New York: Knopf, 1985.

The gripping story of the high-ranking Soviet diplomat who became so disillusioned with the Communist system that he offered his services to U.S. intelligence as a way out.

Sontag, Sherry, and Christopher Drew. *Blind Man's Bluff: The Untold Story of American Submarine Espionage.* New York: PublicAffairs, 1998.

The mind-boggling history of underwater spying during the Cold War, so ingenious and brazen that it hardly seems real.

Stevenson, William. *A Man Called Intrepid: The Secret War.* New York: Ballantine Books, 1977.

The long suppressed story of how Sir William Stephenson, head of British Security Coordination in New York from 1940 to 1945, did everything in his power—sometimes legally, sometimes not—to get America into the war and to coordinate U.S. and British intelligence efforts against Germany and Japan.

Stiller, Werner. *Beyond the Wall: Memoirs of an East and West German Spy.* Washington, DC: Brassey's (U.S.), 1992.

One of the few available inside looks at how the superb East German foreign intelligence service operated, articulately told by a bright young Stasi case officer who defected to the West in 1979.

Thomas, Evan. *The Very Best Men—Four Who Dared: The Early Years of the CIA.* New York: Simon & Schuster, 1995.

The compelling stories of four of the early giants of U.S. intelligence: Frank Wisner, Desmond FitzGerald, Tracy Barnes, and Richard Bissell.

Trepper, Leopold. *The Great Game: The Story of the Red Orchestra.* London: Sphere Books, 1977.

The autobiography of the master spy who ran the Soviet intelligence networks in Nazi-occupied Europe during World War II and who, if there were ever to be a Hall of Fame for spies, would be a charter member.

Warner, Roger. *Back Fire: The CIA's Secret War in Laos and Its Link to the War in Vietnam.* New York: Simon & Schuster, 1995.
A detailed account of the CIA's large but little-known paramilitary operation in Laos in the '60s and early '70s, with unforgettable portraits of the CIA officers who served there.

Weinstein, Allen, and Alexander Vasiliev. *The Haunted Wood: Soviet Espionage in America—The Stalin Era.* New York: Random House, 1999.
The shocking story of Soviet espionage in the United States in the '30s and '40s, carefully researched and written by one of today's best writers on intelligence subjects.

Winks, Robin W. *Cloak & Gown: Scholars in the Secret War, 1939–1961.* New York: William Morrow, 1987.
A well-documented study of the early years of collaboration between spies and professors.

Wise, David. *Spy: The Inside Story of How the FBI's Robert Hanssen Betrayed America.* New York: Random House, 2002.
The best, by far, of the many Hanssen books, a valiant attempt to unlock the psyche of a man who is still a relative mystery to FBI and CIA psychological profilers.

Winterbotham, F. W. *The Ultra Secret.* New York: Dell, 1974.
The full story, told by the man who ran the operation, of perhaps the greatest intelligence triumph of all time, the British success in breaking Germany's codes during World War II.

Wolf, Markus. *Man Without a Face: The Autobiography of Communism's Great Spymaster.* New York: Random House, 1997.
The surprisingly candid memoirs of the mastermind behind the East German foreign intelligence service, the toughest service the West faced in the Cold War.

Yardley, Herbert O. *The American Black Chamber.* Indianapolis, IN: Bobbs-Merrill, 1931. Reprinted, 1981.
The still enthralling account of how a mathematical genius broke foreign codes for the War Department and the State Department from 1917 to 1929 and moved the United States, at least temporarily, into the exciting world of SIGINT.

COMMENTATORS

Allen, David S.
David Allen is associate professor and chair, Department of Journalism and Mass Communication, at the University of Wisconsin–Milwaukee. A former journalist, he is the author of the book, *Democracy, Inc.: The Press and Law in the Corporate Rationalization of the Public Sphere*. He is the coeditor, with Robert Jensen, of the book *Freeing the First Amendment: Critical Perspectives on Freedom of Expression*. His research has appeared in journals such as *Communication Law & Policy*; *Journal of Mass Media Ethics*; *Free Speech Yearbook*; *Journalism: Theory, Practice, and Criticism*; and *Angelaki: Journal of the Theoretical Humanities*. From 2002 to 2003 he served as chair of the Media Ethics Division of the Association for Education in Journalism and Mass Communications.

Anderson, Terry H.
Terry Anderson is a professor of history at Texas A&M University. He has taught in Malaysia and Japan and was a Fulbright professor in China and the Mary Ball Washington professor of American history at University College Dublin in 2001 and 2002. He has written numerous articles on the Vietnam War era. He is the co-author of *A Flying Tiger's Diary* (with fighter pilot Charles Bond Jr.) and the author of *The United States, Great Britain, and the Cold War, 1944–1947*; *The Movement and the Sixties*; *The Pursuit of Fairness: A History of Affirmative Action*; and *The Sixties*.

Bohn, Michael K.
Michael Bohn was a career naval intelligence officer. His assignments included operational and scientific intelligence analysis, support to covert intelligence operations, and intelligence analysis management. He conducted reviews of U.S. counterespionage operations and assessed methodologies to identify U.S. citizens spying for foreign countries. He was director of the White House Situation Room during the Reagan administration, with access to the most sensitive intelligence collection operations of the U.S. government. He is the author of *Nerve Center: Inside the White House Situation Room*

and *The Achille Lauro Hijacking: Lessons in the Politics and Prejudice of Terrorism.*

Bosley, Jackson W.

Jack Bosley is an Indiana native. He has a background in Oriental studies at Stanford University's Graduate School. He served in World War II in the 82nd, 101st, and 17th Airborne Divisions. He was recalled for duty in the Korean War and was detailed to the CIA. He served in several Asian countries as a CIA case officer. His duties included political and economic reporting, end-use observation of foreign and military aid, and monitoring the military preparedness of friendly nations.

Botea, Roxana

Roxana Botea is a second-year Ph.D. student and teaching assistant in the Political Science Department at the Maxwell School in Syracuse, New York. Her sub-fields are international relations and public administration. She is originally from Romania. She completed her undergraduate studies at Arizona State University as a Presidential Scholar, graduating *summa cum laude* in economics and Spanish. Her interests include foreign affairs, defense policy, international security, counterterrorism, and intelligence. She is cofounder of the Student Association on Terrorism and Security Analysis, an international and interdisciplinary graduate student association dedicated to the critical analysis of terrorism, counterterrorism policy, and related national and international security issues. She also interns with the National Security Studies Program, a professional and training program for the Department of Defense hosted by the Maxwell School.

Boyles, Stephanie L.

Stephanie Boyles is a wildlife biologist for People for the Ethical Treatment of Animals, the world's largest animal rights organization, with more than 800,000 members and supporters dedicated to animal protection. She graduated from the College of Notre Dame of Maryland with a B.A. in biology and philosophy in 1994. She received an M.S. in environmental science from Christopher Newport University in 2005. She worked as a field intern at Patuxent Wildlife Research Center in Laurel, Maryland; a research assistant and lab manager at Johns Hopkins University, Duke University, and North Carolina State University; and a wildlife field research assistant for Virginia Tech before accepting a position with PETA in 1998. As the wildlife biologist at PETA, she focuses on human-wildlife conflict resolution, specifically helping federal, state, and local agencies, corporations, and businesses develop humane, cost-efficient wildlife control policies and procedures. She and her family live in the Hampton Roads area of Virginia.

Brekke-Esparza, Lauraine
Lauraine Brekke-Esparza has served as city manager of Del Mar, California, since January of 1993. Before that, she was assistant city manager in Ventura, California, for seven years. Other positions included seven years with the Seattle City Council, the last three of which were as executive director responsible for legislative analysis. She was also the director of executive administration for King County, Washington, for four years. She has a B.A. in history and political science from Rosemont College in Pennsylvania and a master's degree in public administration from the University of Washington.

Brewer, Ray
Ray Brewer served in the CIA for twenty-nine years as an information management officer. He is now retired and living in Alabama.

Brown, Philip
Phil Brown served from 1965 to 1996 in the U.S. Information Agency Foreign Service. He had public diplomacy assignments in French Africa, the Soviet Union, and France. During his tours in Moscow, he served as press attaché from 1978 to 1981 (the Brezhnev years) and as public affairs officer from 1987 to 1990 (the Gorbachev period). He was also press attaché at the American Embassy in Paris from 1981 to 1986. In Moscow, he was an occasional paddle tennis partner of Jim Olson.

Clearfield, Abraham
Abraham Clearfield was born in Philadelphia. He received a B.A. and an M.A. in chemistry from Temple University and a Ph.D. from Rutgers University. After a year in the research laboratories of the Army Quartermaster Corps, he worked for the Titanium Alloy Manufacturing Company as a chemist, rising to the rank of senior scientist. In 1963 he joined the faculty of Ohio University in Athens, where he became a full professor in 1967. He joined the faculty of Texas A&M University in 1976. He has won the Southwest Research Award of the American Chemical Society and the Sigma Chi Distinguished Scientist Award. He was awarded an honorary Ph.D. from Oviedo University in Spain. He has published nearly 500 research papers, holds twenty patents, and has edited three books. He lives in College Station, Texas, with Ruth, his wife of fifty-five years. He is a member of Congregation Beth Shalom in Bryan, Texas, and has taught Jewish history courses.

Corbin, Louise
Louise Corbin joined the CIA as a teaching assistant at the language school. Later, while overseas, she provided technical support to agent operations.

At CIA headquarters, she was a staff officer in the Soviet/East European Division and worked on operations against Soviet and East European targets. In Vienna, she was the CIA representative at the Confidence and Security Building Measures negotiations.

Corbin, Richard L.

Dick Corbin served for twenty-eight years in the CIA's Directorate of Operations, focusing largely on the Soviet Union. His duties included five overseas tours. He retired from the CIA in 1995. Since 1999, he has been working with the U.S. Department of Energy to improve its counterintelligence program.

Culbertson, Eugene

Eugene Culbertson is a retired senior intelligence service officer in the CIA's Directorate of Operations. He had postings at CIA headquarters in addition to twenty-two years of clandestine service overseas in Europe, Africa, and the Middle East.

Drogin, Bob

Bob Drogin covers intelligence and national security in the Washington bureau of the *Los Angeles Times*. He previously worked as a foreign correspondent for the *Times* in Southeast Asia, South Asia, and Africa, and has reported on international developments from more than forty countries. He has won or shared numerous awards for his journalism, including a Pulitzer Prize. He has also worked abroad for a United Nations agency.

Edger, David N.

Dave Edger retired from the CIA following a thirty-five-year career in clandestine operations. During his career, he served in numerous executive positions in Washington, including associate deputy director for operations, where he was the senior officer who supervised the worldwide operations of the CIA's Clandestine Service. He also served in various operational and executive positions around the world and was involved in all phases of the CIA's mission. His principal areas of expertise include human source collection, counterterrorism, and paramilitary operations. After retirement from the CIA, he founded 3CI Consulting LLC, a company that provided security and counterterrorism advice to major American corporations, academic institutions, and organizations. He is the author of *Intelligence Operations in Business*, a guidebook for executives. He has spoken widely across the United States and has appeared often on radio and television programs. He has been a visiting professor at the University of Oklahoma for three years, teaching courses in intelligence, diplomacy, and political science.

Everett, Randy W.

Dr. Randy W. Everett, M.D., was born in 1956 and raised in Colorado and Utah. He attended Utah State University and Brigham Young prior to graduating from Baylor College of Medicine in 1984. He completed his urology residency at USC/Los Angeles County Medical Center in 1990 and then settled in Fort Collins, Colorado. His wife Ruth Ann and he are the parents of five sons. He is a former scoutmaster and is currently a bishop in the Church of Jesus Christ of Latter-day Saints.

Feaver, Peter D.

Feaver (Ph.D., Harvard, 1990) is the Alexander F. Hehmeyer Professor of Political Science and Public Policy at Duke University and director of the Triangle Institute for Security Studies. He has written several books on American civil-military relations, most recently *Armed Servants*, (Harvard, 2003), and *Choosing Your Battles* (Princeton, 2004, coauthored with Christopher Gelpi). He is presently directing a research project looking at the willingness of the American public to pay the human costs of war.

Forbey, Sarah

Sarah Forbey earned a master's of international affairs degree in national security studies from the George Bush School of Government and Public Service at Texas A&M University. Her research interests include Central Asia and the Caucasus. She holds a master's degree in film from the University of London and has written on French cinema and animation. She is committed to the ethical conduct of U.S. foreign policy.

Gerber, Burton

Burton Gerber served thirty-nine years as an operations officer in the CIA, much of that time overseas. In retirement, he volunteers at a number of organizations and speaks on ethics at universities and in other venues. With Professor Jennifer Sims, he is coeditor of *Transforming U.S. Intelligence*, a book published by Georgetown University Press. He is a member of the Council on Foreign Relations, the Royal Society for Asian Affairs, and the Order of Malta. He received a B.A. with high honors from Michigan State University.

Gerstenschlager, Burke

Burke Gerstenschlager is a writer, poet, and teacher of Latin and Western humanities. He received his B.A. at the University of Texas in Austin and his Master of Divinity at Yale University Divinity School. He is interested in the various interpretations of the Bible in popular Americana, contemporary theology about virtue ethics and postmodernity, and gender roles in Greco-Roman culture and the early Christian church. He resides in New Haven, Connecticut.

Graving, Richard

Richard Graving is professor of law at South Texas College of Law in Houston and adjunct professor at the George Bush School of Government and Public Service at Texas A&M University. For more than fifty years he has practiced and taught in the fields of international and comparative law, with more than twenty years of overseas residence, including Argentina, England, Mexico, and Spain. He is a graduate of the University of Minnesota (B.A. 1950) and Harvard Law School (J.D. 1953). He is a member of the bars of Minnesota, New York, Pennsylvania, and Texas. He is an Army veteran and a forty-year member of the American Society of International Law.

Gronbeck, Bruce E.

Bruce Gronbeck is the A. Craig Baird Distinguished Professor of Public Address and the director of the University of Iowa Center for Media Studies and Political Culture. Working from Iowa's Department of Communication Studies, he is a specialist in political rhetoric, media, and culture. He is the author or editor of ten books as well as dozens of book chapters and articles. He has been president of the National Communication Association and a Fulbright lecturer in Sweden, Finland, and Italy. He holds honorary degrees from Concordia College in Minnesota, Uppsala University in Sweden, and Jyvaskyla University in Finland.

Grunwald, Henry

Henry Grunwald was editor-in-chief of Time, Inc., from 1979 to 1987 and a member of the company's board of directors. Before that, from 1968 to 1977, he was managing editor of *Time* magazine. He served as U.S. ambassador to Austria from 1988 to 1990, having been appointed by President Reagan and reappointed by President Bush. After his return from Vienna, he wrote essays and articles. His autobiography *One Man's America* was published by Doubleday in 1997. *Twilight: Losing Sight, Gaining Insight* was published in 1999, and a historical novel, *A Saint, More or Less*, was published by Random House in 2004. Born in Vienna, he came to America at the age of seventeen. He started with *Time* as a copy boy while enrolled at New York University. He joined the magazine full-time after his graduation. He died in 2005.

Guido, John

John Guido is the director of law enforcement and security programs at the National Emergency Response and Rescue Training Center at Texas A&M University. A former FBI senior executive, he directed international operations and was a member of the FBI executive board. During his thirty-year FBI career, he served in a variety of investigative and management positions at FBI headquarters, in three domestic field offices, and as the legal attaché at the American Embassy in London. He is a graduate of the State Department Foreign Service Institute Senior Seminar and the FBI Executive Development Institute. He has served as a member of the International Association of Chiefs of Police International Advisory Committee and is currently working with the Terrorism Committee. He is a former U.S. Navy officer and a Vietnam veteran.

Hannesschlager, Mike

Mike Hannesschlager was the executive director of the Texas Christian Coalition from 2001 to 2005. He lobbied for pro-life, pro-family legislation, and organized Christians at the grassroots. Before the elections of 2004, he distributed millions of pieces of nonpartisan voter education material across Texas. He is now a student in the national security track at the George Bush School of Government and Public Service at Texas A&M University.

Hedley, John

John Hollister Hedley, Ph.D., served for more than thirty years in the CIA. He edited the President's Daily Brief, briefed the PDB at the White House, served as managing editor of the National Intelligence Daily, and was chairman of the CIA's Publications Review Board. Now retired, he has taught intelligence at Georgetown University and worked part-time on contract for the Center for the Study of Intelligence and the National Intelligence Council.

Herrington, Stuart

Colonel Stu Herrington retired from the U.S. Army after thirty years of active duty. He specialized in counterintelligence, human intelligence, and interrogation of prisoners and detainees. He has a B.A. from Duquesne University, an M.A. from the University of Florida, and an honorary doctorate of humane letters from Duquesne University. He served in Vietnam, Operation Just Cause (Panama), and Operation Desert Storm. In the last two assignments he was commandant of strategic interrogation centers for high-value prisoners. Since his retirement, he has visited Guantanamo in 2002 and Iraq in 2003 to evaluate interrogation procedures. He is the author of *Stalking the Vietcong: Inside Operation Phoenix* and *Traitors Among Us: Inside the Spy Catcher's World*.

Inman, Admiral Bobby R.

Admiral Bobby Inman graduated from the University of Texas in 1950 and from the National War College in 1972. He served in the U.S. Navy from 1951 to 1982, when he retired with the permanent rank of admiral. While on active duty, he served as director of the National Security Agency and deputy director of central intelligence. After retirement from the Navy, he was chairman and chief executive officer of the Microelectronics and Computer Technology Corporation in Austin, Texas, for four years and chairman, president, and chief executive officer of Westmark Systems, Inc., a privately owned electronics industry holding company for three years. He also served as chairman of the Federal Reserve Bank of Dallas from 1987 through 1990. His primary activity since 1990 has been investing in startup technology companies. He was appointed as a tenured professor holding the Lyndon B. Johnson Centennial Chair in National Policy at the University of Texas in 2001.

Jebb, Colonel Cindy R.

Colonel Cindy Jebb is professor and director of comparative politics and security studies in the Department of Social Sciences at the U.S. Military Academy. She has served in numerous command and staff positions in the U.S. and overseas, to include tours with the 1st Armored Division, III Corps, and the National Security Agency. During 2000 and 2001, she served as USMA Fellow at the Naval War College, where she taught the graduate-level course on strategy and force planning. She is the author of *Bridging the Gap: Ethnicity, Legitimacy, and State Alignment in the International System* (Lexington, 2004) and *Mapping Macedonia: Idea and Identity,* coauthored with P. H. Liotta (Praeger, 2004). Her book *The Fight for Legitimacy: Democracy Versus Terrorism,* also coauthored with P. H. Liotta, is forthcoming. She received a Ph.D. in political science from Duke University in 1997, an M.A. in political science from Duke in 1992, an M.A. in national security and strategic studies from the Naval War College in 2000, and a B.S. from the United States Military Academy in 1982.

Jensen, Robert

Robert Jensen is an associate professor of journalism at the University of Texas in Austin. He completed his Ph.D. in media law and ethics at the University of Minnesota. Before that, he worked for a decade as a professional journalist. He is the director of the Senior Fellows Program, the honors program of the University of Texas College of Communication. He is involved in a number of activist groups working against U.S. military and economic domination of the rest of the world. He is the author of *Citizens of the Empire: The Struggle to Claim Our Humanity* and *Writing Dissent: Taking Radical Ideas from the Margin to the Mainstream*, and coauthor of *Pornography: The Production and Consumption of Inequality.*

Lake, Joseph E.

Ambassador Joseph E. Lake is a research associate at the John Goodwin Tower Center for Political Studies at Southern Methodist University and a consultant on international affairs, management, and information technology. He served as U.S. ambassador to Albania and Mongolia as well as deputy assistant secretary of state. He is the former director of international affairs for the City of Dallas. He has appeared on CNN, PBS, the Discovery Channel, radio and television news programs, World Net, Mongolian Television, and Taiwan Television. During his thirty-five-year career in the Department of State he served ten years in East Asia, six years in West Africa, and five years in the Balkans. In the United States he served in the office of the secretary of state and at the U.S. Mission to the United Nations.

Lee, Kyu Mani

Kyu Mani Lee, Ph.D., was an intelligence officer for the Korean Air Force from 1965 to 1970. He was director of mental health for the State of Kansas from 1988 to 1992 and superintendent of Larned State Hospital in Kansas from 1992 to 2001. He now lives in Colorado.

Lieser, Mary Lee

Mary Lee Lieser worked at CIA headquarters and overseas as an analyst in the Directorate of Operations, beginning in 1961 and, with breaks, until 1994.

Lieser, William D.

Bill Lieser was born in California. He received a B.A. in political science from the University of California in Berkeley in 1963 and an M.A. in international relations from Boston University in 1968. He joined the CIA as a junior officer trainee in 1963. He served abroad as an operations officer and manager for twenty years, working primarily against Soviet and Warsaw Pact targets. He was chief of liaison with the House of Representatives in the DCI Office of Congressional Affairs from 1993 to 1995 and a senior inspector in the Office of the Inspector General from 1995 to 1997. He retired from the CIA in January 1997 and is currently self-employed as a travel consultant.

Life, Richard

Captain Richard "Dick" Life, U.S. Navy (retired), was raised in small towns in West Virginia and Ohio. He was an Eagle Scout and an athlete. He grew up in a very conservative Southern Baptist family, but after graduating from the U.S. Naval Academy in 1962 he married a Catholic and converted. The Lifes have six children; two were born to them and four are Korean orphans they adopted. His twenty-nine-year Navy career began in diesel submarines. He had deployments to the Mediterranean and also conducted special infiltration missions along the South Vietnamese coast. His final twenty-four years in the Navy were in naval intelligence. He served primarily as an overt human intelligence collector with tours of duty in Vietnam, Moscow, West Germany, and the United States. He retired from the Navy in 1991 and now volunteers for various church- and State Department–funded programs that focus on creating economic and political stability in former Communist countries. He has taught political science courses at the University of Northern Colorado and lectures frequently on foreign affairs, national security issues, leadership, and ethics.

Mason, Harry
Professor Harry Mason joined the Patterson School at the University of Kentucky in 2004 after a forty-two-year career in intelligence. He served in domestic and foreign assignments with the CIA and related organizations. He was promoted to deputy director for intelligence community programs and budgets in the Carter and Reagan administrations. He was a consultant and president of a security company before joining the Patterson faculty.

███, John

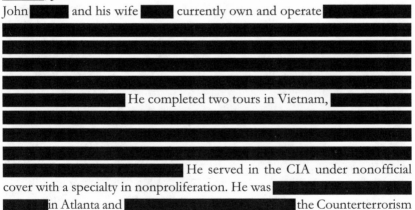

John ███ and his wife ███ currently own and operate ███ ... He completed two tours in Vietnam, ... He served in the CIA under nonofficial cover with a specialty in nonproliferation. He was ███ in Atlanta and ███ the Counterterrorism Center, an organization established after September 11, 2001, to prosecute the war on terror, principally in Afghanistan and Yemen. He is the recipient of the Intelligence Medal of Merit (two awards), George Bush Award, and Director's Award. He retired from the CIA as a member of the Senior Intelligence Service.

Mathis, Margaretta
Margaretta Mathis is a doctoral candidate at the University of Texas at Austin.

She graduated from Ohio Wesleyan University with a B.A. in politics and government and has a master's of international management from Thunderbird, the Garvin School of International Management. She has international experience in education, business, nonprofit, and public-private partnership in Europe, Russia, and Nigeria. She has held positions as division director for the Governor's Community Policy Office in Arizona, staff representative in the office of Senator John McCain, and researcher for international trade legislation at the Committee on Ways and Means in the U.S. House of Representatives. She serves on the executive council of Prepare America, an organization that connects colleges across America to enhance first-responder capacity for homeland security.

Meacham, Margaret
Margaret Meacham is working on a Ph.D. in higher education administration at the University of Texas in Austin. She has worked for the last ten years in administration for the Texas Tech Medical Center in Lubbock and has worked with many ethical issues involved with teaching, research, and clinical patient care.

Miller, J. Michael
Archbishop J. Michael Miller, C.S.B., has been the secretary of Catholic education and titular archbishop of Vertara at the Vatican in Rome since November 2003. He was born in Ottawa, Canada, and was ordained a Catholic priest by Pope Paul VI in 1975. He was president of the University of St. Thomas in Houston, Texas, from 1997 until assuming his present duties in Rome.

Mills, Gena
Gena Mills is a retired CIA operations officer who served for thirty years, with eight overseas tours in six countries, ranging from Southeast Asia to the Soviet Union, Eastern Europe, and Latin America. During her career, she served in increasingly responsible management positions, both at CIA headquarters and at CIA stations abroad, participating in and overseeing clandestine intelligence operations. Her decision to retire "early" was in part based on "changes [she] observed in the Agency and increasing legal hurdles and constraints which were being placed on virtually every aspect of clandestine collection, making it more difficult to fulfill traditional tasks for which the Agency had long been responsible."

Mills, Robert
Robert Mills is a retired CIA operations officer with twenty-eight years of operational and managerial experience in both overseas and domestic

activities. His service included tours of duty in Asia, Latin America, Europe, and the Near East, including two tours in denied areas. His experience extended to both collection and counterintelligence operations.

Moyar, Mark
Dr. Mark Moyar is an associate professor at the U.S. Marine Corps University. He also teaches distance education courses for the George Bush School of Government and Public Service at Texas A&M University. He received his B.A. *summa cum laude* from Harvard University and his Ph.D. from Cambridge University. During his studies, he had the opportunity to work with two of the leading historians of intelligence, Ernest May of Harvard and Christopher Andrew of Cambridge. In 1997, he published a book on the Phoenix Program, a counterinsurgency initiative during the Vietnam War. The first volume of his two-volume history of the Vietnam War has been completed and will be published by the Free Press.

Nelson, Tom
Pastor Tom Nelson is from Waco, Texas. He attended the University of North Texas from 1969 to 1973, where he was a varsity football player. He became a Christian in 1972. After attending the Dallas Theological Seminary, he became the pastor of Denton Bible Church in Denton, Texas, where he has been since 1977. He is a frequent speaker for the Fellowship of Christian Athletes and Campus Crusade. He and his wife of thirty years have two sons. One son is with the U.S. Secret Service and the other plays professional baseball with the St. Louis Cardinals. He has written five books and does several conferences a year on the biblical perspective of love, sex, and marriage from the Book of Solomon.

Peters, Ralph
Ralph Peters is a retired U.S. Army officer and the author of twenty books. With experience in sixty countries, he has written extensively on military, intelligence, and strategic issues. A frequent guest on the broadcast media, he is a columnist and essayist who contributes to a range of newspapers, magazines, and policy journals in the United States and abroad. He is also a prize-winning, best-selling novelist whose historical fiction appears under the pen name Owen Parry. His most recent book is *New Glory: Expanding America's Global Supremacy*.

Pfaff, Charles A.
Lieutenant Colonel Charles A. "Tony" Pfaff, a former assistant professor of

philosophy at the United States Military Academy, has authored several articles on the subject of military ethics and the ethics of intelligence, including "The Ethics of Espionage" in the *Journal of Military Ethics* and "The Ethics of Complex Contingencies" in *The Future of the Army Profession, 2nd edition*. He graduated from Washington and Lee University with a B.A. in economics and philosophy and from Stanford University with an M.A. in philosophy. He currently serves as a foreign area officer on the Joint Staff.

Pimentel, Stanley A.

Stan Pimentel retired from the FBI in September of 1996 after almost thirty years of service. He served as the FBI's legal attaché at Mexico City from October 1991 until his retirement. He had previously served as the FBI's legal attaché in other Latin American posts and as chief of the Foreign Liaison Unit at FBI headquarters. He is currently a consultant on Latin American matters. Transaction Periodicals published his case study of Mexico entitled "The Nexus of Organized Crime and Politics in Mexico" in the spring 1999 issue of *Trends in Organized Crime*, in conjunction with the National Strategy Information Center. This case study was published in Spanish by Editorial Grijalbo in Mexico in a book entitled *Organized Crime and Democratic Governability: Mexico and the Border* by Professors John Bailey and Roy Godson.

Pogacnik, Jason

Jason Pogacnik is a graduate assistant at the Daniel Patrick Moynihan Institute for Global Affairs at Syracuse University's Maxwell School, where he is currently involved in crisis management and leadership profiling projects. He graduated *magna cum laude* from Georgetown University's School of Foreign Service in 2003. At the Maxwell School, he is completing a joint program leading to an M.A. in international relations and a master's of public administration. His interests include international security, crisis management, counterterrorism policy, intelligence, U.S. foreign policy, political leadership, and Balkan politics. He is cofounder and president of the Student Association on Terrorism and Security Analysis, the first international and interdisciplinary graduate student association dedicated to the critical analysis of terrorism, counterterrorism policy, and related national and international security issues.

Porter, Michael

Michael Porter is a professor of communication at the University of Missouri in Columbia.

Powers, Thomas

Thomas Powers is the author of *The Man Who Kept the Secrets: Richard Helms and the CIA*. He also wrote *Heisenberg's War: The Secret History of the German Bomb*. He writes frequently for *The New York Review of Books*, *The New York Times Book Review*, *Harper's*, *The Nation*, *The Atlantic*, and *Rolling Stone*. He won a Pulitzer Prize for national reporting in 1971.

Prince, Howard T.

Howard T. Prince, Ph.D., is the director of the Center for Ethical Leadership in the Lyndon B. Johnson School of Public Affairs at the University of Texas in Austin. He served twenty-eight years in the U.S. Army before retiring with the rank of brigadier general. He is a highly decorated veteran of the Vietnam War and was wounded twice while serving in an infantry battalion with the 1st Cavalry Division. He served as the professor and head of the Department of Behavioral Sciences and Leadership at the U.S. Military Academy in West Point from 1978 to 1990. He was the founding dean of the Jepson School of Leadership Studies at the University of Richmond in Virginia, where he served from 1990 to 1997.

Revell, Oliver

Oliver "Buck" Revell served in the FBI as a special agent and senior official from 1964 to 1994. In 1987, he was in charge of a joint FBI/CIA/U.S. military operation (Goldenrod) which led to the first apprehension overseas of an international terrorist. He was in charge of the Dallas Division of the FBI at the time of his retirement in 1994. He retired with the rank of associate deputy director. He is the author of *A G-Man's Journal: A Legendary Career Inside the FBI—From the Kennedy Assassination to the Oklahoma City Bombing*. He is the founder and president of Revell Group International, an international security firm based in Dallas, and also chairman of Visiphor Corporation of Vancouver, Canada.

Rodriguez, Russell

Russell Rodriguez is a student in the master of public service and administration program at the George Bush School of Government and Public Service at Texas A&M University, where he has also earned the graduate certificate in advanced international affairs from the Bush School. He holds a B.S. in sociology from Texas A&M. He plans to enter public service upon graduation.

Ruby, Tom

Lieutenant Colonel Tom Ruby is an assistant professor of joint warfare studies on the faculty of the Air Command and Staff College, Air University, Maxwell AFB, Alabama. He instructs courses in joint aerospace operations, joint campaign planning, and morality in warfare. He is a graduate of the Joint Military Intelligence College, where he received his M.S. in strategic intelligence and was named a distinguished graduate. He also completed the Air Command and Staff College, where he was named outstanding contributor. In May 2004 he earned his Ph.D. in political science from the University of Kentucky. In fall 2004, he served on the staff of the Multi-National Force in Iraq, in Baghdad, where he helped conduct the commanding general's number one priority by coauthoring a strategic campaign process review ahead of Iraq's first democratic elections.

Salazar, John
John Salazar has a B.A. in Latin American Studies. He served for nine years in the Peace Corps, three years as a volunteer and six years on the Peace Corps staff. He then joined the U.S. State Department, where he served for twenty years, retiring in September 2002 as a senior foreign service officer. He is currently president of the Central Texas Foreign Service Association.

Scherer, Christopher
Christopher Scherer is an attorney in private practice in California. In addition to a law degree, he holds degrees in theology and religious studies.

Smith, Haviland
Hav Smith served in the CIA from 1956 to 1980. He was educated at Exeter, Dartmouth (A.B. 1951), and the University of London. He was in the U.S. Army from 1951 to 1954. In the CIA, he was a case officer, supervisor, and station chief. His overseas assignments included Prague, Berlin, Beirut, and Tehran. At CIA headquarters, he supervised worldwide recruitment efforts against the USSR and Eastern European countries. He was also executive assistant to DDCI Frank Carlucci and chief of the counterterrorism staff. His foreign languages are French, German, Russian, and Czech. He lectures and writes extensively on the Middle East, terrorism, the intelligence community, and the role of intelligence in foreign policy. He and his wife live in Vermont. In addition to lecturing and writing, he fishes, skis downhill, hikes, bikes, grows peppers, makes hot sauces, turns bowls on his lathe, gathers mushrooms, and canoes on the rivers.

Sullivan, John
John Sullivan was a polygraph examiner with the CIA for thirty-one years. From 1971 to 1975 he was assigned to Vietnam. During his career, he traveled

around the world and, he says, "has probably met more spies than any man alive." After retiring from the CIA in 1999, he authored *Of Spies and Lies: A CIA Lie Detector Remembers Vietnam* and *Gatekeeper: Memoirs of a CIA Polygrapher.*

Tarlow, Peter E.

Dr. Peter Tarlow has been the rabbi at Texas A&M University's Hillel since 1983. In that capacity he has worked with Jewish students and faculty, taught courses on Jewish ethics, and served as chaplain for the College Station Police Department. He is an expert in the impact of crime and terrorism on the tourism industry, event risk management, and tourism and economic development. He has a Ph.D. in sociology from Texas A&M University. He also holds degrees in history, Spanish and Hebrew literatures, and psychotherapy. Since 1990 he has been teaching courses on tourism, crime, and terrorism to police forces and security and tourism professionals throughout the world. He has been an adviser on tourism development and security to the Hoover Dam, the Bureau of Reclamation, the U.S. Customs Service, the Salt Lake City 2002 Winter Olympics, the U.S. National Park Service, and numerous other U.S. and international organizations.

Tatyrek, Aaron

Aaron Tatyrek is a political science and Russian major at Texas A&M University. He has been involved in the Student Conference on National Affairs, the Student Senate, and MSC Conversations. He is keenly interested in Sino-American and Russo-American relations. After graduation, he intends to pursue a graduate degree in international relations.

Tumlin, Geoffrey R.

Geoffrey Tumlin is the assistant director of the Center for Ethical Leadership in the Lyndon B. Johnson School of Public Affairs at the University of Texas at Austin. He has a Ph.D. in communications studies from the University of Texas. Upon graduating with a B.S. from the United States Military Academy at West Point, he was commissioned as an infantry officer in the Army and spent the majority of his military service with the renowned 25th Light Infantry Division in Hawaii. His areas of expertise are leadership studies and interpersonal communication. He has taught various college courses in leadership, communication, management, and interpersonal interaction. Prior to joining the Center for Ethical Leadership, he served as a leadership and communications consultant for numerous organizations, including Shell Oil, Wyeth Pharmaceuticals, Riata Luxury Apartment Homes, Blue Star Management, Highland Park Independent School District, and the Elgin,

Illinois, Police Department. He currently teaches a large undergraduate course at the University of Texas titled "Fundamentals of Ethical Leadership."

Williams, John
John Williams served in the U.S. Information Agency from 1968 until his retirement in 1996. He received B.A. and M.A. degrees in journalism from the University of Michigan in 1966 and 1968 respectively. His assignments with USIA included Spain, Argentina, Poland, New Zealand, Austria, and Bolivia. He attended the U.S. National War College in 1985, where he received the best research paper award for "Public Diplomacy Aspects of the Intermediate-Range Nuclear Force Deployments in Europe." He was assigned to the Public Affairs Office of the secretary of defense from 1995 to 1996. Since his retirement from the government, he has worked in the private sector as a public relations and media relations adviser. Since 2001 he has been the media director for the National Training Systems Association.

Zandstra, Laura
Laura Zandstra is a sophomore majoring in international studies at Texas A&M University. She is specializing in the politics of Africa and the Middle East. In addition, she is working on a minor in French. Her outside activities include reading, golf, and working as a summer camp counselor. She lives in College Station, Texas.

Ziesche, Barbara
Barbara Ziesche emigrated with her family from Germany to the United States in 1960. She grew up in Colorado and went to Colorado State University, where she majored in German and minored in French. She taught at middle schools and high schools for twenty-seven years.

INDEX

academic issues scenarios: credentials fabrication, 154–157; operational use of academics, 93–97; plagiarizing dissertation, 157–169; use of P-sources, 97–100

Agee, Philip, 41–42, 56, 129–130, 255n28

agents: "agent" defined, 229n1; breaking promise to scenario, 190–194; personal and impersonal handling of, 247n13

Allen, David S., on scenarios: journalism cover, 74–75; operational use of journalist, 79–80; press placements, 149–150; protection of code breaking, 186; spying on friendly countries, 169

Ames, Aldrich, 114, 258n38

Amit, Yossi, 170, 254n27

Anderson, Terry H., on scenarios: bogus website, 198–199; foreign officer visitors, 216; hit team, 59; kidnapping and torture, 68–69; prostitute for terrorist, 102; spying on friendly countries, 170; truth serum, 71; unauthorized cover, 195; use of P-sources, 99–100

Angleton, James Jesus, 40, 231n5

Aquinas, St. Thomas, 30

Aristotle, 17–18

assassination. *See* hit team scenario

Augustine, Saint, 21, 30

Bible, 15–17, 30

biological attack scenario, 203–206

Bismarck, Otto von, 25–26, 27

Black Chamber, 36

blackmail. *See* homosexual blackmail scenario

Bohn, Michael, on scenarios: Romeo operations, 117; spying on overseas Americans, 166–167; tampering with U.S. mail, 182–183; torture training, 86; use of P-sources, 99

Bosley, Jack, on scenarios: coercive pitch, 121–122; forging documents from friendly countries, 208; industrial espionage, 175–176; kidnapping and killing defector, 127–128; truth serum, 71

Botea, Roxana, on scenarios: backdoors to computer systems, 200; homosexual blackmail, 47; industrial espionage, 176–177; interrogation, 219; opera-tional use of academics, 96

Boyles, Stephanie, on kamikaze dolphin scenario, 164

Brekke-Esparza, Lauraine, on scenarios: fake diagnosis, 143; kamikaze dolphins, 164; seduction and compromise, 114; unauthorized cover, 195

Brewer, Ray, on scenarios: bogus website, 198; child prostitute, 104; drugging foreign diplo-mat, 146; protection of code breaking, 186; spying on friendly countries, 169

bribing foreign government scenario, 179–182

Brown, Philip, on scenarios: drugging foreign diplomat, 146; election tampering, 111; evidence fabrication, 133–134; operational use of journalist, 77; press placements, 152

Buckley, William, 86–87

Bush, George W., 65–67, 69, 87

car pickups, 250n19

Carter, Jimmy, 41

case officer, CIA: defined, 229n1; recruitment cycle and, 25, 236n2

Castro, Fidel, 39, 60

Catechism of the Catholic Church, 22, 30

Central Intelligence Agency (CIA), 35, 52, 66, 233n10, 241n2, 248n14; FBI and, 3–4, 248n14; Officer In Residence Program, 12–13, 235n14; pay scale of, 230n3; predecessor groups to, 36–37; primary directorates of, 244n8; recruitment and, 25, 230n2, 236n2, 246n11; stations of, 245n10; women in, 7, 115–119, 232n8

child prostitute scenario, 103–105

Church Committee, 41, 75, 96, 240n2

Cicero, Marcus Tullius, 18–20

Clarridge, Duane "Dewey," 5, 85

Clearfield, Abraham, on scenarios: exposing unwitting person to risk, 162; false flag, 55; humanitarian aid worker cover story, 89; spying on United Nations, 172; terrorist act for bona fides, 107

Clinton, Bill, 241–242n2

code breaking, protection of scenario, 186–190

coercive pitch scenario, 120–123

COINTELPRO, 40

collateral damage scenario, 210–215

Communism, U.S. attitude toward spying and, 36–39

compartmentation, 89, 246n12

computer systems, backdoor to scenario, 199–203

Congress for Cultural Freedom, 152–153

Corbin, Louise, on scenarios: election tampering, 110; fake diagnosis, 144; feeding drug habit, 124–125; homosexual blackmail, 47

Corbin, Richard, on scenarios: evidence fabrica-tion, 133; exposing unwitting person to risk, 162; hit team, 57; L-devices, 136; prostitute for terrorist, 101–102

countersurveillance, 260n43

cover stories scenarios, 87–93

covert action, 239–240n1, 250n20

Cox Report, 50, 242n4

Crowell, William, 202

220; operational use of academics, 94; Romeo operations, 117–118
Jedburgh teams, 141, 256n33
Jensen, Robert, on scenarios: election tampering, 111; journalism cover, 75
John (CIA officer), on scenarios: backdoors to computer systems, 201; breaking promise to agent, 192; L-devices, 136–137; tampering with U.S. mail, 183–184
John Paul II, Pope, 29–31, 131
journalism scenarios: cover story, 72–76; operational use, 77–81

Kant, Immanuel, 24–25
Kennedy, John F., 41, 60
Kennedy, Robert F., 60
KGB: Clayton Lonetree and, 11–12, 233n12, 234n13; drugs and, 147–148; Romeo operations and, 118–119; successor organizations to, 243n5
kidnapping scenarios: and killing defector, 126–131; and torture by surrogates, 67–70
Kisevalter, George, 6, 231n7

Lake, Joseph E., on scenarios: humanitarian aid worker cover story, 88; human rights violations, 83; industrial espionage, 176; terrorist act for bona fides, 106
Lee, Kyu Mani, on scenarios: backdoors to computer systems, 200; bogus website, 198; L-devices, 136; plagiarizing dissertation, 159; spying on friendly countries, 169–170
lethal devices scenario, 135–138
Lieser, Mary Lee, on scenarios: bribing foreign government, 180; child prostitute, 104; homosexual blackmail, 47–48; missionary cover, 91–92; protection of code breaking, 187–188
Lieser, William, on scenarios: collateral damage, 211; plagiarizing dissertation, 158; Romeo operations, 118; spying on overseas Americans, 166; torture, 64
Life, Richard, on scenarios: bribing foreign government, 180; false flag, 55; foreign officer visitors, 216–217; kidnapping and killing defector, 128; prostitute for terrorist, 101
Lipka, Robert, 56
Lonetree, Clayton, 9, 11–12, 233n12, 234n13
Lumumba, Patrice, 39, 60

Machiavelli, Niccolo, 22–24
mail tampering scenario, 182–185
Mason, Harry, on scenarios: academic credentials fabrication, 156; backdoors to computer systems, 200; breaking promise to agent, 192; election tampering, 110; forging documents from friendly countries, 208; hit team, 58; journalism cover, 74; protection of code breaking, 186; torture training, 86; use of P-sources, 98
Mathis, Margaretta, on scenarios: collateral damage, 212; homosexual blackmail, 48; insertion operations, 140; interro-gation, 219; press placements, 150; protection of code breaking, 187; seduction and compromise, 113; torture, 64–65; Trojan horse, 50
Maugham, Somerset, 255n29
McCain, John, 66, 215
McCarry, Charles, 255n29

McGehee, Ralph, 42
Meacham, Margaret, on scenarios: collateral damage, 211; forging documents from friendly countries, 208; homosexual blackmail, 48; insertion operations, 140; interrogation, 219–220; press place-ments, 150; protection of code break-ing, 187; seduction and compromise, 113; torture, 64; Trojan horse, 50–51
MHCHOAS, 41
military officers (anonymous), on scenarios: biological attack, 204; collateral damage, 212; human rights violations, 83–84; insertion operations, 140–141; kidnapping and killing defector, 129
Miller, Archbishop J. Michael, on hit team scenario, 59
Mills, Gena, on scenarios: academic credentials fabrication, 156; biological attack, 205; false flag, 54; foreign officer visitors, 216
Mills, Robert, on scenarios: insertion operations, 139; operational use of academics, 94; Trojan horse, 51–52; use of P-sources, 99
Mindszenty, Cardinal Joszef, 147–148
Ministry for State Security (MSS, China), 49–52, 242n3
missionary cover scenario, 90–93
MKULTRA, 40, 148
Mossad (Israel), 254n27
Moyar, Mark, on scenarios: academic credentials fabrication, 155; election tampering, 110; evidence fabrication, 132; terrorist act for bona fides, 107; torture, 65

National Committee for a Free Europe, 153
National Security Agency (NSA), 239n1
Nelson, Tom, on scenarios: child prostitute, 104; collateral damage, 210–211; hit team, 57; missionary cover, 91; torture, 64
"nonofficial cover," 232n9

Office of Strategic Services (OSS), 36–37
Officer In Residence Program, CIA, 12–13, 235n14
"official cover," 232n9
Ogorodnik, Aleksandr, 137–138
Olson, James M. (author): background of, 1–2; CIA recruitment of, 3–5; CIA service of, 5–7, 9–12, 246n11; family of, 6, 7–9; teaching career of, 11–13
Olson, Meredith, 6–9, 12–13, 105, 233–234n12, 233n11, 246n11
one-time pads, 260n41

Penkovsky, Oleg, 6, 231–232n7
People's Liberation Army (PLA), 157, 257n36
Peters, Ralph, on scenarios: biological attack, 205; child prostitute, 104; coercive pitch, 121; false flag, 54; kamikaze dolphins, 164
Pfaff, Tony, on scenarios: bribing foreign government, 180; coercive pitch, 122–123; evidence fabri-cation, 132–133; homosexual blackmail, 48
Philby, Harold "Kim," 81, 141, 256n34
photo reconnaissance. See IMINT
psychological operations (psyops), 262n47
Pike Committee, 41, 240n2
Pimentel, Stanley, on scenarios: feeding drug habit, 125; hit team, 58–59; prostitute for terrorist, 102; spy-ing on United Nations, 173; truth serum, 71
plagiarizing dissertation scenario, 157–169
Pogacnik, Jason, on scenarios: academic credentials

About the Author

JAMES M. OLSON spent his entire career in the Directorate of Operations of the Central Intelligence Agency. He served as chief of counterintelligence at CIA headquarters in Langley, Virginia, and also in field assignments in Moscow, Vienna, and Mexico City. He is the recipient of the CIA's Distinguished Career Intelligence Medal, the Intelligence Medal of Merit, and the Donovan Award. He retired from the CIA in 2000 and now teaches courses on intelligence and national security for the Master's Program in International Affairs at the George Bush School of Government and Public Service of Texas A&M University. He is the author of "The Ten Commandments of Counterintelligence," which appeared in the fall-winter 2001 issue of *Studies in Intelligence*. He and his wife Meredith live in College Station, Texas.